Horse Racing's
Top 100
Moments

Horse Racing's
Top 100
Moments

BY THE STAFF OF BLOOD-HORSE PUBLICATIONS

EP
ECLIPSE
PRESS

LEXINGTON,
KENTUCKY

Library of Congress Control Number: 2006900681

ISBN-13: 978-1-58150-139-1
ISBN-10: 1-58150-139-0

Printed in China
First Edition: 2006

Distributed to the trade by
National Book Network
4720-A Boston Way, Lanham, MD 20706
1.800.462.6420

A Division of
Blood-Horse Publications
Publishers Since 1916

How shall we rank thee upon glory's page,
Thou more than soldier, and just less than sage?

— Thomas Moore, 1779–1852

Table of Contents

Introduction

SECRETARIAT WINS the Belmont Stakes by an eye-popping thirty-one lengths. D. Wayne Lukas captures six consecutive Triple Crown races. Man o' War suffers a shocking defeat by a horse appropriately named Upset. In the past hundred years or so, horse racing has seen its share of exciting, devastating, uplifting, and groundbreaking moments, and *Horse Racing's Top 100 Moments* examines the best of the best.

In 2005 the staff of Eclipse Press and *The Blood-Horse* magazine brainstormed to come up with a list of racing's greatest moments. We recognized five categories — racing, breeding, auctions, innovations, and oddities — and identified more than two hundred potential moments.

We then selected a panel of racing experts to rank the moments:

• Edward L. Bowen, the widely respected Turf historian and the author of seventeen books about racing.

• Timothy T. Capps, the former editor of *The Thoroughbred Record* and racing executive.

• Morton Cathro, a former reporter, editor, and columnist for the Oakland *Tribune*.

• Alice Chandler, an internationally known breeder and a leader in numerous racing industry organizations.

• Steve Haskin, the award-winning senior correspondent for *The Blood-Horse* magazine and the author of several books about horse racing.

• Joe Hirsch, the venerated Turf writer who chronicled the sport for five decades.

• John McEvoy, an award-winning author and racing historian.

• William Nack, the award-winning writer for *Sports Illustrated* and author of the definitive biography of Secretariat.

Before we sent the list off to the panel, we arranged the choices alphabetically and provided space for write-in moments. The eight panelists embraced the assignment, with one acknowledging that the challenge was so fascinating he dreamed of it at night.

It didn't take long for the results to come in. We had designed a point system to determine the final ranking, and some of the results were indeed surprising. Some of us had assumed that Secretariat's Belmont tour de force would finish in first place. Yet that singular moment ranked fourth. The exploits of other horses surpassed Big Red for the second and third spots. Creation of the Breeders' Cup was determined to be the No. 1 greatest moment. Although not the unanimous choice of the panelists, the Breeders' Cup finished nearly twenty points ahead of the second greatest moment, the Seabiscuit–War Admiral match race.

Interestingly, innovations such as the photo-finish camera, film patrol, and starting gate finished in the top twenty. We wondered how the panelists weighed their importance against other top moments in the sport.

"I probably gave more weight to historic developments — introduction of pari-mutuel wagering, the film patrol, modern starting gate, public address system, photo finish camera — without which subsequent racing achievements would not have been possible," McEvoy said.

For Bowen, comparing dramatic, enthralling moments against those having lasting impact "involves a mental juggling similar to that of historians tracking, say, the presidency. What seems humdrum at the time might be seen in retrospect to have hastened a domino effect of lasting significance," he said.

"How you compare Secretariat's Belmont to a technological breakthrough like the starting gate that influences races day by day for decades is probably as much a matter of impression as judgment."

Panelists also had to weigh events they had witnessed firsthand with those that had occurred before their time or beyond their purview.

Capps explained the challenge: "It was a classic head versus heart scenario: My heart pulled me in the direction of the horses and their performances; my head, in the direction of the business changes that redefined racing from its 'Sport of Kings' imagery to a consumer-driven business."

Although most of the moments are positive and even heart-warming, some are decidedly not — breakdowns, bankruptcies, and deaths — though still worthy of inclusion for their contribution to racing's broad panorama.

Said Nack: "I tended to play that kind of stuff down, though it was hard to ignore the Ruffian breakdown — in a nationally televised event. It engaged me emotionally as few other racing events ever did."

Completing the exercise left the panelists impressed by racing's grandeur and history and

> "How you compare Secretariat's Belmont to a technological breakthrough like the starting gate that influences races day by day for decades is probably as much a matter of impression as judgment."
>
> Edward L. Bowen

feeling good about the sport on the whole. "It was like turning and looking inside this giant magical egg, into a kind of make-believe kingdom where memory and desire still mix and all the passing days and years in the sport seem so wonderful and worthwhile," Nack said.

Ranking the moments also underscored how the sport has changed and been changed by forces more powerful than the competitive fires of man and horse.

"Racing is basically a sport that has beauty and competition at its core, but the industry is affected by matters as wide ranging as the public's shifting reactions to gambling, the rapid transition of technologies that dictates how the public follows its sports, the declining connection to the horse in many aspects of society, and frequent disparity between legislators' ambitions and wisdom," said Bowen. "Through it all, the Thoroughbred — and the lure of the race and the gamble — has prevailed."

Written by staff and correspondents of *The Blood-Horse, Horse Racing's Top 100 Moments* is a fond tribute to the sport's finest and most significant days in the sun. *The Editors*

IT WAS AN IDEA whose time had come, concluded John Gaines, early in 1982 — create a combination Super Bowl and NCAA tournament for Thoroughbred racing. The best would be lured to an autumnal showdown by unprecedented purses, each age and sex category given its proper moment at center stage, and the excitement and prestige of the event would attract a national television audience and, hence, increase public interest in Thoroughbred racing.

Gaines, master of Gainesway Farm in Kentucky and one of the arch thinkers and power brokers of the Turf since the early 1960s, put his energy as well as his intellect into establishing this banner day for Thoroughbred racing. He traveled the country explaining, cajoling, probably intimidating — he was not unfamiliar with the tactic — in meetings with racetracks and horsemen and horsemen's groups. Although stuck with the arcane name Breeders' Cup — with all its confusing implications — the idea for this annual red letter day resonated with the sundry and varied strata that make up the Thoroughbred racing industry.

The Breeders' Cup offered many positives. For one, it would create a virtually irresistible magnet for horses with championship aspirations to come together for meetings late in the year. For racing fans and industry participants whose experience in the game is

1 The Inaugural Breeders' Cup

limited to the past two decades or less, the impact of this kind of race day might be lost. Prior to the Breeders' Cup, while certain races, such as the Jockey Club Gold Cup, had the potential to bring the best horses from East and West together, there was no assurance that such year-end climactic meetings actually would occur or even be in trainers' and owners' plans. The Breeders' Cup races could not guarantee such match-ups, of course, but they certainly would create incentives difficult to resist. None of the seven races envisioned would have a purse less than $1 million, and this in a day when the Arlington Million had pioneered the seven-figure purse only the year before Gaines began his campaign.

Even a pot of gold at the end of the rainbow will have its critics, if they have to contribute to the pot. The ideas for funding of what was projected as a $13-million day of racing involved contribution of a season's fee for each stallion, which when nominated would mean his foals could be nominated as well, each for an individual payment (eventually set at five hundred dollars).

John Gaines (inset), the creator of the Breeders' Cup; Wild Again (inside) edges Gate Dancer and Slew o' Gold to win a dramatic inaugural Breeders' Cup Classic

next year when Seth Hancock signed on to nominate the stallions at prestigious Claiborne Farm.

The idea was saved, and the Breeders' Cup beckoned from the future — with the autumn of 1984 selected for the inaugural running.

D.G. Van Clief, scion of a racing family visible through its involvement in the auction house Fasig-Tipton Company and in Nydrie Stud in Virginia, was the inspired choice to head the Breeders' Cup. Young, energetic, polished, and articulate, Van Clief steered the ship through the roughest waters. Anyone not satisfied with the

The Breeders' Cup has seen many great moments since 1984, including Arazi's 1991 Juvenile victory at Churchill Downs

A hue and cry countered the enthusiasm many felt for the idea. On October 9, 1982, *The Blood-Horse* remarked that "the Breeders' Cup is in trouble. Its detractors are many, for myriad reasons, and as of this writing it seems about to be buried under layer upon layer of criticism. The idea is too good to let die."

Compromises were struck, and within the month the scene looked brighter. Among concerns to be addressed was the issue that only the large breeders and owners would benefit because they would likely stand the sires of the winners and/or own those winners. This fear was assuaged in part by a sideline program that would supplement purses of existing stakes throughout the year, these extra monies available only to Breeders' Cup nominees that won or placed in those races.

The compromise could be seen in two lights: (1) It destined the Breeders' Cup to drain off millions upon millions of dollars into a shotgun program that had little to do with the original intent, or (2) it saved the whole endeavor from dying while yet unborn. At any rate, with that deal struck and with Gaines — a controversial personality and lightning rod — agreeing to step aside, a sufficient number of stallion managers pledged their support. A key moment occurred early the

Breeders' Cup under such management virtually had to be somehow determined to be a naysayer for the sake of being a naysayer. Van Clief stood the test of time and today is president of Breeders' Cup Limited and commissioner and CEO of the affiliated National Thoroughbred Racing Association.

Eight racetracks, eager to stage the first running, bid for the event. Hollywood Park in California won the prize — and the logistical headaches of the pioneer. Hollywood had the advantage of almost certain good weather, and NBC came on board to televise the entire program live.

Marje Everett, who ran Hollywood Park at the time, was no less controversial a character than Gaines. Traditionalists had harshly criticized her for her earlier management of Arlington Park in Chicago, and her gambits at Hollywood Park included construction of the Cary Grant Pavilion, a posh building situated at a location that made watching horse races awkward.

Nevertheless, Mrs. Everett was a proven commodity as a manager dedicated to the game. Moreover, her connections to glamorous personalities was a fillip other tracks could hardly match. At the gala party on the eve of the event, Frank Sinatra sauntered onto the stage to sing for a crowd through which Elizabeth Taylor, Jimmy Stewart, John Forsythe, Joan Collins, Gregory Peck, and Diahann Carroll mingled.

A crowd of 64,254 turned out for the first Breeders' Cup on November 10, 1984, while millions more watched the action unfold on television. The first Breeders' Cup race was the Juvenile for colts, in which Chief's Crown solidified his claim to the Eclipse Award as champion of the division. The runner-up was future Preakness winner Tank's Prospect and third was future Kentucky Derby winner Spend a Buck, underscoring the class of horse the races attracted.

An unforeseen plus for the Breeders' Cup was how quickly and fervently the key European owners adopted it as a cherished year-end goal, even though it meant prolonging their season beyond such races as the Prix de l'Arc de Triomphe in France and Champion Stakes in England. The first running of the $2-million Breeders' Cup Turf found Daniel Wildenstein's wondrous mare All Along returning to North America, where the previous year she had won the Rothmans International (in Canada), Turf Classic, and Washington, D. C., International in separate invasions to earn Horse of the Year honors.

All Along was beaten in the Turf, but her neck loss came against Lashkari, a 54-1 shot representing another of the most important owners in Europe, the Aga Khan. The Breeders' Cup was central to the world stage from its inception, and the participation of top European stables has remained one of its hallmarks.

In its first rendition, the Breeders' Cup Day climax, the $3-million Breeders' Cup Classic — then the richest race in the world — saw drama above and beyond expectation. Slew o' Gold, the elegant darling of the older horses, was odds-on in the mile and a quarter race. The 31-1 Wild Again, supplemented by Black Chip Stable for $360,000, led from soon after the start and proved brave and ready for the sternest of tests through the stretch. Gate Dancer, an erratic colt whose tendency toward distraction led trainer Jack Van Berg to fit him with colorful ear coverings, cavorted through the stretch to challenge, squeezing Slew o' Gold between himself and the frantic pacemaker.

Wild Again prevailed in a lapped-upon finish that Slew o' Gold's jockey, Angel Cordero, described as himself and his mount being the "ham in a ham sandwich." Gate Dancer, Preakness winner from the spring, was second across the wire but was disqualified and placed third.

The victory led to a signature image that has lingered. This was the moment captured when Wild Again's jockey, Pat Day, lifted his cap and eyes toward the heavens.

The Breeders' Cup — later to adapt the hyped slogan "World Thoroughbred Championships" — had been launched in dramatic style. After twenty-two runnings, racing's championship event has become entrenched as a beacon for the best horses of America and abroad and a true test of champions. *ELB*

In the 2004 Breeders' Cup, Ghostzapper validated his dominance in the Classic

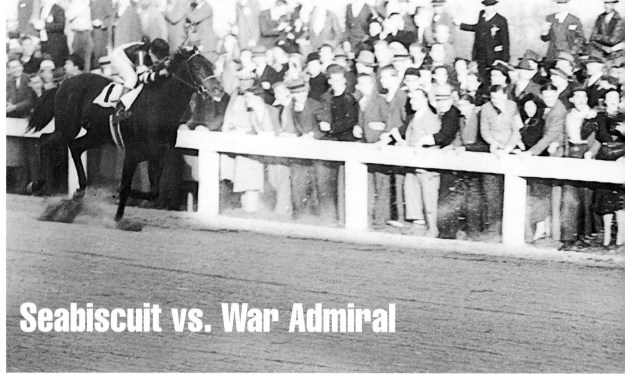

Seabiscuit vs. War Admiral

MANY OF HORSE RACING's oft-repeated stories have one or two elements that elevate them to the category of memorable — but very few contain the competition, contrast, and crescendo of the match race between Seabiscuit and War Admiral in the 1938 Pimlico Special.

Both horses descended from Man o' War, though neither physically resembled the great racehorse. War Admiral, a son of Man o' War, was diminutive like his mother, Brushup. He shared her rich brown coat and smooth, shapely conformation. Seabiscuit was a gangly, plain bay with no markings, not particularly impressive to the eye. His pedigree did little to improve on his looks nor did his awkward gait. He was by the hot-tempered Hard Tack, and his dam was the never-raced Swing On.

War Admiral came out of the gate full force as a two-year-old, winning his first two races for his owner and breeder — sportsman and East Coast landholder Samuel D. Riddle, whose family had made its fortune in the textile industry. Riddle had been unimpressed by the colt, lamenting his likeness to his dam. In the shadow of the powerful and heady Man o' War, whom Riddle also owned, War Admiral seemed even smaller than 15 hands.

But a small stature meant nothing to the colt.

He finished in the money in his remaining four races as a two-year-old, including a particularly brilliant victory in the six-furlong Eastern Shore Handicap against staunch competitors Maedic and Bottle Cap. Despite this eye-opening achievement, his best was yet to come as a three-year-old.

Riddle had long shunned racing "out West" and had never had a Derby contender. He and his trainer, George Conway, reconsidered this embargo when War Admiral scored an easy win in the mile and one-sixteenth, $10,000-added Chesapeake Stakes, a major Derby prep race.

The lone Riddle team member with Derby experience was jockey and Shepherdsville, Kentucky, native Charley Kurtsinger. He not only had ridden Twenty Grand to victory in the Derby six years earlier but also had done so in record time (2:01 4/5).

Not to be completely outdone by his own success and proving Riddle's decision to race "out West" a wise one, the jockey piloted War Admiral to a one and three-quarters-length win in the Run for the Roses in 2:03 1/5. The Derby time was second only to Kurtsinger's trip on Twenty Grand.

With the relationship of the Derby and Preakness not yet set in stone in 1937, the latter race was only a week later. War Admiral cooled out of the Derby so well that he was placed on a

train to Baltimore that night and arrived the next day. This time, Riddle, who had stayed home from the Derby due to illness, was present to see War Admiral win by a head over Pompoon in a homestretch battle.

Three weeks later Riddle was front and center to witness America's fourth Triple Crown being bestowed upon his horse, who had won the Belmont Stakes by three lengths despite shearing off a portion of the hoof wall of his right foreleg as he bolted away from the gate. As War Admiral had run, blood from the gaping wound spattered his underbelly, an image many present that day could not forget, both for its visual acuity and for the heart the little horse showed.

The injury was not career ending, and War

Admiral finished out the year with nary a blemish on his perfect record — eight wins in eight races.

Meanwhile, Seabiscuit, who was bred and owned by Wheatley Stable, was making waves on the West Coast.

As a juvenile, he had started an amazing thirty-five times, sometimes in claiming races, and had not managed to break his maiden until his eighteenth race. His trainer, the legendary Sunny Jim Fitzsimmons, had not thought much of Seabiscuit. After the horse had raced ten times as a three-year-old, Fitzsimmons entered Seabiscuit in a claiming race for a tag of $4,500. No one claimed the colt, but a few days later Charles S. Howard, a bicycle repairman and salesman who traded two wheels for four and grew the country's largest Buick dealership in San Francisco, came looking for a nice allowance runner.

His trainer, "Silent" Tom Smith, whose reticence convinced many he lacked a tongue, persuaded Howard to buy Seabiscuit for $7,500. The colt ended his sophomore season with nine wins in twenty-three starts, some of them small stakes. Like War Admiral, though, the best lay ahead.

As a four-year-old in 1937, Seabiscuit began amassing wins as Howard barnstormed his West

In the winner's circle: owner Charles Howard, jockey George Woolf, trainer Tom Smith, and Pimlico's Alfred Vanderbilt

15

Coast favorite on a cross-country racing campaign to prove the horse was as good as any other the East could proffer. Seabiscuit ended the year with wins in ten major stakes races, parting Easterners with their money as he took the Brooklyn, Yonkers, and Massachusetts handicaps. His victories pitted him against War Admiral for Horse of the Year, with the Triple Crown winner taking the honor while Seabiscuit garnered leading earner.

Their mutual success, coupled with the fact the two horses had never crossed paths, led racing fans to clamor for a meeting to determine superiority. Howard saw the historical significance (and bragging rights) of such a meeting and decided it should come in a match race, with no outside interference. It took some convincing for Riddle, who told reporters he had no interest in demeaning War Admiral's reputation in a contest with a Western colt.

Thus began a bidding war among racing's coterie for the distinction of hosting what newspapers were dubbing the greatest match race since Man o' War defeated Sir Barton in 1920. Chicago's Arlington Park offered a $100,000 purse but stipulated the addition of a third horse. On the same day, Belmont Park came forth with a similar offer, sans the extra horse. Suffolk Downs

entered the bidding a few days later, but its offer included pitting the horses in a full field and providing a $70,000 purse.

Riddle and Howard agreed to race at Belmont on May 30, Decoration Day, going ten furlongs and carrying 126 pounds. As racing fans and pundits eagerly anticipated the match-up, Belmont made plans to accommodate the overflow crowd, including securing extra trains for transportation. Meanwhile, rumors circulated that both horses were not in top form. The rumor about Seabiscuit proved true, and six days before the race Howard withdrew his charge. The only solace Belmont officials could gather from the ruins was the assurance that War Admiral would instead run in the Suburban, scheduled for May 28. Their hopes were once again extinguished, and tempers ignited, when trainer Conway scratched War Admiral, citing wet conditions from earlier rain as the cause.

Throughout the summer, opportunities for the two horses to meet came and went as both went about the business of racing. At one point they both ended up entered in the Massachusetts Handicap. At the last moment permissible, forty-five minutes before post, trainer Smith found heat in one of Seabiscuit's legs and withdrew him from the race. War Admiral finished fourth to Hal Price Headley's Menow.

Heading to the post: War Admiral (center) and Seabiscuit (right)

Finally, it was announced October 5 that Riddle and Howard had signed an agreement, with each posting five thousand dollars in earnest money, to race on November 1, opening day at Pimlico in Maryland. And they would do so for the comparatively paltry figure of $15,000 to the winner of the nine and a half-furlong race, with the two competitors carrying 120 pounds. Both owners agreed if the track were muddy, as determined by a "neutral" party, the race would be postponed. Howard also conceded to Riddle's insistent request for a walk-up start.

In the interim Seabiscuit ran in the Laurel Stakes and was beaten by the filly Jacola, taking some of the sheen off of the upcoming match race. Seabiscuit's regular jockey, John "Red" Pollard, had also suffered a debilitating riding accident earlier in the year and had not healed sufficiently to ride. Even with Pollard's absence and Seabiscuit's defeat in the Laurel, Howard remained imperturbable.

"I'm not worried in the least," he told reporters. "I know we are going to whip War Admiral."

Despite moving the race to a Tuesday to avoid splitting Pimlico's seams, a record crowd of 40,000 arrived to witness the showdown. So many fans showed up, including Hollywood movie stars and nearby Washington, D.C., politicos, that Pimlico had to open its infield to accommodate the overflow. The legendary Clem McCarthy could not fight his way through the crowd in time to get back to the announcer's booth, so he called the race for NBC from the finish line instead.

Known for his fearless riding style, the "Iceman" George Woolf had the mount on Seabiscuit in the stead of his good friend Pollard. Kurtsinger, having been out several months with an injury, was back on War Admiral.

At 4 p.m. the two rivals walked up to the line. After two false starts, George Cassidy, who had been brought in from New York to start the race, dropped the flag, and the horses were off. Seabiscuit leapt away like a Quarter Horse, leaving racing fans slack jawed at the sight. Many had assumed War Admiral, known for his powerful starts, would gain the edge from the beginning. Seabiscuit, though, immediately took the lead,

Seabiscuit trains for the match race

snapping off the first quarter in :23 3/5 and coming over to the rail two lengths ahead of War Admiral.

Turning into the backstretch, Kurtsinger began urging his colt. The crowd roared as War Admiral closed on his rival, at one point getting his head in front. Seabiscuit, not to be overtaken, stepped up to the challenge, and the two horses raced in lock step, Man o' War's blood boiling to the surface in both. The horses continued battling around the final turn and well into the stretch.

Heading for home, Seabiscuit began to pull away. By the time the horses reached the final furlong pole, Seabiscuit had established an indomitable lead over the tiring War Admiral. He emerged the victor by four lengths, running the race in a Pimlico record of 1:56 3/5. Seabiscuit, who had gone off at 2-1 to War Admiral's 1-4, paid $6.40 to backers.

Seabiscuit's victory and his vast heart made it impossible for Easterners to shrug off their West Coast competitors. Though War Admiral won more races that year, Seabiscuit's victory over the little colt left an indelible impression and garnered Horse of the Year honors. *RB*

Kelso's Five Horse of the Year Titles

"THEY DON'T MAKE 'em like they used to." It's cliché, but how else can you describe Kelso? Other horses may have been faster, carried more weight, or excelled at a particular distance, but no other horse was so consistently good for so long.

Kelso raced for seven years, eight if his abbreviated season at age nine is counted, and for five of those years, from 1960 to 1964, he dominated the ranks, winning thirty-five of his fifty-three starts. He also collected a Horse of the Year title in each of those years for an unprecedented and likely to be unmatched record.

Bred by Maryland horsewoman Allaire du Pont, Kelso was foaled at Claiborne Farm in Kentucky. As a foal, he was sent with his dam to his owner's Woodstock Farm near Chesapeake City, Maryland. Kelso had become a handful by the time he was to be broken, and his bad temperament was a major factor in his being gelded as a yearling. Gelding him didn't help his disposition, but he managed to learn his lessons anyway.

After an abbreviated two-year-old season of only three starts (one win, two seconds), Kelso was in danger of being sold due to a suspicious tendon. But no one was interested. About the same time, Mrs. du Pont hired Carl Hanford as trainer for her stable. After seeing Kelso work impressively, Hanford persuaded Mrs. du Pont to hold on to the gelding for a while longer. "The way he's been working, he might be any kind," Hanford told her.

The trainer certainly had no idea what he was about to unleash on the racing world. In Kelso's first start for Hanford, the three-year-old gelding zipped six furlongs in a Monmouth Park allowance to win by ten lengths. Kelso followed with a twelve-length score at Aqueduct. After a lackluster

eighth in the Arlington Classic, in which Kelso raced bottled up behind horses most of the way, the gelding seemed determined not to lose again. He made six more starts that year, winning all of them, including the two-mile Jockey Club Gold Cup (his first of five), mile and a quarter Hawthorne Gold Cup, and mile and five-eighths Lawrence Realization. He was a lock for 1960's Horse of the Year, following Armed (1947) as the second gelding to earn that title since the year-end awards were officially designated in 1936, and for champion three-year-old male.

While his four-year-old season was not as perfect-seeming as his three-year-old one, Kelso still dominated in key races. He captured the Met Mile, Suburban, and Brooklyn to win New York's Handicap Triple Crown; added an eight-length score in the Woodward (first of three); and won his second Gold Cup. He also made his turf debut that year, finishing second to T. V. Lark in the Washington, D.C., International, at Laurel Park. The International, which brought together race-horses from around the world and was a precursor to races such as the Arlington Million and Breeders' Cup Turf, would prove a frustrating obstacle for Kelso over the next few years. Of course, Kelso took home Horse of the Year honors for the second straight year, as well as champion older horse.

After a nice winter vacation Kelso returned to the races in May of his five-year-old year. He was entered in the Met Mile under 133 pounds, a weight he had carried to victory the year before in the Suburban. However, this was his first race off a layoff; he was conceding ten pounds to 1961 Kentucky Derby winner Carry Back and from thirteen to twenty-five pounds to the rest of the field. In an uncharacteristic performance Kelso simply failed to fire and finished a dull sixth. Carry Back was the winner.

Kelso rebounded with an allowance score; then he finished second in the Suburban and Monmouth handicaps to Beau Purple and Carry Back, respectively. Kelso's jockey for these races was Bill Shoemaker, who had replaced the retired Eddie Arcaro, Kelso's regular rider since the fall of 1960. Shoemaker's finesse riding style didn't mesh with Kelso's headstrong ways, so Carl

Hanford looked for another jockey and found a match in Ismael "Milo" Valenzuela, who had won the 1958 Derby and Preakness aboard Calumet Farm's Tim Tam.

In their first pairing, Kelso and Valenzuela won a turf allowance at Saratoga. Next, Kelso ran fourth, with Don Pierce aboard (Valenzuela had another commitment), in another turf allowance,

The mighty Kelso (opposite, with Ismael Valenzuela) dominated New York racing in the 1960s with victories in such races as the Woodward (above) and Suburban (left)

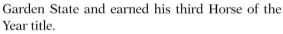

Kelso wins his first of five Jockey Club Gold Cups (above); In retirement, he gained a new career as a show jumper (below)

this one at Atlantic City. But once Valenzuela was back on board, he and Kelso won three straight, including easy scores in the Woodward and Gold Cup. After a second-place finish to old nemesis Beau Purple in the Man o' War Stakes on a soft turf course, Kelso tried for the Washington, D.C., International again. And once more he found himself the runner-up, this time to Match II, who became the only horse ever to pass Kelso in the stretch to win a race. Kelso had grabbed the lead early after dueling Beau Purple into submission and couldn't hold on over the deep turf course. Many observers called it Kelso's greatest performance; that his gameness and courage were on full display in the losing effort. He closed out the season with an easy win in the Governor's Plate at

Garden State and earned his third Horse of the Year title.

For his six-year-old season Kelso didn't receive his customary lengthy winter vacation. Instead he was sent to Florida for the Hialeah and Gulfstream meets, with mixed results. In four Florida starts, he came away with victories in the Seminole and Gulfstream Park handicaps, the latter under 130 pounds. He continued in 1963 in much the same vein, winning his next seven starts, including the Nassau County under 132 pounds, the Suburban under 133, and the Aqueduct under 134 — plus another easy win in the Gold Cup. Again, he was slated for the D.C., International, and once again he finished second, this time to the top turf runner Mongo.

At age seven in 1964, Kelso was the undisputed king of racing. He had received an incredible fourth Horse of the Year title for his brilliant 1963 season, and fans looked forward to seeing their hero race again. In fact, Kelso's popularity had led to a fan club with its own newsletter, *Kelsoland*, and he received fan mail at his own mailbox at Woodstock Farm. Racetrack officials courted Mrs. du Pont and Hanford to try and get the champion to make an appearance. Hollywood Park was one of these tracks, and Kelso's connections finally agreed to send him west. The trip ended up a disaster, from mechanical problems and delays on

the plane ride out to a loud-speaker near Kelso's stall at Hollywood that kept him tightly wound. The old gelding never settled down and ran like it, finishing unplaced in the Los Angeles Handicap and Californian Stakes.

Returned east, Kelso got a win under his belt in allowance company at Aqueduct, then finished second in the Suburban and Monmouth. The third-placed horse in the Monmouth was four-year-old Gun Bow, who would become perhaps Kelso's greatest and most testing rival. Gun Bow won their next meeting, the Brooklyn, in which Kelso was bumped at the gate and didn't factor in the race. But in the September 7 Aqueduct Handicap, the two horses met again, both carrying 128 pounds. Kelso prevailed by three-quarters of a length. In their next battle Gun Bow edged the old man by a nose in the Woodward. Then came the Washington, D.C., International.

On November 11, 1964, six international runners lined up against Kelso and Gun Bow at Laurel Park for the mile and a half International. But it might as well have been a match race. Gun Bow, the slight second choice to favored Kelso, jumped out to an early daylight lead with Kelso tracking him. Down the backstretch Kelso made his move, catching Gun Bow with a mile run in 1:34 4/5. The two competitors hit a mile and a quarter in 2:00 (Northern Dancer's Kentucky Derby-winning time that year) with Kelso a half-length in front and eight lengths separating the two from the rest of the pack. Then the gallant old gelding began to pull away, exerting his domi-

Allaire du Pont and her champion

nance once more. He bounded to the finish four and a half lengths in front of his rival in time of 2:23 4/5. The time was an American record and slashed two and two-fifths seconds off the Laurel course record.

After the race Allaire du Pont called Kelso's International victory his most exciting triumph, while an ecstatic Carl Hanford said the win "was tremendous." The International victory cinched Kelso's fifth title for Horse of the Year, but it also was his last major hurrah. He would race again at eight, winning three of six starts, but his glory days were past. Retired in early 1966, Kelso spent his twilight years at Woodstock Farm, still receiving fan mail and visitors. He died in 1983 at age twenty-six, a king to the last. *JM*

4 Secretariat's Belmont

FEW EVENTS, WHETHER IN SPORTS or any other endeavor, serve as a yardstick of greatness by which all others are measured. Although most people consider Secretariat's victory in the 1973 Belmont Stakes such a yardstick for Thoroughbred racing, history has shown that premise to be incorrect.

What Secretariat accomplished on that uncharacteristically hot June afternoon cannot be used as a measuring tool in any way, just as no mere mortal could measure his own feats of strength against those of Hercules. For on that one day, Secretariat, like Hercules, was driven by the gods. The combination of his thirty-one-length victory and American-record time of 2:24 for the mile and a half was so far beyond the guidelines that determine greatness that no one dares aim for it or even dreams of coming close to it.

It mattered little that only five opponents challenged him or that his main rival, Sham, fell apart

midway through the race and never raced again. This was all about Secretariat, who basically was running a match race against immortality. Every tick of the clock and every widening length brought him closer to the gates of the pantheon.

Secretariat's feats prior to the Belmont were extraordinary, including a Horse of the Year campaign as a two-year-old, and track-record-breaking performances in the Kentucky Derby and Preakness (that latter record recognized by the

Daily Racing Form following an electronic timer malfunction). Not only did he break Northern Dancer's Kentucky Derby record by three-fifths of a second, he accomplished the rare feat of running each quarter-mile faster than the one before.

A feeling of great anticipation that history was about to be made electrified the days preceding the Belmont. But it had been twenty-five years since Calumet Farm's Citation swept the Triple Crown, and the failed attempts by two of the

sport's most popular stars — Majestic Prince in 1969 and Canonero II in 1971 — were still fresh in everyone's minds.

And, despite Secretariat's record-breaking performance in the Kentucky Derby, there was the question of whether a son of Bold Ruler could get the grueling mile and a half. As the race grew closer, the pressure mounted for owner Penny Tweedy and trainer Lucien Laurin. They had combined to win two legs of the Triple Crown the previous year when Riva Ridge captured the Derby and Belmont, but a sloppy track, which the colt detested, likely cost him his place in history.

Secretariat, who had been syndicated by Tweedy and Claiborne Farm's Seth Hancock for a record $6,080,000 earlier in the year, was rapidly becoming a national hero. Following the Preakness, his photo appeared on the covers of *Time*, *Newsweek*, and *Sports Illustrated*. Two-thirds of the Triple Crown would not be enough this time. It was all or nothing for the handsome chestnut colt known as "Big Red."

On June 1, eight days before the Belmont, trainer Lucien Laurin sent Secretariat out for his final, serious work for the Belmont, and the big colt made it look easy, going three-quarters in 1:11 3/5.

Belmont day brought temperatures in the high eighties and a brisk breeze. In addition to that for Sham, there was some minor support for My Gallant, who had finished a well-beaten third in the Derby and Preakness before defeating older horses in a mile and one-eighth allowance race at Belmont, and for C.V. Whitney's late-closing Pvt. Smiles. The fans sent Secretariat off as the 1-10 favorite, with Sham at 5-1.

As co-host Jack Whittaker said at the opening of the CBS telecast, "There may be some people who do not know who or what Secretariat is — people who have been marooned on Pacific islands or lost in Amazonian jungles."

Secretariat made his way on to the track, greeted by exercise rider Charlie Davis aboard stable pony Billy Silver. When the crowd of more than

Secretariat in the Belmont paddock

55,000 caught their first glimpse of Big Red, they let out a loud cheer. It would be the first of several joyous outbursts on this day.

Despite the hot weather Secretariat was cool and calm in the post parade and warming up never turned a hair. Finally, it was post time, and the big colt walked into the gate with no problem. The crowd grew still, as if gathered at a launch site, waiting for a rocket to be sent into orbit.

A roar from the stands announced the start of the race. Secretariat broke sharply from the rail, and jockey Ron Turcotte, not wanting to get pinched back on the inside, gave the colt his head and he soon was on the lead, with Sham right alongside. As they rounded the first turn, Laffit Pincay on Sham decided to test Big Red early and took over the lead, inching away by a half-length.

Turcotte again let out a notch on Secretariat, who powered to the lead. Sham stayed with him, and for a short while it looked as if it were going to be a match race between the two big horses, who had put in a testing half-mile in :46 1/5. But then Secretariat began to ease clear, first by a length, then two, then three. With each stride, the distance between him and Sham increased. The three-quarters in 1:09 4/5 seemed almost surreal, even over the lightning-fast track. When Secretariat hit the mile marker in 1:34 1/5, opening up a seven-length lead, it became obvious the colt was going to attempt to do what had never been done before — sprint the entire mile and a half of the Belmont.

Midway on the turn, Secretariat was so far in front, track announcer Chic Anderson could only take a wild guess at the number of lengths. It was then that he made his still-famous call, "Secretariat is moving like a tremendous machine!"

This was a machine that had only two speed settings — fast and faster. Secretariat kept pouring it on. He blazed the mile and a quarter in a track-record 1:59 flat, hugging the rail as he turned into the stretch. In front of him was the portal into immortality. Off to the right, the packed grandstand was now a wall of noise. Everywhere, arms were flailing, hands were clapping, and fists were pumping in celebration. Down the stretch, the solitary figure of Secretariat seemed to be in another time zone than his rivals. The crowd knew they

Penny Tweedy leads in the Triple Crown winner

were witnessing history but wouldn't have a true measure of it until the final time was posted.

Turcotte took a look at the tote board and saw he was well on his way to shattering the track record of 2:26 3/5 set by Gallant Man in 1957. Shortly after Secretariat crossed the finish line, Anderson took a look at the tote board and announced prophetically, "Secretariat has accomplished the unbelievable task of breaking the track record by two and three-fifths seconds. That is a record that may stand forever."

In mentioning Secretariat's vanquished foes, Anderson said, "You can't be embarrassed by being beaten by the greatest horse in this century."

Secretariat returned to a hero's welcome. People shoved and squeezed their way closer to the winner's circle, many armed with cameras to record the historic moment. When Turcotte took off his cap and waved to the crowd, the roar from the grandstand rose to a glorious crescendo.

So ended the greatest performance in Thoroughbred history; one that transcended the Sport of Kings and raised the equine genus to another level. If there is one indelible image of racing, it is the footage of Secretariat, his bright chestnut coat and blue-and-white silks faded by the years, charging down the stretch in the 1973 Belmont. More than three decades later, it remains as magical as ever: a moment frozen in time. *SH*

5 Hollywood Park Introduces First Film Patrol

EVERY FRACTION OF A SECOND counts in horse racing. So in 1941, the ability to capture every instant of a race on film changed the sport forever. Stewards could suddenly make informed decisions about claims of foul and positions along the rail by replaying races over and over.

Aptly for the filmmaking state, California inaugurated the practice.

Hollywood Park ushered in the film patrol on May 23. Each of eight patrol judges, stationed at eighth-mile intervals around the one-mile track, held a motion-picture camera attached to a pair of binoculars. The device, called the binocular camera, was created by Lorenzo Del Riccio, a camera innovator who worked in the film industry. As the horses approached the observation post of each judge, he began taking pictures until the horses were a little more than a sixteenth of a mile beyond his post. "As they pass immediately before him he lowers the glasses to watch the race with the naked eye, but keeps the camera going," reported *The Blood-Horse*.

After the last race the films were developed and pieced together. The sixteen-millimeter film was spliced and viewed by the stewards the following morning and then made public. Hollywood's system was refined in 1945 when cameras were

Stewards review film from a race

installed in towers, which freed stewards from manning the cameras.

Nunzio Pariso was the first jockey suspended for an infraction caught on film: crowding on the last turn at Hollywood. From watching the race live, stewards believed he had contributed to the dangerous crowding on the last turn, and a review of the pictures confirmed their impression that Gold Bubble, with Pariso up, was responsible.

At the end of the fifty-one-day season, Hollywood officials deemed the film patrol a suc-

cess. The presiding steward reported that Marshall Cassidy, a New York steward who was in California evaluating the system, was also happy with the experiments. He predicted that other tracks would adopt the practice.

Cassidy was right. The film patrol quickly became an essential part of life at the racetrack, although some tracks, such as Churchill Downs and Ak-Sar-Ben, took well into the 1950s to purchase their own systems. Rockingham Park used a helicopter patrol in addition to filming the races

Recording the action from a film tower; (opposite) jockeys watch a head-on reply

close-up. Hollywood Park, in addition to the towers arrayed around the track, also had a system called performance observer. This involved twelve trained spectators following one horse as opposed to watching the race as a whole.

The film patrol initially seemed intrusive to some jockeys, but they came to see it as a help as it made everyone watch his step and ride more safely. Also, being able to watch themselves ride improved their ability. Mostly, however, it did help sort out what was foul and what was fair.

In October 1969, for example, Belmont Park had a string of five foul claims in one day. Twenty-two jockeys appeared at the theater to see the reruns of the inquiry-marked races about an hour before the next day's first post. Racing officials used the film's features to explain their decisions on punishments and excuses, running the film forward, backward, and in slow motion and stop action.

Today some stewards often watch the race live, while others watch on monitors that show both a pan shot of the race and a head-on view. Next, all the stewards review each race on film after it is run to make sure no infractions took place. Some race cameramen sit in towers that might capture the first turn or other important parts of the track; some tracks have different cameras set up for the turf track, all to capture each second and angle of every race.

A few high-profile cases in recent history have proved the value of the film patrol. In 1999 jockey Billy Patin was suspended from riding for five years after Arkansas racing officials ruled he had used a "battery" in an upset in the Arkansas Derby aboard a gelding named Valhol. In that instance, film footage showed a dark object falling from Patin's hand after he passed the finish.

Film has also cleared jockeys. After the 1995 Kentucky Derby, Kentucky racing officials examined videotape of an alleged handoff of a "battery" between Gary Stevens on winner Thunder Gulch and Pat Day, aboard third-place horse Timber Country. After scrutinizing the film, stewards decided they were merely looking at a victory handshake, and both riders were exonerated. The film patrol, which started as a novelty, now stands as a crucial part of racing. *EMG*

6

Nashua vs. Swaps

THE NASHUA VERSUS SWAPS match race of August 31, 1955, stirred up a public lather seldom witnessed in sports. The event had about four months to grow from concept to reality — public requirement almost — and it was lush with the elements of good drama. There were a villain and a hero, and which was which generally depended on the observer's geographical loyalties.

To the Easterner, accustomed to great stables landing great prizes with royally bred horses, Swaps was the villain for knocking Nashua off his perch by winning the Kentucky Derby and spoiling the Triple Crown. To the Westerner, long accustomed to knocks on his homebreds, Nashua was the villain inasmuch as he was a symbol of all that Eastern prejudice.

To the Easterner, the breeder-owner and trainer of Swaps were the antitheses of how a Thoroughbred outfit ought to be run. Rex Ellsworth and Mesh Tenney wore cowboy hats, tended to treat horses like other animals, did not seem impressed by socializing, and disdained some of the traditional cadences of the backstretch. Tenney might sleep in a stall and from time to time be seen astride one of Ellsworth's Thoroughbreds in a Western saddle.

To the Westerner, Nashua's Belair Stud outfit, inherited by dashing William Woodward Jr., typified the attitude that success in Thoroughbred racing was the birthright of a certain kind of sportsman and that interlopers were not welcome. Even the horse seemed arrogant, with his needlessly close finishes and high-fashion pedigree.

If there were characters in the play that were above ill will, they were probably Nashua's trainer, Sunny Jim Fitzsimmons, and the star jockeys, Eddie Arcaro and Bill Shoemaker. Fitzsimmons

was a national sporting treasure, and one did not have to know much about him to be struck by this severely bent old gentleman with the kind eyes and distant history of struggle and sustained excellence. As for the riders, Arcaro had ridden with such prominence on both coasts and in between that he added little to the East versus West taste that the affair had otherwise. To a lesser extent, the same was true of Shoemaker.

Nashua was bred by Woodward's father, William Woodward Sr., who was associated with the Hanover National Bank, owned historic Belair Stud in Maryland, raced abroad as well as here, and had his horses raised in the Bluegrass, at the Hancock family's Claiborne Farm. Woodward's diary mentioned such things as dining with the king of England and shopping for Chippendale furniture while abroad to see his horse run in the Epsom Derby.

Nashua's sire, Nasrullah, was a plum American breeders long had coveted, and one of the most dynamic of that set, Arthur B. "Bull" Hancock Jr., had finally secured him. By the time Nashua and others in the stallion's first American-sired crop were foaled, Nasrullah was the reigning leader on the English sire list. The dam of Nashua, Segula, was a stakes-placed daughter of Woodward Sr.'s and Fitzsimmons' 1939 Derby–Belmont winner Johnstown, one of the brace of classic winners they campaigned in the 1930s. The second dam, Sekhmet, was by the French classic winner and leading sire Sardanapale.

For all the contrasts of Nashua's and Swaps' backgrounds, insofar as pedigree was concerned, there was less difference in fact than in image. Khaled, sire of Swaps, had been bred by the Aga Khan, same as Nasrullah. Khaled was a high-class English stakes winner by Hyperion, who at that time represented the ultimate in international pedigree fashion inasmuch as he had a decade's head start on Nasrullah.

Despite the class and fashion of Khaled's background, Ellsworth and Tenney managed to introduce a rag-tag image. Khaled was alternated between breeding and racing (without further success) after his importation and before his eventual permanent retirement to Ellsworth's stark California ranch.

Nashua (left) atones for his Derby loss to Swaps (opposite, below) in their Chicago match race

The dam of Swaps was Iron Reward, by the expensive Beau Pere, and the next dam was Iron Maiden, destined to foal a Kentucky Derby winner for Calumet Farm in Iron Liege.

At two, Nashua struck early and in the highest context of top-level Eastern racing. He won six of eight as a juvenile in 1954, including such cher-ished targets as the Hopeful Stakes at Saratoga and the Futurity at Belmont Park. He was voted the champion two-year-old colt.

The following winter, despite Nashua's stub-bornness, Arcaro forced him to win the Flamingo Stakes and Florida Derby in Florida. Then, with Arcaro suspended, Ted Atkinson rode him in the

Swaps turns back the powerful rush of Nashua in the Derby

Wood Memorial, in which Nashua surged ahead just in time to defeat his top rival of the previous year, Summer Tan.

Swaps generated a *Sports Illustrated* headline about California's having a glint in the eye when he won the Santa Anita Derby. Earlier he had turned in a promising juvenile campaign, winning the moderately important June Juvenile and two other races from six starts. At three he was a different colt, hinting of brilliance in two starts before the Santa Anita Derby. Then, in his debut at Churchill Downs a week before the Derby, he was so startling in winning a six-furlong prep that on Derby Day he prevailed for some time as betting favorite. Eventually, Nashua

With Swaps back in California, Nashua makes easy work of the Preakness

was the top pick at 6-5, but Swaps was second choice over Summer Tan, who had won the previous year's Garden State Stakes by nine lengths. So, it could not be truly said that Derby fans and racegoers overlooked Swaps.

Shoemaker put Swaps on the lead early, and the powerful rush of Nashua to challenge was turned back. Swaps soared to victory. It was not a major upset in terms of odds, but to many fans it was a stunner.

Nashua resumed winning in the East and Midwest, and Swaps returned to California, where he repeatedly ramped up a status as the state-bred hero too good to have been imagined.

The knights of East and West were summoned to the place epitomizing the Midwest, Chicago, for the match. Ben Lindheimer, head of Washington Park in the city of "broad shoulders," lured them with a $100,000 purse, winner-take-all. The conditions were Derby conditions: one and a quarter miles with 126 pounds up. A crowd of more than 35,000 turned up for the weekday match.

Past performances invited the presumption that the sleek Swaps would set the pace, but Arcaro came out of the gate whoop-de-doing on the husky Nashua and guided him to a path the great rider perceived as the best available footing. Nashua led early, turned back Swaps several times, and raced home by six and a half lengths. To the East, justice had been served. To the West, a travesty had been visited upon the worthy.

The horses had hardly cooled out before word that Swaps had been slightly lame began to pick at the fabric of the moment.

Nashua prevailed as Horse of the Year that season, but Swaps' astounding streak of track, American, and world records the following year earned him that title at four. Thus, like many other match races, the Nashua–Swaps affair could be labeled inconclusive, with neither side's adrenaline subsiding as a result of its having taken place.

On August 31, 1955, however, in the froth and fervor of its lead up and unfolding, it was a race like no other. *ELB*

Dr. Fager's World-Record Mile

ALTHOUGH DR. FAGER's world-record mile in 1:32 1/5 was a summit that attracted the nation's top climbers, no one was able to reach it for nearly three decades.

It finally was conquered in 1997, and has been bettered several times since, but those records were all achieved over the rock-hard turf courses in Southern California and at Belmont Park. It wasn't until 2003 that the Doctor's world record was equaled on the dirt, but that was accomplished under twenty-one fewer pounds. So, here we are after thirty-seven years and Dr. Fager's record mile, under 134 pounds, still has not been broken.

When Dr. Fager arrived at Arlington Park on August 22, 1968, two days before the Washington Park Handicap, everyone knew the world record for the mile was in danger of being broken. After all, the Arlington Speedway had seen the record fall several times, the latest being the great Buckpasser's 1:32 3/5 mile two years earlier in the Arlington Classic.

Buckpasser had become the first horse ever to crack the 1:33 mile. His record, however, nearly was broken two months later when Bold Bidder, carrying 120 pounds, captured the Washington Park Handicap in 1:32 4/5.

By the summer of '68, Dr. Fager had established himself as one of the fastest Thoroughbreds of all time, and his wild nature on the track and hell-bent-for-leather approach to racing was the perfect formula for an all-out assault on the record. He ran with a reckless abandon never seen before. Sure, there were Thoroughbred rockets such as Swaps and other brilliant free-running horses, but Dr. Fager looked and ran as if he should have been leading a herd of wild mustangs across the Great Plains.

He had already run the fastest mile ever in New York by a three-year-old, equaled the track record

for a mile and a quarter at Aqueduct under 132 pounds, and shattered the track records for a mile and one-eighth and a mile and a quarter at Rockingham Park. He had also come within a fifth of a second of the seven-furlong record at Aqueduct under a 130 pounds, a record he eventually would destroy by a full second carrying a staggering 139 pounds.

So, there was a reason the eyes of the racing world were focused on Arlington Park on August 24. Dr. Fager was being asked to carry 134 pounds, but weight never seemed to faze him or his trainer, John Nerud. Nerud never ducked weight, and, in fact, would later tell New York Racing Association racing secretary Tommy Trotter to assign Dr. Fager 145 pounds for his career finale, the seven-furlong Vosburgh Handicap, in order to send Dr. Fager home with a bang never before heard. Trotter couldn't justify putting that much weight on the horse and settled for "only" 139 pounds.

Tartan Farm owner William McKnight always gave Nerud free rein to run the stable's racing and breeding operation, and Nerud took advantage of it by building one of the most successful operations in the country. He knew in Dr. Fager he had a horse that would leave a long-lasting legacy, and

Dr. Fager flies to a world-record mile (below); trainer John Nerud walks with his speedy star to the track for a workout

Dr. Fager winning the Whitney prior to his record-setting effort

the Washington Park Handicap was the race in which the son of Rough'n Tumble—Aspidistra would show off his true greatness.

Dr. Fager and Nerud arrived in Chicago in the middle of an oppressive heat wave, and the horse began to get a bit on edge. Dr. Fager was prone to colic, having suffered several bouts in the past, and Nerud knew he had to watch him very closely. The afternoon before the race he sat with the horse, talking to him and keeping him as relaxed as possible. That night he walked him around the shed to keep him moving. Dr. Fager settled down and the next day was ready to set the racing world on fire.

Fortunately, the sweltering heat broke on race day, thanks to a cool wind that whipped through the Chicago area. Nerud and jockey Braulio Baeza did not talk about records before the race. Nerud always believed in giving his horses as easy a race as possible and never set out to break a

record. This day would be no different.

A field of ten was entered, and if there was any horse even remotely capable of competing with Dr. Fager it was the California invader Racing Room, who was in receipt of eighteen pounds. Racing Room had brilliant speed going short or long and was equally at home on dirt or turf.

It was apparent that Dr. Fager would not have an easy lead, with the presence of former world-record holder Hedevar, who had helped run Dr. Fager into the ground in the previous year's Woodward Stakes, setting the race up for Hedevar's stablemate and Dr. Fager's arch rival Damascus. Also in the field was the three-year-old Kentucky Sherry, who had run the co-fastest opening six furlongs and equaled the fastest opening half-mile in the history of the Kentucky Derby.

But Dr. Fager had always shown the ability to come from off the pace in one-turn races. Although he broke on top, when Hedevar,

were expecting the battle of all battles, with Alydar trying to stop his nemesis from becoming racing's eleventh Triple Crown winner.

Despite his dominance over Alydar in the win-loss column, Affirmed remained linked with his rival as if a single entity. Their names slid smoothly over the tongue like some classic comedy team. Saying one name without the other was like saying Abbott without Costello or Laurel without Hardy. The only way Affirmed would be able to separate himself from Alydar was to write his own chapter in the history books, and that could only be accomplished by sweeping the Triple Crown.

But even the enormity of that feat would be lessened slightly, with Seattle Slew having captured racing's prestigious triad the year before, and with Secretariat's record-breaking tour de

Locked in eternal combat: Affirmed (on the rail) and Alydar

Affirmed leads his rival to the wire in the Kentucky Derby

force in 1973 still fresh in everyone's mind. This one would have to be special: a race so memorable it would find its own niche in racing lore.

Alydar's trainer, John Veitch, felt he had to try something new, especially after the Preakness, when Alydar appeared to have Affirmed measured only again to come up just short. Affirmed seemed to use his ears as antennae, and whenever he sensed danger, an ear would jut out in that direction. That's when his rider Steve Cauthen knew Affirmed had honed in on the enemy. In the Preakness, just when it appeared as if Alydar finally was going to get by Affirmed, out came Affirmed's right ear. Alydar, despite drawing seven and a half lengths clear of third-place finisher Believe It, was unable to make up another inch on Affirmed, who dug in to win by a neck.

For the Belmont, Veitch decided to remove Alydar's blinkers in the hope it would give the Calumet colt the slight edge he was missing. Neither Veitch nor Affirmed's trainer, Laz Barrera, was about to take it easy with his respective horse, despite the hard race in the Preakness. Each knew the Belmont was going to be decided in the trenches, as had most of the other battles between the two colts, and going a mile and a

half, both would have to be dead-fit and sharp.

The previous year Veitch had worked three-year-old filly Our Mims the full mile and a half distance prior to her victory in the twelve-furlong Coaching Club American Oaks. He saw no reason not to do the same with Alydar. Ten days before the race Alydar worked a mile and a half in 2:43 3/5, then came back four days later and drilled a strong six furlongs in 1:12 3/5. There was no doubt about his fitness. To hone his colt's sharpness, Veitch had Alydar blow out three furlongs the day before the Belmont in :35 flat in the slop.

Barrera gave Affirmed a series of long gallops to build his stamina. Nine days before the race the trainer worked the colt a mile in 1:40 1/5, then gave him a five-furlong drill in 1:01 six days later.

The stage was set for one of the most anticipated battles in many years. Only three others showed against the dynamic duo, with the hard-knocking Darby Creek Road the only one given any chance to pose even a remote threat. The crowd of more than 65,000 made Affirmed the 1-2 favorite, with Alydar at even money.

Affirmed, as expected, broke sharply and went right to the lead. Alydar, directly inside Affirmed, moved up to challenge, and it became obvious that his jockey, Jorge Velasquez, was going to make a race of it early. After establishing his position within striking range of his rival, Velasquez took a slight hold of Alydar, enabling Affirmed to open a length lead around the first turn. The opening quarter in a slow :25 played to Affirmed's advantage, as he was already in control of the race.

Turning into the backstretch, Affirmed was still ambling along on the lead, with a snail-like half in :50 under his belt. Velasquez, sensing the urgency of the situation, decided it was time to turn the Belmont into a match race. He moved Alydar up to Affirmed's throatlatch, and the battle everyone had been hoping for was on.

With almost a mile still to go, Velasquez seemed content to keep Alydar a neck off Affirmed. The opening three-quarters were run in a lethargic 1:14, but the pace was now quickening, with both horses drawing five lengths clear of the others. Alydar continued to put pressure on Affirmed, and the pair went the next quarter locked together in :23 2/5 to reach the mile marker in a solid 1:37 2/5.

At the quarter pole Alydar moved in for the kill, but Velasquez was well aware this was no ordinary prey. Both Cauthen and Velasquez went to a series of right-handed whips. Alydar pulled on even terms with Affirmed nearing the three-sixteenths pole. If he were ever going to crack the thick shell of Affirmed, it would be now, going a mile and a half. Both colts were still at each other's throat passing the eighth pole, a dozen lengths ahead of Darby Creek Road. The crowd was going wild. This was everything they had hoped for and more.

Inside the eighth pole Cauthen switched the whip to his left hand and rapped Affirmed a half-dozen times to the wire. Alydar, still under a right-handed whip from Velasquez, was fully stretched, straining to get by a stubborn Affirmed. But Affirmed, as he had done so often, refused to be beaten and held on to win by a head, completing the mile and a half in 2:26 4/5, the third-fastest Belmont ever run at the time. In

Affirmed and Alydar in the stretch run of the Preakness

all the excitement, the fact that he had become racing's eleventh Triple Crown winner was almost forgotten.

Nearly three decades later, the 1978 Belmont still is considered by many the greatest race ever run. Although it secured Affirmed's place in history, the colt's true worth to this day is measured not by that race or his other victories but by his unwavering courage time after time against a foe who forced him to be great. *SH*

10 Woody Stephens' Five Belmonts

AS YOU ENTER the Belmont Park clubhouse, you can't help but notice the large painting and numerous trophies on display beneath a large arch, under which is inscribed "Woody's Corner."

This well-deserved shrine is dedicated to Woodford C. "Woody" Stephens, whose feat of five consecutive Belmont Stakes victories remains one of sports' greatest achievements.

The painting by Anthony Alonso that dominates the display shows Stephens aboard his pony, along with his five Belmont winners.

To win America's most grueling race, with its mile and a half distance, is an accomplishment any trainer would be proud of. But to win it five years in a row, as Stephens did from 1982 to 1986, is beyond comprehension. Just to have a horse entered in five consecutive Belmonts is amazing.

Stephens, who was inducted in the Racing Hall of Fame in 1976, won the race with horses on the lead the whole way, coming from just off the pace, and coming from far back. He won it on fast, muddy, and sloppy tracks, and won for four different owners. Remarkably, only one of the five horses went off as the favorite.

Stephens' remarkable run started with Henryk de Kwiatkowski's Conquistador Cielo, who won by fourteen lengths in the slop. The following year Stephens won with August Belmont IV's Caveat, who came from eleventh to win going away by three and a half lengths. In 1984 he sent out Kentucky Derby winner Swale, owned by Claiborne Farm, to win by four lengths as the 3-2 favorite. Stephens outdid himself the following year, finishing first and second with Brushwood Stable's Creme

Fraiche and de Kwiatkowski's Stephan's Odyssey. Stephens completed his streak the way it began, with a victory by a de Kwiatkowski-owned horse in the slop. That horse was Danzig Connection, who paid a generous eighteen dollars to win. As the horse crossed the finish line, track announcer Marshall Cassidy saluted his trainer's feat by saying "Congratulations, Woody Stephens."

The 1982 Belmont hardly seemed like a logical spot for Conquistador Cielo, who had put on a dazzling display of speed only five days earlier, winning the one-mile Metropolitan Handicap by seven and a quarter lengths over older horses in a scorching 1:33. Prior to that, he had won a one-mile allowance race at Belmont by eleven lengths in 1:34 1/5.

Stephens, who was sixty-eight at the time, was known as a patient trainer and not one prone to audacious moves with his horses. Conquistador Cielo had suffered a saucer (or stress) fracture as a two-year-old, but the injury healed the following winter with the help of an electro-therapy machine.

Following the Met Mile, Stephens went back to the test barn to observe the colt, and when he saw how well he had cooled out, the astute trainer started thinking about running him right back in the Belmont. When everything went perfectly over the next few days, Stephens made the decision to run.

In the field were Kentucky Derby winner Gato Del Sol, Preakness winner Aloma's Ruler, and Preakness runner-up Linkage, who surprisingly was sent off as the 2-1 favorite.

The race turned out to be no contest, as Conquistador Cielo, under Laffit Pincay Jr., took over the lead after a quarter-mile, turned back a challenge with a half-mile to go, then opened a big lead and kept widening it, winning under a hand ride. Gato Del Sol finished a distant second.

Stephens, who had won the Kentucky Derby with Cannonade in 1974 and the Preakness with Blue Man in 1952, had completed his own Triple Crown.

In 1983 Stephens sent out a horse that was the complete opposite of Conquistador Cielo. Caveat, who was a son of Cannonade and owned primarily by Belmont in partnership with the colt's breed-er, Ryehill Farm, had no early speed, coming from thirteenth to finish second in the Arkansas Derby and again from thirteenth to win the Derby Trial Stakes. Going into the Kentucky Derby, he had already started eighteen times. In the Run for the Roses, Caveat came from seventeenth to finish third, beaten only two and a quarter lengths by Sunny's Halo.

Given Caveat's running style, Stephens skipped the Preakness, prepping his horse for the Belmont with an allowance victory at Belmont. Caveat went off as the second choice in the Belmont, only ten cents to the dollar behind Slew o' Gold.

With Pincay aboard, Caveat unleashed a power-ful run from some eighteen lengths back and at the quarter-pole was on the rail and only a length and a half behind pace-setting Au Point and Slew o' Gold, who had been tracking him throughout.

When Angel Cordero Jr., on Slew o' Gold, brought his colt in on Au Point, closing up the

Creme Fraiche (1985) and Danzig Connection (1986) hole on the rail, Pincay had a choice to make: take up and go around and risk clipping Au Point's heels or stay where he was and try to get through. He chose the latter. When the hole closed even further, Caveat went crashing into the rail. But he quickly recovered and burst to the lead before drawing off to a convincing score.

Stephens had become the first trainer to score back-to-back Belmont victories since Lucien Laurin with Riva Ridge and Secretariat in 1972 and '73.

The 1984 Belmont looked like a great spot for Stephens' third straight Belmont, something that hadn't been accomplished since Frank McCabe won the 1886, '87, and '88 runnings.

Although Swale had run an inexplicably poor race in the Preakness after winning the Derby easily, he still was sent off as the 3-2 favorite in what was considered to be a weak field. With Pincay aboard, Swale went right to the front and was never in any danger as he set slow fractions before drawing clear to defeat 26-1 shot Pine Circle. With a final time of 2:27 1/5, he joined Stage Door Johnny as the fourth-fastest Belmont winner of all time.

Not bad for a horse considered the stable's second-stringer. When two-year-old champ Devil's Bag failed to duplicate his brilliance at three and

was retired before the Derby, it was Swale, a six-time stakes winner himself at two and three, including grade I wins in the Florida Derby, Belmont Futurity, and Young America Stakes, who stepped in to replace him.

Tragically, Swale died only a week after the Belmont, rearing and falling over while being bathed. The exact cause of death, thought at first to be a heart attack, was never announced, although there were eyewitness claims that the horse was electrocuted by a fan that had fallen off a window sill and landed in the puddle of water in which Swale was standing.

By 1985 Stephens had already been talking about retirement for several years. But as he continued to send out top-class stakes horses, he kept those thoughts in the back of his head, especially after finishing second in the 1985 Kentucky Derby with 13-1 shot Stephan's Odyssey.

In the Belmont, Stephens sent out the potent entry of Stephan's Odyssey, with Pincay aboard, and Creme Fraiche, ridden by Eddie Maple. Creme Fraiche, a gelded son of Rich Cream, had put a major scare into Kentucky Derby winner Spend a Buck, falling a neck short of upsetting him in the rich Jersey Derby, with a $2-million bonus on the line for Spend a Buck. The son of Buckaroo had skipped the Preakness to try for

Garden State Park's big bucks, awarded to any horse sweeping the Cherry Hill Mile, Garden State Stakes, Kentucky Derby, and Jersey Derby.

Even without Spend a Buck, the Belmont still drew a strong field. In addition to the Stephens entry were the record-breaking Preakness winner Tank's Prospect and Preakness runner-up Chief's Crown, the defending two-year-old champion. El Basco, a close third in the Jersey Derby, also received a good deal of support.

But as the field charged down the stretch, it was Creme Fraiche and Stephan's Odyssey who had drawn clear of the pack. All Stephens could think watching them battle was, "If they dead-heat, then I'll have five Belmonts."

In the final yards, however, it was Creme Fraiche who edged away from his stablemate to win by a half-length. It was another four and a half lengths back to Chief's Crown in third. Stephens had now ventured into virgin territory with his fourth straight Belmont victory.

For Stephens, the thought of winning five consecutive Belmonts pretty much evaporated in the fall of 1985 when his best young horse, Young America runner-up Danzig Connection, finished a dismal twelfth in the Breeders' Cup Juvenile. X-rays following the race revealed a bone chip in the colt's right foreleg. Following arthroscopic surgery, the son of Danzig, whom Stephens also had trained, was put back in training the following winter, breezing for the first time on March 8.

Danzig Connection made it back to the races and was beaten in a pair of allowance races before winning the Peter Pan Stakes, Belmont Park's nine-furlong prep for the Belmont Stakes. Still not having proven himself in top-class company, he seemed to be a cut below Kentucky Derby winner and Preakness runner-up Ferdinand, who actually was made second choice in the Belmont behind Arkansas Derby winner Rampage, who had finished an unlucky fourth in the Derby.

Stephens had pretty much resigned himself to the fact that his Belmont streak was about to come to an end, especially with Ferdinand appearing to be a natural mile and a half horse. "You have to be awful lucky to have a horse to run in the Belmont five times, much less win it,"

Stephens said the week before the race. But when the track came up a sea of slop on Belmont day, Stephens thought that the California-based Ferdinand, trained by Charlie Whittingham, might be at a disadvantage, not having run over a wet track before. Suddenly, there was hope.

With Chris McCarron aboard, Danzig Connection sat right off the pace set by Mogambo. Ferdinand, closer up than usual, was a threatening presence in third. At the quarter-pole,

Swale winning the 1984 Belmont

Danzig Connection held a slight lead over John's Treasure and Ferdinand, who looked primed for the kill. Ferdinand battled to the eighth pole but couldn't get by the stubborn Danzig Connection, who drew clear, winning by a length and a quarter, with John's Treasure just getting up for second over Ferdinand.

Stephens had done it — five consecutive Belmont Stakes victories. He did manage to get a horse to the 1987 Belmont, but Gone West was geared more toward eight- and nine-furlong races, and he tired after making a brief bid on the far turn, finishing sixth.

The next time you're at Belmont, stop by "Woody's Corner." It is much more than a painting and a collection of trophies. It is a corner of history. *SH*

11

Regret Wins the Kentucky Derby

REGRET COULD BE AN ICON for the Kentucky Derby — after all, many contend, her 1915 decisive victory against the boys launched the heraldry that makes the Run for the Roses much more than a horse race.

Colonel Matt Winn, general manager of Churchill Downs at that time, knew how to wring every drop of ink from the press and create a sensation when the opportunity presented itself. He easily spotted the exponential effect of a talented, undefeated filly bred and owned by mining tycoon Harry Payne Whitney taking on the country's best three-year-old colts.

Winn went so far as sending a letter to Algernon Daingerfield of The Jockey Club in New York City imploring him to persuade Regret's owner to include the Whitney horses in the Kentucky Derby "as the names of Regret and such horses would do us a lot of good in an advertising way."

Whitney acquiesced and agreed to send Regret by freight train from his farm in Red Bank, New Jersey, to Louisville, Kentucky. The horse's trainer, James Rowe Sr., and jockey, Joe Notter, would accompany the well-bred filly, who had been born in the very shadow of Monmouth Park at Brookdale Farm.

By Broomstick and out of Jersey Lightning, Regret descended from the important producer Maria West, who stamped the best of her runners with the same rich chestnut coat and blazed face Regret wore. The family of Shelby West, a Louisville horseman, had brought Maria across the Blue Ridge Mountains from Virginia in the pre-Civil War days. Regret herself was of moderate build, deep-chested but still feminine enough to be mistaken for a colt only occasionally.

As a two-year-old in 1912, Regret raced just three times, all within a two-week period in August and all stakes sprints for juveniles. She took the Saratoga Special over seasoned performers in her debut and followed it up with victories in the Sanford Memorial and Hopeful stakes.

After her opening trifecta, Regret was given almost nine months off from active competition but not from training for the Derby, despite the prolonged wintry weather in the Northeast.

"There was a hedge alongside the training track, and a late snowstorm left six- and eight-foot drifts," her jockey, Notter, told racing writer Charles Hatton years later. "Whitney hired every man he could get to shovel snow so Regret could work out."

Six days before the Derby, Rowe and Notter arrived in Louisville with Regret and a stable pony in tow. Rather than getting a room at the fancy Galt House, the two men wanted to keep a close eye on their Derby hopeful.

Rowe and Notter stayed in the stall next to Regret all week. The filly had not done so well shipping to Louisville. Her appetite waned for

several days as she was "in love" (polite parlance for being in season). In her last work she only went the Derby distance of a mile and a quarter in 2:08 and change. Midweek it began to pour, rain seeping in through cracks in the barn, dampening the spirits of the small entourage.

"We were all perfectly miserable," Notter told a reporter years later. "Mr. Rowe was beginning to wonder if he should run Regret ... I told him not to worry. The mare will be all right. We will be in front before the others can get on stride."

Derby day dawned clear and bright. All the hoopla over the showdown between the filly and the colts drew a crowd of 40,000 to Churchill Downs. Patrons arrived in open-air streetcars, Model Ts, horse and buggies, and on foot. Magnolias bloomed beside the streets, with signs advertising lager strangely juxtaposed next to the fragrant white blossoms. Men wore three-piece suits and matching hats, while colorful, heeled pumps peeked out from beneath women's skirts, getting their first glimpse of daylight as hemlines began rising that year.

But the lady who drew the most attention that day was Regret, who seemed to know she was the belle of the ball. As she waited, albeit a little nervously, in the paddock, bettors watched her carefully, seeking visible evidence that the lady was

Regret wears the Derby roses; (opposite) Regret with James Rowe (on left) and H.P. Whitney

Regret at Saratoga; trainer James Rowe

capable of beating the boys. The race had drawn fifteen colts to take on Regret, the largest Derby field ever at the time.

"The comments were as various as were the opinions of the thousands who pushed their way in and out of the betting enclosure to register their sentiments in the form of pari-mutuel tickets," wrote racing journalist J.L. Dempsey, who surmised that the volume of betting was nearly double the amount handled on any of the previous forty Derbies.

Kentucky hardboots must have liked what they saw because Regret was made the 2.65-1 favorite at post time.

She did not disappoint. She headed for the front of the pack, as Notter had predicted, and stayed there, under restraint, all the way to the

wire, finishing the race in 2:05 2/5. Pebbles sat in second the entire time, but never threatened, finishing two lengths behind Regret. Sharpshooter, another two lengths behind Pebbles, took third, also having retained his position through the mile and a quarter race.

"It turned out to be one of the easiest victories of my entire riding career," Notter told a reporter after he had retired. "It was so easy, in fact, that I can't count it among my greatest racing thrills."

For Whitney, though, the victory confirmed Regret's standing as his favorite Thoroughbred, quite an achievement considering Whitney's immense success as an owner and breeder.

As the Derby winner jogged back to the stand, the crowd gave her another great roar of

applause, for her accomplishment as a Thoroughbred and as a filly. Officials warmly offered Whitney congratulations as he strode up to admire the horse he had bred.

"The glory of winning this event is big enough, and Regret can retire to the New Jersey farm any time," Whitney told the press. "I told Rowe I didn't care if she never won another race if she could only land this one. I have seen much bigger crowds than this one in the East and abroad, but

Handicap at Saratoga but did not race again that year. She had battled respiratory ailments off and on, which gave her slight wind problems. She lost her first race the following year, finishing last in the Saratoga Handicap, then easily won in allowance company in her only other start at four.

Her best effort turned out to be in the 1917 Brooklyn Handicap, when the five-year-old mare succumbed in the last stride to her stablemate,

Genuine Risk in 1980 becomes the second filly to the win the Derby

I never saw a more enthusiastic one. It's great."

Everyone was impressed with the filly's victory. A new brand of cigars, with Regret's name on the box and her image engraved on the bands, appeared in Louisville the very next day.

Years later Winn told Hatton: "Regret's victory made the Derby. It was when Mr. Whitney brought her out here from the East and she won that the race began to be nationally interesting and important."

As for Regret, after returning to New York from Louisville, she won the Saranac

the nine-year-old gelding Borrow, who won in 1:49 2/5, at the time an American record for nine furlongs. The field that year included two other Kentucky Derby winners — Old Rosebud and Omar Khayyam — and the outstanding handicappers Roamer and Stromboli.

Though this was notably her best race, it is not the one that stands in perpetuity. Regret hung her star as the first filly to win the Derby, and for sixty-five more years, no other filly until Genuine Risk in 1980 matched that achievement, making it burn brighter each passing year. *RB*

D. Wayne Lukas Wins Six Straight Triple Crown Races

GRINDSTONE CLOSED RELENTLESSLY through the Churchill Downs homestretch, just getting up in the final strides to edge Cavonnier by a scant nose to win the 1996 Kentucky Derby. The victory had plenty of sentimental value as it was the first Derby win in numerous attempts for the colt's owner, Lexington businessman and philanthropist W.T. Young. But Grindstone's win held even greater historical value: It was the sixth consecutive victory in a Triple Crown race for trainer D. Wayne Lukas — a record likely never to be matched.

For racing pundits it almost seemed a given that Lukas would have a top contender for the classics; after all, the former basketball coach seemed to have an endless supply of good runners for a string of deep-pocketed owners. In fact, in the 1996 Derby he entered four other horses along with Grindstone, with Peter Mitchell's Prince of Thieves finishing third.

But only three years earlier Lukas had been in the midst of a major training slump. He failed to win a grade I race during a thirty-month period, costing him clients and nearly bankrupting him. He was dogged by bad publicity surrounding the breakdown of Union City in the 1993 Preakness. And then in December 1993 a runaway Tabasco Cat ran down and seriously injured Lukas' son and assistant trainer, Jeff, who was trying to stop the colt.

Ironically, it was Tabasco Cat, a shiny chestnut son of Storm Cat, who helped turn the stable's fortunes around. Owned by Young, who had remained loyal to Lukas, in partnership with David Reynolds, Tabasco Cat entered the 1994 Preakness Stakes off a sixth-place finish behind winner Go for Gin in the Derby. The third choice behind Go for Gin and Derby third Blumin Affair, Tabasco Cat received a smart ride from Pat Day and got up to win by three-quarters of a length over the Derby winner. The victory was an emo-

tional one for Lukas and his first in the race since
Tank's Prospect in 1985.

"I'd long ago tried to separate this horse from
what happened to Jeff. It would have been unfair
to hold it against him. Still, it's only right that we
dedicate this race to Jeff," said Lukas after the
Preakness.

But Tabasco Cat wasn't finished. He returned to
take the Belmont Stakes by two lengths, again

over Go for Gin, to give Lukas his first victory in
the mile and a half classic.

In 1995 Lukas hit the Triple Crown trail armed
with several legitimate contenders. Topping the
list was Timber Country, a handsome chestnut
son of Woodman. Winner of the 1994 Champagne
Stakes and Breeders' Cup Juvenile, Timber
Country had been named champion two-year-old
colt, and although he was winless in his Derby

Thunder Gulch pulls an upset in 1995, helping make Lukas a familiar presence in the Churchill Downs winner's circle

preps, he had still finished well enough for Lukas to remain confident in the colt's chances. Also high on the stable roster was the filly Serena's Song, who had finished a narrow second to champion Flanders in the 1994 Breeders' Cup Juvenile Fillies. She had won all four of her starts along the Derby trail, including the Jim Beam Stakes over the boys. Lukas entering a filly in the Derby came as no surprise; he had won his first

Run for the Roses with the roan filly Winning Colors in 1988.

But it was the overlooked, or perhaps underestimated (bettors made him 24-1), Thunder Gulch who took the roses. Timber Country was third, while Serena's Song finished well back after setting the pace.

A chestnut son of Gulch owned by Michael Tabor, Thunder Gulch had come into the Derby with victories in the Fountain of Youth and Florida Derby under his belt. Gary Stevens, who, like Lukas, had won his first Derby with Winning Colors, was aboard.

Even with the "wrong horse" winning the Derby, Lukas had quietly built a three-race win streak in Triple Crown events. Both Thunder Gulch and Timber Country headed on to Pimlico for the Preakness, and this time, the "right horse" won. In the two weeks between the Derby and Preakness, Lukas tried some new tactics with Timber Country, including getting him in the bit earlier and keeping him focused. The changes paid off as the colt got past his stablemate in the stretch and held off the determined local hero, Oliver's Twist. This time Thunder Gulch was third.

The trio moved on to Belmont Park for the Belmont Stakes. However, a virus knocked Timber Country out of the race, and it was up to Thunder Gulch to carry the stable's hopes, which he did in fine fashion, capturing the Belmont by two lengths as the favorite. Lukas' fifth straight win in a classic, an unprecedented achievement much like Woody Stephens' five consecutive Belmonts in the 1980s, also gave the trainer a personal Triple Crown.

And with Grindstone's Derby victory, Lukas set the bar even higher, at six straight classic wins. However, the streak had to end at some point. Grindstone was retired due to injury soon after

the Derby, and Editor's Note, who had finished sixth in the Derby for Lukas and W.T. Young, became the stable's Preakness hope. He closed late to get third but wasn't going to catch winner Louis Quatorze, trained by Nick Zito. But for that loss, Lukas might have had back-to-back Triple Crown wins, albeit with different horses, for Editor's Note returned to win the Belmont, giving the trainer his third straight win in that race.

Lukas' dominance couldn't last forever, and Cavonnier's runner-up Derby finish had heralded the arrival of trainer Bob Baffert, who would pick up the mantle of Triple Crown Trainer with Silver Charm and Real Quiet. But in 1999 Lukas returned to the Triple Crown spotlight with Charismatic, who captured the Derby and Preakness before finishing third in the Belmont and pulling up immediately after the race. And a year later, Lukas stood once more in the Belmont winner's circle, celebrating his fourth victory in the Belmont Stakes, after longshot Commendable crossed under the wire first.

Whether D. Wayne Lukas makes it to the winner's circle of a Triple Crown race again, what he accomplished from 1994 to 1996 will long remain one of the most amazing training feats the sport of horse racing has ever seen. *JM*

Tabasco Cat wins the 1994 Preakness (left); Timber Country (below left) takes the 1995 Preakness while Thunder Gulch comes back to win that year's Belmont

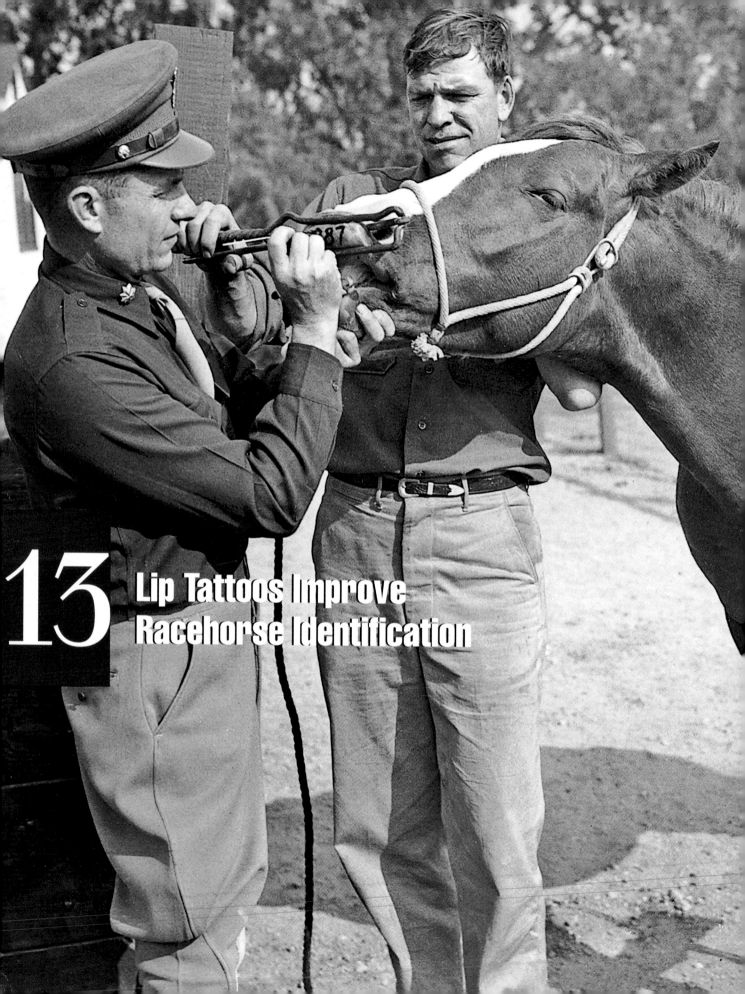

13 Lip Tattoos Improve Racehorse Identification

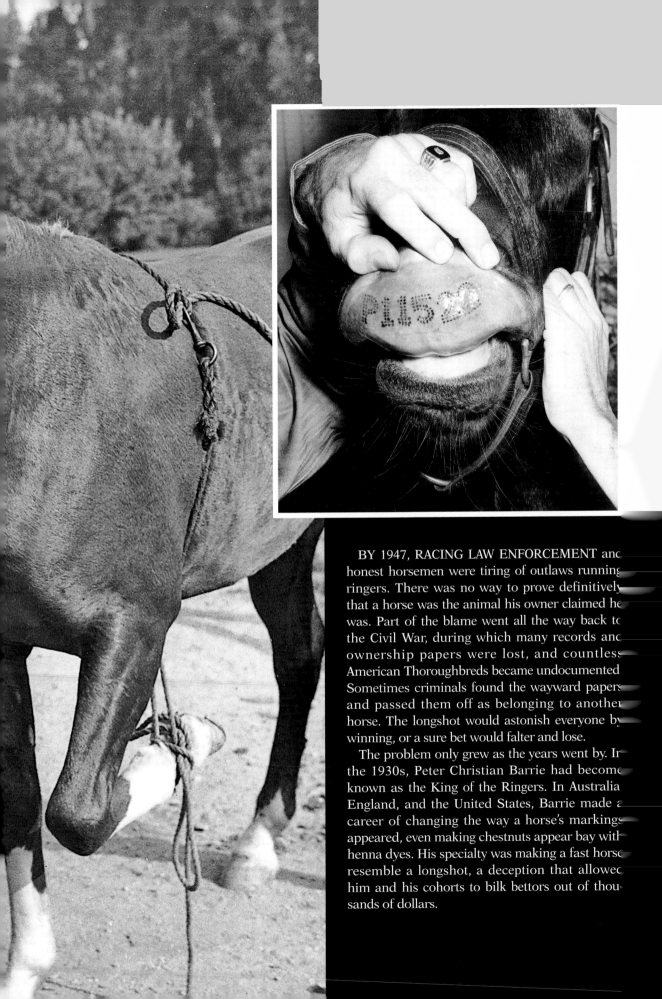

BY 1947, RACING LAW ENFORCEMENT and honest horsemen were tiring of outlaws running ringers. There was no way to prove definitively that a horse was the animal his owner claimed he was. Part of the blame went all the way back to the Civil War, during which many records and ownership papers were lost, and countless American Thoroughbreds became undocumented. Sometimes criminals found the wayward papers and passed them off as belonging to another horse. The longshot would astonish everyone by winning, or a sure bet would falter and lose.

The problem only grew as the years went by. In the 1930s, Peter Christian Barrie had become known as the King of the Ringers. In Australia, England, and the United States, Barrie made a career of changing the way a horse's markings appeared, even making chestnuts appear bay with henna dyes. His specialty was making a fast horse resemble a longshot, a deception that allowed him and his cohorts to bilk bettors out of thousands of dollars.

A horse identifier verifies a tattoo number

Because of Barrie's antics, and those of many others, racing officials began to devise measures to improve racehorse identification. After World War II the newly established Thoroughbred Racing Protective Bureau, a subsidiary of the Thoroughbred Racing Associations, set out to prevent this type of fraud and build public confidence. The new Thoroughbred Racing Protective Bureau staff included former FBI men, who began fingerprinting everyone working in racing, "from stable boys to Alfred Gwynne Vanderbilt," as the *New York Times* said. They also gave horses their own equivalent of fingerprints — identification numbers tattooed under their lips so officials could check whether the horse running was in fact the horse its papers said it was.

Owners originally objected to tattooing because of the pain it would cause their horses as well as

the difficulty of imprinting uniform figures on thousands of racers. But by 1947 Dr. J.G. Catlett and Walter Turnier of the New York and Hialeah Park horse identification bureaus had developed small sets of needles that registered a single digit or letter in one quick administration instead of by a series of punctures, one painful prick at a time. Catlett and Turnier created a set of three-quarter inch characters, made up of small clusters of needles that outlined the desired symbols. With their system, the spot to be tattooed was washed with ink, and then the letter or figure was swiftly perforated into the horse's lip flesh.

It took about two minutes for a set of four digits and a letter to be applied to a horse's lip. The new method yielded uniform markings, even on a first try, and could be done by people who had never tattooed horses before. By the time *The*

Blood-Horse reported on the new system on February 15, 1947, between three hundred and four hundred Thoroughbreds already had been branded by this method, and the results seemed "satisfactory."

The acceptance of lip tattooing never wavered once instituted at the racetracks. Seeing a way to protect their valuable investments, some of the sport's biggest names immediately jumped on board. Isabel Dodge Sloane lined up her two-year-olds to receive their tattoos as soon as the process became available, and William Helis and Alfred Vanderbilt were quick to have all of their horses tattooed.

Now, every racing day, horse identifiers are hard at work, peeling horses' lips back to read the tattoos inside. The identifier carries a copy of each entered horse's foal registration records from The Jockey Club. This includes the horse's ID number, birth date, breeder, owner, lineage, coloring, and markings.

To determine whether a horse can race, the identifier might have to scrutinize tattoos that have sometimes faded with age. Tattoos also help the identifier if the wrong horse is accidentally brought out or a certificate contains an error, as well as if an unscrupulous trainer or owner is trying to run one horse in another's place.

Thoroughbreds aren't the only horses to receive tattoos. Standardbred tattoos have letters, numbers, and a star, while Thoroughbreds are now a letter and five numbers. Arabians, Appaloosas, and Quarter Horses that race have lip tattoos as well. To have a Thoroughbred tattooed, the owner only needs a registration certificate from The Jockey Club. The Thoroughbred Racing Protective Bureau still adminis-ters the tattoo program, keeping on file information for each tattooed Thoroughbred. Branding reports contain details about the horse and a photograph of the tattoo. Horse identifiers who need help naming a Thoroughbred can access the files, and so can owners looking for background information on their horses.

If 1947 was one watershed year in horse identification, the industry soon may be facing another. The future of American racehorse identification could lie inside the horses, rather than under their lips: Racehorses foaled in Great Britain have had a microchip implanted into their necks since 1999. *EMG*

An example of tattooing today

The Arrival of Intertrack Wagering

TODAY, MORE THAN 85 percent of the money wagered on horse racing comes through simulcasts — the transmission of signals from racetracks to other racetracks, off-track wagering outlets, and account-betting services. Before 1982 almost all pari-mutuel handle was generated on track.

That major shift in where dollars and revenue originate is one of the most important developments in racing in the past thirty years. Industry officials say there's no looking back, but they also acknowledge simulcasting has created its own set of challenges.

In the days before simulcasting, most patrons

TODAY, MECHANIZED STARTING GATES are an everyday sight in horse racing, so common that many racegoers take them for granted. But until 1939 horses entered in a race were started by less exact methods. Before Clay Puett and his mechanized starting gate came along, racetracks used ropes, ribbon, or wooden barriers. A jockey's skill or starter's stammer could affect the outcome of a race, and starts were often dangerous events, all too easily becoming a crowded tangle of hooves, arms, and legs.

Puett had been a rider and understood the perils of starting a race. In 1931 he took a job as a starter at the Spudd Rodeo in Greeley, Colorado, and realized that he had no control over lining up and sending off the field. Frustrated, he decided to try to make a starting gate. He told riders, many of whom he knew from his jockey days, "I'm going to put you guys in and let you out when I want you to."

Puett debuted one style of gate at the races during the rodeo-style Frontier Days festival in

A start at Bay Meadows from one of Clay Puett's earlier gates

Cheyenne, Wyoming. It failed, but he kept at his project, trying breastplates and chains across the front of the stalls. Neither worked. He kept tinkering with his creations and took the gate to small races in Wyoming and Colorado. In 1935, when he was working as the starter at Exhibition Park in Vancouver, he used his own devices, which became prototypes of the 1939 model. "No one believed at that time you could lock up Thoroughbreds," he told *The Backstretch* magazine in 1994. "They were too high strung. Trainers, owners, starters, and jockeys said I was barking up the wrong tree, that starting gates would never work, but I knew horses. I grew up on horses. I was convinced it was possible to teach a horse to race out of a closed gate."

With Puett's gates, the horses were completely enclosed in individual stalls. The front of each stall had two doors, which met in the middle in the form of a wide V, and were covered with a heavy wire screen.

Clay Puett

Padded tailboards held horses in the stalls; there was no padding on the forward gates. The gate did not save labor, as three or four assistant starters were still necessary, but riders and trainers alike approved of the jockeys being in charge once the horses were loaded.

The electric latch that kept the gates closed was modeled after bomb release mechanisms installed in contemporary Army planes. It was four inches wide, two and a half inches deep, and eight inches high. The latch had a clear plastic front so a starter could see inside and worked just like a gun trigger; a magnetic switch made by Canon tripped the trigger. Each stall had a lock so the horse couldn't break out. Later the gates were made with an electromagnetic lock that enabled the stalls to open when the electric current was shut off, reversing the original process.

On July 1, 1939, the gate debuted in Canada. In a letter to *The Blood-Horse*, one observer described the event: "I witnessed the use of this gate while visiting in Vancouver recently. Nothing has been introduced to racing in the past 20 years that has given such unanimous satisfaction to the public, horsemen, and racing officials as this new gate, which absolutely eliminates the abuse of horses at the gate. It is amazing how notoriously bad horses 'give up' once they step into their stalls. Average time at post for 147 races at Vancouver has been 30 seconds."

The gates next appeared in California, and then the East. Pimlico was the first Eastern track to use the Puett gate. On October 28, 1939, *The Blood-Horse*'s J.A. Estes observed that horses new to the gate tended to kick at the device but soon become discouraged since they could not hurt the gate or themselves.

Estes did notice one drawback in the new gate system during a start he described as "too good." He had seen all the horses come out together in a large field. One horse propped slightly after taking one jump, and the others went away in line. The horses on the outside began angling toward the inner rail and in the resulting throng a jockey was brushed off his horse and hurt. Estes thought that if the horses had been more staggered at the start, the accident

probably would not have happened.

All in all, however, the response to the gates was positive. Estes asked horsemen for their opinions: "I talked with several trainers, including some who are more or less famous for their severe criticisms, and found not one with any reservations in his approval. Such unanimity on a race course is amazing."

Improvements made over the years included multiple lock devices and the ability for the gates to be moved up or down about eight inches, depending upon the starter's decisions about the horses' experience. Today, Puett's company, True Center Gate in Phoenix, Arizona, still manufactures gates, and an award bearing Puett's name is given to innovators by the University of Arizona.

Puett remained actively involved with his innovation until his death in 1998. At age ninety-four in 1994, he was still visiting racetracks and talking about his gates, which were the subject of a special display at the Kentucky Derby Museum. As Puett once told a reporter: "I live and breathe starting gates." *EMG*

The Puett gate

16 Kentucky Tracks Institute Pari-Mutuel Betting

PARI-MUTUEL BETTING PROBABLY was destined to become the norm for North American racing, but an act of revenge hastened its arrival. The year was 1908, and former Louisville mayor Charlie Grainger headed the New Louisville Jockey Club, which owned Churchill Downs. On January 1 that year, the group that came to political power in Louisville had defeated the group Grainger supported, and the combat had been so bitter that the winners determined to exact vengeance.

As described by Colonel Matt Winn, who had been managing Churchill Downs for about a half-dozen years (*See No. 19*), the feelings went so deep that city hall sought to shut down the racetrack and destroy its most prized event, the Kentucky Derby, by outlawing bookmaking, the track's means of taking wagers. However, the fortuitous discovery of an amendment to Kentucky law paved the way for pari-mutuel wagering. Once established in Kentucky, pari-mutuel wagering caught on in other racing states.

Winn, a former tailor, had seen every Derby since its inaugural in 1875 and, while the race was not yet the national event it would later become, Louisville citizens revered it as a local tradition.

Winn recalled the sequence years later in the book *Down the Stretch*, his life story as told to Frank G. Menke. The knockout punch city hall chose to throw was aimed at gambling, then under attack in various states as a so-called reform movement swept the nation. Bookmaking was the prevalent form of action at Churchill Downs at the time, and the new group in power decided that bookmaking was illegal. Winn countered that there was no law against bookmaking, which had begun somewhat spontaneously in 1882 and caused no official ever to object.

City hall pushed through a law banning bookmaking, and the sheriff of Jefferson County pledged that deputies would throw out bookmakers if they tried to operate at the scheduled spring race meeting.

With Winn's long connection to the Derby, he recalled a brief attempt in 1878 to offer a new-fangled form of wagering via pari-mutuel machines. Perhaps, he thought, this form of betting could be re-instituted and the racetrack could survive.

The pari-mutuel system had been devised in France in the 1860s by Pierre Oller. Owner of a perfume shop in Paris, Oller liked to bet on horse races but determined the bookmakers were not giving him a fair shake. The "mutuel" system meant offering the public the chance to bet among themselves and thereby set the odds themselves. The bets were placed in a mutuel pool and winning payoffs were determined by how many bettors picked the right horse. The racecourses took a percentage, initially 5 percent. This form of wagering became so well accepted that it replaced bookmaking as the officially recognized form of betting at Paris racecourses.

Winn's hopes that he could use the mutuel machines were dashed at first by a check of an old law that banned "Keno, faro, or other machine (used) ..." in wagering. He was confident that at the time the old law was passed, the phrase "other machine" referred to roulette, but he also knew the current city fathers would extend interpretation to the mutuel machines.

Bookmakers gave way to pari-mutuel betting in Kentucky in the first part of the twentieth century

71

The ban of book-making put the Kentucky Derby in jeopardy

It turned out, however, that another wrinkle saved the day.

Colonel M. Lewis Clark, the Louisvillian who masterminded the establishment of a racetrack in his home city, drew heavily on the image and conduct of European racing in crafting his idea of what he could create at home. Clark had brought over some prototype mutuel machines prior to the first Kentucky Derby in 1875, but they went unused until three years later, when Winn remembered seeing them.

Winn and Grainger did further checking of the statute books, which revealed an 1878 amendment to the betting rule stating, "This act shall not apply to persons who may sell combination, or French pools, on any regular race track during the races thereon." (The mutuel system was sometimes referred to as "French pools" or as "Paris mutuels" before general adaptation to the phrase "pari-mutuel.")

Apparently, Winn figured, it had taken Clark three years before "he succeeded in cajoling some friendly lawmakers into inserting the amendment." The machines had been used briefly in the late nineteenth century but were not popular enough for the public or racetracks to crowd out the bookmakers, and the experiment was abandoned.

Winn and Grainger determined that reviving the mutuels could be more easily defended to city hall than trying to go to auction pools (as opposed to bookmaking), but there was the problem of finding and repairing the old machines. Eventually, they were recovered, from Churchill Downs storage, a pawnshop, and a souvenir collector. Four machines, however, would not be sufficient.

Winn knew that Kentucky had been just one of several racing locales, including New York, that had experimented with the Paris mutuels. So, he contacted horse and track owner Phil Dwyer to locate more. Another pair of the battered and rusty machines was dispatched to Kentucky. (The failure of the machines to catch on in New York had come in spite of positive publicity occasioned by Nackajack paying $1,178 for a five-dollar bet in a race at Jerome Park as early as 1872. The bookmakers offered only between 5-1 and 20-1 as opposed to the mutuel price of 234-1.)

Despite Winn and Grainger's having discovered the amendment specifically permitting pari-mutuel betting, city hall and the sheriff angrily vowed to shut down any form of gambling that took place at the track. By then, the race meeting was growing near. Churchill management sought an immediate court ruling on the validity of the old amendment, but an overloaded court docket

would put them on familiar footing, although they would be facing unfamiliar tight turns tucked into the one-mile dirt track. There was nothing he could do about that. He could, however, give them options as to style of shoeing, not insisting that only slick plates touch his turf.

Europe had not yet converted to starting gates, so he decreed that his race would commence via a walk-up start. He also made the race one and a half miles, a distance hardly unknown to top American horses but more familiar to Europeans.

Schapiro could not skew everything in favor of the adventurers he was seeking. Teletimer technology and the racing commission presumably checked any thought he might have had about a clockwise trail, as was more common in Europe than the American counterclockwise racing. One additional plum he advertised, though, was that the invaders could be flown in at the last minute, easing fears about a delayed equine equivalent of "jet lag," which is often experienced by horses a few days after long flights.

As a horse race, the inaugural Washington, D.C., International was an interesting affair. Wilwyn, an English horse who had not established himself in the top levels at home but had fashioned an impressive ten-race winning streak, was steered from well behind by jockey Manny Mercer and prevailed by one and three-quarters lengths. The American horse Ruhe was second, but the next two, Zucchero and Niederlander, were Europeans. The favorite in the field of seven, America's Greek Ship, was worn down by the pace, which produced a final time of 2:30 4/5. The time was some five seconds better than the course record, but it was not a distance widely employed on Laurel's grass.

Winning owner Robert Boucher, a hops grower from Kent, was struck by the scene. "I shall never forget the tremendous sporting spirit of the crowd that had bet against my horse, but cheered him home." (Wilwyn paid fifteen dollars.)

Maryland icon Humphrey Finney declared the event "the greatest thing for racing in the Maryland area since the Seabiscuit-War Admiral race (1938)."

Schapiro had made his point, and it flew in the face of some conventional wisdom. *The Blood-Horse* headline and subheads of the lead article on the race revealed a pre-race skepticism: "A Remarkable Train of Events. Wilwyn Holds his Form and Sets Track Record, Laurel Brings off the Impossible—a Successful International Race."

Beneath this declaration, the noted racing journalist Joe Palmer began his exercise in contrition: "When you're wrong, you'd better admit it quick, before somebody else points it out …

"I took what might be called a dim view of the Washington, D.C., International … I couldn't have been farther wrong."

Palmer concluded his report: "Laurel got away with an international race, which is the most remarkable thing of all."

The following year another European, Worden II, won the event, and then in 1954 C.V. Whitney's Fisherman became the first American to win it. Honors went to South America in 1955, with El Chama of Venezuela triumphant.

In 1956 Whitney initiated a reverse international pattern when he sent Fisherman and Career Boy to challenge the great Ribot in France's Prix de l'Arc de Triomphe. By 1958 Schapiro's race got an extraordinary boost when the champion of Europe, Arc winner Ballymoss, came over for his race, which also featured two invaders from the Cold War-era Soviet Union.

The Laurel race waxed, waned, and disappeared, but international racing had a foothold that would grow more and more entrenched. Today, when intercontinental fields enter the gate at the Breeders' Cup, the Dubai World Cup, the Japan Cup, or the Hong Kong Cup, the name John Schapiro probably is rarely spoken. A half-century and more ago, however, it was he who showed the way. *ELB*

18 Samuel D. Riddle Purchases Man o' War

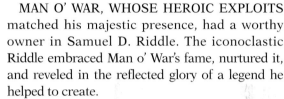

Man o' War as a young horse

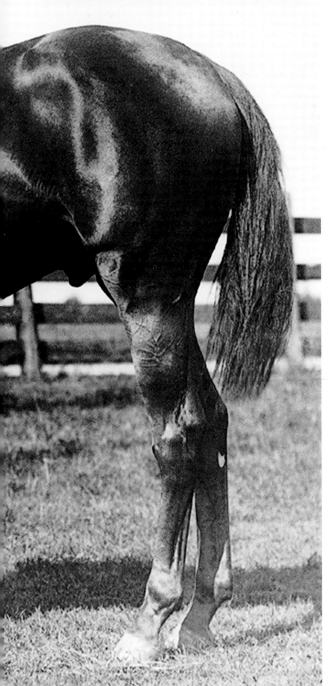

MAN O' WAR, WHOSE HEROIC EXPLOITS matched his majestic presence, had a worthy owner in Samuel D. Riddle. The iconoclastic Riddle embraced Man o' War's fame, nurtured it, and reveled in the reflected glory of a legend he helped to create.

That he came to own the Horse of the Century at all resulted in forces larger than both Man o' War and Riddle.

August Belmont II bred the son of Fair Play—Mahubah and intended to race the strapping colt as he had his sire, but World War I intervened. The most powerful man in racing, Belmont served as chairman of The Jockey Club, was a guiding force of the new Belmont Park, and bred scores of stakes winners at his Nursery Stud in Kentucky. Among his many business accomplishments, Belmont helped found the New York subway system.

When his country called, though, the titan sought a commission and served in Spain with the Quartermaster Corps, securing supplies for the Allies. War kept Belmont from home longer than anticipated, so he reluctantly decided to sell his yearling crop of 1918. The already named Man o' War was a late addition, for his breeder liked the looks of the colt and his pedigree.

Nursery Stud initially offered the yearlings for sale privately, but no takers emerged and the youngsters were shipped to Saratoga Springs, New York, a few days before the auction on August 17, 1918.

Ensconced in his summer home at the Spa was Riddle. The grandson of a textile manufacturer, Riddle was born in 1861 in Glen Riddle, Pennsylvania. He grew up to be an ardent sportsman who enjoyed foxhunting and the 1,700 acres of his Glen Riddle Farm. Riddle cut a fine figure though he was widely regarded as opinionated and even bombastic. "Riddle was a medium-sized mustachioed fellow variously described as 'aristocratic,' having the manner of an English general, and resembling an old Roman senator," Man o' War biographer Edward L. Bowen writes.

Breeder August Belmont II (below) and owner Samuel D. Riddle (right)

Riddle and trainer Louis Feustel went to see the Belmont draft before the sale. "... when Red poked his big head through the door my heart skipped a little ... You see, I rode once and I've trained. I know them, if I do say it," the New York *Herald-Tribune* quoted Riddle as saying.

According to different reports, Riddle either had to have Man o' War at any cost or his wife Elizabeth insisted for the sake of Feustel, who was keen for the colt. Feustel had galloped Man o' War's grandsire, Hastings, had worked for Fair Play's trainer (Sam Hildreth), and himself had trained Mahubah.

On the block late in the sale, the high-headed chestnut was sold to Riddle for five thousand dollars. One of the many stories that followed Man o' War's purchase was that Riddle thought the colt might make a fine hunter. Yet he would have been a rather expensive one, based on the auction's average price of $1,038. Golden Broom brought the top price of $15,600 from Walter M. Jeffords, whose wife was a niece of Riddle's wife. The two men enjoyed a friendly rivalry, but the families operated Faraway Farm in Lexington, Kentucky jointly for many years. Man o' War and Golden Broom would have a short-lived rivalry of their own, with the expensive Jeffords colt besting the Riddle trainee in a series of yearling dashes.

Yet once the youngsters made it to the races there was no question which was the superior racehorse. Man o' War excelled from the outset, winning nine of ten races as a juvenile and carrying 130 pounds six times. In his only loss, to Upset in the Sanford Memorial Stakes at Saratoga, Man o' War fell victim to traffic and bad luck amid some speculation that the race had been fixed (*See No. 29*).

Riddle's notion of sophomore racing did not include a mile and a quarter under 126 pounds in the early spring, so Man o' War did not venture to his birth state for the Kentucky Derby. He returned to the races as a three-year-old in the Preakness Stakes, his first of eleven consecutive victories and each race a command performance. He won the Belmont Stakes by twenty lengths — certainly a rueful day for his breeder — the Lawrence Realization by a hundred lengths, and the Potomac Handicap under 138 pounds. He was asked for an effort only once when John P. Grier reportedly headed him in the stretch of the Dwyer Stakes.

In his last race Man o' War made Sir Barton, winner the previous year of the as-yet unofficial Triple Crown, look like a plodder. The champion never raced in Kentucky, but he was paraded at the old Kentucky Association track in Lexington on his way to Faraway Farm, where he would soon become Kentucky's greatest tourist attraction.

Riddle initially allowed Man o' War to be bred only to mares owned by him and the Jeffordses, but he eventually eased his policy. Opinion has encompassed both extremes: that Riddle mismanaged Man o' War's stallion career and that he orchestrated it beautifully. In any case, Man o' War enjoyed a distinguished record in the stud, siring the outstanding stakes winners Crusader, War Relic, and American Flag and the Triple Crown winner War Admiral. In all, he sired sixty-four stakes winners, or 17 percent.

His sire record mattered little to the thousands of people who journeyed to Faraway Farm for a look at the big red horse. During the last sixteen years of his life, he enjoyed the daily devotion of his groom, Will Harbut, who entertained tourists with his recitation of Man o' War's exploits. For Harbut and fans everywhere, Man o' War was "de mostest hoss."

Man o' War died in 1947 at age thirty, and his funeral was broadcast nationally over radio (*See No. 80*). Riddle had commissioned an oversized statue from sculptor Herbert Haseltine, who completed it several year's after the horse's death. Today, the remains lie at the Kentucky Horse Park with the sculpture standing sentry and welcoming visitors at the entrance.

Riddle survived Man o' War by less than four years, dying of complications from a stroke in early 1951. *JD*

Man o' War with beloved groom Will Harbut

19 Matt Winn Saves Churchill Downs and the Derby

THE KENTUCKY DERBY's stature as the world's most famous horse race owes much of its enduring popularity to Louisville entrepreneur Matt J. Winn.

In the fall of 1902, the successful forty-one-year-old businessman was approached about putting together a group to buy the then financially troubled Churchill Downs. He initially balked but consented for the sake of rescuing the Derby.

Winn had witnessed the first Kentucky Derby in 1875 from the back of his father's merchant wagon, parked in the infield. He started his career as a traveling representative for a wholesale grocer, then parlayed his sales acumen into a partnership with his friend and tailor, Ed Langan. The pair expanded Langan's business into a profitable shop that also served as a regular haunt for other businessmen, sportsmen, and politicians.

In addition to his work, which supported a family of nine daughters, Winn enjoyed a leisurely lifestyle that included frequent forays to Churchill Downs, where he pursued his interest in betting.

Winn's success and connections within the business community led friend and former newspaper editor Charlie Price to approach him in late 1902 about purchasing Churchill Downs.

At the time, Churchill was owned by a group of investors who had purchased it in 1894 and spent $100,000 for a new grandstand that included the now-famous Twin Spires. But those efforts were not enough to keep the track solvent, and Price began shopping for a buyer. With no takers, Price told Winn the track could be obtained for $40,000.

But Winn was reluctant to accommodate Price,

The original clubhouse

The iconic Twin Spires

according to the book *Down the Stretch: The Story of Colonel Matt J. Winn*.

"This is a rash and reckless thing you are asking me to do," Winn recalled telling his friend. "My first impulse after giving thought to Charlie's proposition was to turn it down. I reasoned that if two different groups of seasoned race track executives, operating over a span of 27 years, could not make Churchill Downs a profitable enterprise, what magic had I which could revolutionize the sequence in history?

"I'd say 'no' and make it stick for a thousand years if it involved anything but the Derby. But they mustn't stop running that race."

The lure of saving the Derby was enough for Winn to save Churchill Downs. Winn put together a group that included hotel operator Louis Seelbach and Mayor Charles Grainger. The new owners immediately established a "Jockey Club" in which two hundred memberships were sold for a hundred dollars each. Those funds were used to build a new clubhouse, and the spring 1903 meet was the first profitable one in the track's history.

The following year Winn sold his clothing store and was installed as Churchill Downs' vice president and general manager. As part of his philosophy that track management should not own or bet on horses running at Churchill Downs, Winn never wagered again after taking charge.

He then went about performing his "magic," becoming a one-man promotional machine for the Kentucky Derby.

Winn made forays to New York, where he hosted the local media, including prominent writers Damon Runyon and Grantland Rice, at the Waldorf Hotel. His efforts paid off, as the Derby grew in stature. Attendance at the 1947 Derby was a record 102,000.

For his brash hucksterism Winn drew comparisons to P.T. Barnum, the promoter extraordinaire

84

who started the circus that later became the Ringling Brothers and Barnum & Bailey Circus.

Winn proudly used the title of colonel, not because of any military service but as a result of being inducted into the Royal Order of the Kentucky Colonels.

In a 1949 *New York Times* article, Arthur Daley said of Winn, "A fabulous character in every respect ... He could give cards and spades to Barnum and beat him ... The Kentucky Derby is a monument to him. It's his baby and his alone. He will always be a part of it, even more a part of it than the spired towers of Churchill Downs. He alone made it what it is today."

In striving to incorporate tradition and showmanship into the Derby picture, Winn:

• Headed the effort to turn the Derby into a full-fledged festival that provided a multitude of events for Louisvillians and included bands in the infield;

• Continued to stage the Derby during the years of the Great Depression and World War II. The wartime Derbies became known as the "streetcar Derbies" because only locals could attend due to travel restrictions;

• Introduced the traditional garland of roses draped over each year's Derby winner and the gold cup presented to the winning owner;

• Started the tradition of an annual souvenir glass listing the names of all the winners of the classic;

• Began the tradition of having "My Old Kentucky Home" played on Derby Day.

But Winn's influence in Kentucky and national racing circles went beyond the Derby. The track itself flourished as Winn and his partners increased field sizes by boosting purses that previous owners had cut trying to recoup the costs of building the grandstand.

In addition to running Churchill Downs, Winn also assisted in the management of other tracks in Kentucky, Illinois, Maryland, and New York.

At the turn of the century, Winn joined the effort of New York racing promoter James Butler to establish a Thoroughbred track at the former Empire City harness track. Butler's plan was opposed by the powerful August Belmont II and The Jockey Club. Hesitant at first to butt heads with Belmont, Winn finally signed on to what became a successful, albeit bitter, battle.

Another Turf battle that went in Winn's favor came in 1908 when local politicians who disliked Churchill president Charlie Grainger decreed that bookmaking, then the only form of wagering at Churchill, was illegal. Faced again with the prospect of the Derby's cancellation, Winn found a way around the new legislation by installing pari-mutuel machines to take win, place, and show wagers. That year's Derby went on as scheduled. *(See No. 16.)*

With Churchill Downs continuing to show a profit every year under his leadership, Winn died in 1949 at age eighty-eight with the distinction of being the only person to have witnessed seventy-five consecutive runnings of the Derby. *RM*

Winn charms his Derby guests

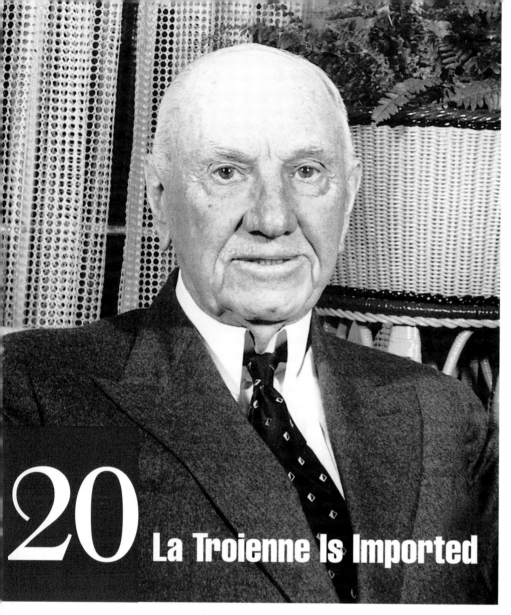

20 La Troienne Is Imported

man purchased more horses.

Success at this level and the growing need to find good racers convinced Bradley to breed his own horses. In 1906 he purchased the original piece of land that formed the heart of his 1,400-acre Idle Hour Farm near Lexington, Kentucky.

A self-made man, Bradley understood how to build a successful enterprise, and he sought to learn from the best. In the world of Thoroughbred breeding no enterprise set the standard more than James R. Keene's Castleton Farm near Lexington. The foundation of Keene's success had been to mate European mares to American stallions. (Colin, Peter Pan, Pennant, Court Dress, and Kingston were bred on this principle.) If that theory had worked so well for Keene, it was good enough for Bradley.

The first lot of European mares came to Idle Hour in 1915. Two of these mares from the family of Padua (whom Bradley also imported) proved to be pearls beyond price. From Padula, a daughter of Padua, Bradley bred Black Servant, whom Bradley favored to win the 1921 Kentucky Derby (the colt was beaten a head by stablemate Behave Yourself, giving Bradley his first of four Derby wins). Black Servant became a useful sire for Bradley. The second mare of great value was Vaila, a granddaughter of Padua, who produced five stakes winners for Idle Hour. Among these was Blossom Time, who, when mated to Black Servant, produced perhaps the best horse Bradley bred, Blue Larkspur (1929 Horse of the Year and Belmont Stakes winner).

Therefore, it is not surprising that Bradley, thirsty for additional success, once more went to the European well. Listed among the entries in the 1930 December sale at Newmarket was La Troienne, a four-year-old cull from the stable of

WHEN IDLE HOUR FARM owner Edward Riley Bradley added a small brown mare to his burgeoning broodmare band, little did he realize the long-lasting effects she would have on racing around the world. In 1930 La Troienne was just another mare with potential; seventy-five years later she is a legend.

In the late 1890s Bradley, on his doctor's advice, entered horse racing. Well, it wasn't exactly on his doctor's advice. Bradley's physician had advised him to "engage in a more active, outdoor lifestyle." Bradley, a gambler and bookmaker, translated this prescription as "buy a racehorse."

Bradley first purchased Friar John, a claiming horse, and the worst thing that can befall a novice in the horse business happened. Friar John won his first race in the Bradley silks. Thus, Bradley's "cure" became his disease, and the budding horse-leading French breeder Marcel Boussac. Four unplaced starts in France over two years followed by two placings in three starts in England did not muster a great deal of attention on behalf of any prospective buyer, even though La Troienne had raced in some pretty good company.

Nor would her conformation stop passersby dead in their tracks to take a second look. She was just another small, plain brown mare, a bit on the delicate side.

Certainly nothing about her immediate pedigree impressed either. Although she was by the great sire Teddy, her dam Helene de Troie had been such a disappointment on the flat (although she had won one race) that she was relegated to steeplechasing, where she proved to be more successful. However, past generations of the family did possess a great deal of class. La Troienne's third dam, Doxa, was a full sister to Absurdity, who had foaled two classic winners, Jest (1913 One Thousand Guineas and English Oaks) and Black Jester (1914 St. Leger). Jest also had produced a classic winner in Humorist, who won the 1921 English Derby. (Helene de Troie later produced a classic winner for Boussac, when her daughter Adargatis won the 1934 Prix de Diane.)

E.R. Bradley's savvy purchase of La Troienne continues to have repercussions

And, then again, La Troienne was in foal to the very handsome Gainsborough, who had won the 1918 English Triple Crown. Those things were enough for Bradley, an inveterate gambler anyway, to take a chance. So, for 1,250 guineas, La Troienne became the property of Idle Hour Farm.

La Troienne's 1931 foal, a filly, disappointed her breeder, and, in an age much less concerned with political correctness, was euthanized because of

Kentucky Derby winner Go for Gin; and numerous grade and group winners around the world.

Baby League, by Bradley's 1926 Kentucky Derby winner Bubbling Over, won only one race but produced 1945 Horse of the Year Busher. This powerful branch of the family would later give rise to 2004 Horse of the Year Mineshaft. Joining these elite are champions Numbered Account, Rhythm, Folklore, and 2004 Kentucky Derby winner Smarty Jones. Other world champions

her faulty leg conformation. But what La Troienne produced afterward — matriarchal "begats" of Old Testament proportion — carved her niche in racing lore.

Sent to Bradley's home stallion Black Toney (whom he had purchased as a yearling from Keene), she produced Black Helen. The size of this bay filly's heart and talent far outmatched her tiny frame, and she earned a championship in 1935 with wins in the Florida Derby, Coaching Club American Oaks, and American Derby. As a broodmare, Black Helen established a precedent for the family. She, like most of La Troienne's daughters, founded a dynasty. Among her many stakes-winning, stakes-producing descendants are champions But Why Not, Oedipus, and Princess Rooney; 1994

descending from this foundation mare include Coloso in Mexico, Dyna Actress in Japan, Woodman in Ireland, and Goldsio in the Slovak Republic.

Big Hurry, a daughter of Black Toney, won the 1938 Selima Stakes, then an important fixture for juvenile fillies. Retired to stud, she stands at the head of the most prolific branch of the La Troienne family. In addition to producing champion filly Bridal Flower (herself a major producer), Big Hurry foaled Allemande, the ancestress of champion mare Relaxing (dam of champion Easy Goer), and No Fiddling, whose champion descendants include Regal Gleam, Caerleon, Tikkanen, Turgeon, and Straight Deal. Another branch of this evergreen belongs to Searching, an excellent race mare. Searching produced champions Affectionately (dam of 1970 Preakness winner and champion Personality) and Priceless Gem (dam of multiple French champion Allez France). Sea Hero, the 1993 Kentucky Derby winner, belongs to this group, as does 2001 Irish champion Mozart.

Bred to Bradley's Blue Larkspur in 1937, La Troienne foaled Big Event, who earned her black type with a second in the 1940 Selima Stakes. From her spring Greentree Farm's useful stallion The Axe II and Harbor View Farm's Francis S., as well as Mexican champion Lindo Sinaloa S.

Businesslike, La Troienne's 1939 foal by Blue Larkspur, also made gigantic contributions to the breed. Although she failed to win, she is the source of the durable race mare Busanda, who foaled the great Buckpasser. This champion and Horse of the Year perpetuated La Troienne's great female legacy by leading the North American broodmare sire list four times. Outstandingly, the 1984 champion juvenile filly, belongs to this branch as do champion and 1993 Preakness winner Prairie Bayou and Polish Navy, the sire of Sea Hero.

La Troienne's 1940 foal, Besieged, was a daughter of Black Toney's champion son Balladier. A winner herself, she heads a viable, though not spectacularly successful, clan. Important runners descending from Besieged include Nasty and Bold and Pembroke.

In 1944 La Troienne foaled her fifth and last stakes winner, Bee Ann Mac. Like her half sister Big Hurry, she won the Selima Stakes. As a broodmare, she was a bit of a failure, although the family did produce the grade III winner Shacane in 2002.

Another daughter of Blue Larkspur appeared in 1945. Named Belle Histoire, she failed to win in three starts but accounted for herself as a producer. This branch, too, has its share of champions: 1972 champion older horse Autobiography; Venezuelan champions Lomaxti (1996 juvenile colt) and Gran Fortaleza (2003 three-year-old filly); and champion French mare and classic winner Bright Sky, winner of the 2002 Prix de Diane.

La Troienne's last daughter was foaled in 1947. By this time Bradley had died and the mare had been included in a package lot that was divvied up among three partners: Robert Kleberg, Ogden Phipps, and John Hay Whitney *(See No. 68)*. La Troienne had gone to Whitney's Greentree Stud and for him she produced Belle of Troy, by Blue Larkspur. Modern family members stemming from Belle of Troy include Green Peace, 1986 champion juvenile colt in Mexico, and grade I winners Proud Appeal, Bail Out Becky, More Than Ready, Ten Most Wanted, and Cutlass Reality.

Idle Hour Stock Farm (opposite) proved fertile ground for Bradley, breeder of four Kentucky Derby winners

Although blessed with nine daughters, La Troienne also produced five sons but only two of note. Biologist, a 1934 son of Bubbling Over, won a minor stakes. The other was Bimelech. The son of Black Toney was champion at two and three. He fell a length and a half short of a Triple Crown, his losing margin to Gallahadion in the 1940 Kentucky Derby. One of Bradley's favorites (almost on par with his favored Blue Larkspur), Bimelech became an influential sire.

La Troienne died in 1954 at Greentree Stud. Arguably no other mare in the twentieth century can compare to this small, plain mare who turned out to be a genetic giant. As of the end of 2005, no fewer than 1,106 stakes winners have descended from her. *TH*

21 Native Dancer's Derby Upset

title Triple Crown winner to his accomplishments.

Bred by Alfred G. Vanderbilt, Native Dancer was a son of the great handicap horse Discovery out of the Polynesian mare Geisha. Vanderbilt would often say he should have bequeathed a more masculine name on the gray colt, who later became known as the Gray Ghost.

Vanderbilt came from a privileged background but did his part for racing, serving stints as the head of Pimlico and Belmont Park. His promotional skills were largely responsible for bringing about the fabled 1938 match race between Seabiscuit and War Admiral. Owner of Sagamore Farm in Maryland, Vanderbilt was a competitive presence on the track, and his highest expectations as a racing man were fulfilled in Native Dancer.

Under the tutelage of trainer Bill Winfrey, Native Dancer showed great promise by December of his first year. But rather than rush the colt, Winfrey refrained from starting him until April 1952. Native Dancer easily won his maiden contest at Jamaica racetrack in New York, then captured his next start, the Youthful Stakes, by a commanding six lengths. The colt's other stakes victories included the Saratoga Special, Hopeful, and Futurity, the latter in which he equaled the world record. His unbeaten nine-race streak earned him co-Horse of the Year honors, a title not bequeathed to a two-year-old colt again until Secretariat in 1972. Well before the voting had been tallied, though, the 1953 Kentucky Derby beckoned as a realistic objective. "It will be interesting to note what sort Native Dancer proves at three," Turf writer Charles Hatton said.

Ankle problems had surfaced late in Native Dancer's juvenile season, and they would plague him through the remainder of his career. His ankles were pinfired for osselets, bony growths in

NATIVE DANCER'S IMPROBABLE DEFEAT to Dark Star in the 1953 Kentucky Derby remains one of the most frustrating upsets in American racing. Although "probably best," according to the trip notes, Native Dancer encountered every conceivable obstacle to fall short by a head in the final stride.

Native Dancer would face testing circumstances in future races, but his Derby loss left the only blemish on his otherwise perfect record. By virtually all accounts, he should have added the

the joints, and they required constant care.

Native Dancer didn't make his first start at three until April, winning the Gotham Stakes at Aqueduct by two lengths. The race was broadcast on national television, winning the striking gray legions of new fans. He next added the Wood Memorial. Then it was on to Louisville.

Dark Star had won the Derby Trial Stakes just days before the Run for the Roses for owner Harry F. Guggenheim, the industrialist who raced under the *nom de course* Cain Hoy Stable. Bred by Warner Jones, whose family had founded Churchill Downs and who would later lead it as chairman, Dark Star nevertheless was ignored by bettors, going off at 25-1. Native Dancer, coupled with Vanderbilt's Social Outcast, was the favorite in the field of eleven at 3-5.

Dark Star immediately assumed the lead while Native Dancer encountered traffic and was pushed back to sixth racing in front of the grandstand. Some observers contend Native Dancer lost the Derby on the first turn when Curragh King bore out, taking the Dancer with him and into the path of Money Broker, who collided with the favorite. Eric Guerin, Native Dancer's regular jockey, had to steady the colt and lost positioning. As Dark Star neared the top of the backstretch, he had eleven lengths to the good of Native Dancer. Guerin found room on the outside and asked Native Dancer to run. The colt responded with a third quarter in :23, an incredible effort.

On the final turn Guerin angled toward the rail in an attempt to save ground. Meanwhile, Dark

Star was tiring from his front-running ways and began to drift off the rail. Just as Guerin tried to slip through the hole Dark Star had created, that colt's jockey, Henry Moreno, closed it up. Guerin yanked his colt to the outside, losing ground again. Yet Native Dancer closed resolutely under Guerin's urging, reaching Dark Star's flank and then his neck. At the wire, the two appeared inseparable and the "photo" sign flashed on the tote board. Moments later, though, Dark Star's number went up.

While conceding that Dark Star had run the race of his life, critics roundly castigated Guerin for his erratic ride. "He took that colt everywhere on the track except the ladies' room," a Churchill Downs board member was overhead saying.

Yet according to Native Dancer biographer Eva Jolene Boyd, Native Dancer's loss was not that simple. "It was more likely a long chain of circumstances beginning with the ankles being fired and culminating in the events that arose from the bumping. The fact that he so very nearly overcame it all speaks volumes for the kind of racehorse Native Dancer was."

Native Dancer avenged his defeat in the Preakness and Belmont stakes. Indeed, the remainder of his career was as perfect as it had been until the Derby. Retired in the summer of his four-year-old season after re-injuring an ankle, Native Dancer left an indelible mark as a stallion. Not only did he sire 1966 Kentucky Derby winner Kauai King, he was the grandsire of the great Mr. Prospector and the broodmare sire of Northern Dancer. Native Dancer died in 1967. *JD*

Harry F. Guggenheim's Dark Star leads the Derby field (opposite) and wears the blanket of roses after holding off Native Dancer at the wire

22 Laffit Pincay Jr. Becomes All-Time Leading Rider

When the Panamanian native rode Irish Nip to career victory number 8,834 at Hollywood Park in Inglewood, California, on December 10, 1999, he ended Bill Shoemaker's nearly thirty-year reign as the world's winningest jockey. But Pincay, who at the time was a fifty-two-year-old grandfather, was just getting warmed up.

Pincay finished 1999 with 170 winning rides, his best year since 1992. He followed that with 203 wins in 2000, five of them coming on a magical October afternoon during the Oak Tree Racing Association meeting at Santa Anita Park when California-bred runners were featured in the Cal Cup stakes program. The third of those five winners, a five-year-old mare named Chichim, gave Pincay career victory number nine thousand, when she won the Louis R. Rowan California Cup Distaff Handicap by a neck.

The momentum kept building, with 225 winners in 2001. Setting a new record with every winner, Pincay continued to excel in 2002, with 205 winners. The trainers who had given up on Pincay only five years earlier — when he struggled to win seventy-five races from 718 mounts — were now lining up to acquire his services.

Pincay started fast in 2003, winning with forty-nine of his first 229 mounts, an impressive 21 percent success rate. But his career came to an undignified conclusion on March 1 in a claiming event on the downhill turf course at Santa Anita, when a horse bolted in front of Pincay's mount, Trampus Too, clipped his heels, and sent both horse and rider to the ground.

FEW ATHLETES IN ANY SPORT are blessed with the kind of determination that Laffit Pincay Jr. displayed during his long march to overtake Bill Shoemaker and become Thoroughbred racing's all-time leading rider.

With his large, muscular frame, Pincay battled constantly to maintain a 117-pound riding weight. And in a game where falling out of favor with trainers can be fatal to a rider's career, Pincay kept the faith in his own abilities when others didn't.

In the immediate aftermath of this accident, in which Trampus Too rolled over Pincay, the Hall of Fame rider thought he would be sidelined only a few days. But the injuries, including two broken bones in Pincay's neck, proved far more serious. He announced on April 29, 2003, that his riding days were over. Career win number 9,530, recorded on a maiden named Seattle Shamus on the same March 1 afternoon he suffered his injury, would be his final winning ride.

Born in Panama City, Panama, on December 29, 1946, Pincay was the son of a successful jockey, but he saw little of his father as his parents divorced when he was an infant. A natural athlete, young Laffit dreamed of becoming a Major League baseball player — an infielder — but his small stature led him to the racetrack, where at the age of fifteen he began galloping horses. Two years later, on May 19, 1964, he rode his first winner, a horse named Huelen, at Presidente Remon racetrack in Panama City.

Pincay, a fierce competitor, eventually caught the eye of Florida horseman Fred Hooper, who brought the rider to the United States in 1966. Pincay's first victory on American soil came aboard Hooper's Teacher's Art at Arlington Park on July 1. After his contract with Hooper expired, Pincay headed west and settled in California.

At the time, Bill Shoemaker was the dean of West Coast riders and was taking dead aim on Johnny Longden's record of 6,032 career wins. Shoemaker earned his 6,033rd victory on September 7, 1970, at Del Mar racetrack.

The Shoe rode for another twenty years, retiring in 1990. Career victory 8,833 came aboard Beau Genius in the Hallandale Handicap at Gulfstream Park in Florida.

By then Pincay had his sights set on Shoemaker's record. He had become the dominant rider of the 1970s, winning Eclipse Awards in 1971, 1973, 1974, and 1979, and gaining induction into the National Museum of Racing and Hall of Fame in 1975. The 1980s saw Pincay register his only Triple Crown race triumphs: Conquistador Cielo in the 1982 Belmont Stakes; Caveat in the 1983 Belmont; and Swale in the 1984 Kentucky Derby and Belmont.

But tragedy struck in January 1985, when Pincay's wife, Linda, who was suffering from

Laffit Pincay's friends and fellow jockeys help him celebrate

depression, committed suicide. Pincay became a single parent to daughter Lisa and son Laffit III. He thought about retiring but refocused his energies, putting together one of the best years of his career, winning 289 races, eighty-six of them stakes, for mount earnings of $13,315,049. At season's end he was awarded his fifth Eclipse Award.

As a new wave of riders emerged in the 1990s, it became more of a challenge for Pincay to pick up live mounts. Business began to decline, much more so than his riding skills.

A new wife, Jeanine, and a new son, Jean-Laffit, were the bright spots for Pincay for much of the 1990s. By the end of 1997, when he had won just seventy-five races, Pincay was still 260 winners shy of Shoemaker's record. He thought of moving his business to Northern California, where the competition would be easier. Instead, he recommitted himself to a healthy, low-calorie diet and intense fitness regime that would have him in perhaps the best physical condition of his life.

Trainers slowly came back around, giving Pincay better mounts, especially in the autumn of 1999 when it became clear that he would, barring injury, break Shoemaker's record. Pincay thought it would be appropriate to break it on December 29, his fifty-third birthday. But he was riding too well. He caught The Shoe on December 9, then passed him the next day, winning a mile and one-sixteenth maiden race on the turf aboard the Richard Mandella-trained Irish Nip. *RP*

23 Nasrullah Imported from England

NASRULLAH, WHOSE BLOOD widely invigorated the North American Thoroughbred, exerted perhaps the greatest influence of any of the imported North American stallions of the twentieth century. Greater than Star Shoot, even though they both topped the general sire list five times. Greater than Sir Gallahad III, a four-time leading sire who sired 1930 Triple Crown winner Gallant Fox in his first Kentucky crop. Greater than Blenheim II, Bull Dog, Mahmoud, Heliopolis, Ambiorix, and Sickle, all leading sires.

Nasrullah, who stood in England and Ireland prior to his importation for the 1951 breeding season, got off to a swift start at Arthur B. Hancock Sr.'s Claiborne Farm near Paris, Kentucky. The leading English/Irish stallion in 1951, Nasrullah topped the sires of two-year-olds list with his first North American racing crop (in 1954) and headed the general sire list the next two years to become the first stallion in history to lead both the North American and English/Irish lists.

In his nine years at Claiborne, Nasrullah sired

such champions as Nashua, Bold Ruler, Bald Eagle, Jaipur, and Never Bend, and such co-champions as two-year-olds Leallah, Nasrina, and Nadir, plus major winners Bug Brush, Delta, Mister Gus, and On-and-On. Nasrullah led the general sire list again in 1959, 1960, and 1962, and the two-year-olds list in 1956 and 1962 (with his final crop).

Nashua, from Nasrullah's initial crop, was champion male at ages two and three, Horse of the Year at three, and a top handicap runner at four. He won the 1955 Preakness and Belmont stakes and overtook Citation as the world's leading money earner. His victory in the 1956 Widener Handicap at Hialeah off works alone is the stuff of legends. Purchased by Leslie Combs II on behalf of a syndicate for a then-record $1,251,200, Nashua became a successful sire at Combs' Spendthrift Farm near Lexington.

Bold Ruler was the next of Nasrullah's true superstars. His rise to the top of the two-year-old ranks came on the same card in which Nashua closed out his career with a second victory in the

Jockey Club Gold Cup at Belmont Park. Bold Ruler won the 1956 Futurity Stakes that day but lost out for championship honors with an unplaced effort in the Garden State Stakes in his next start. The following year he was champion three-year-old male as well as co-Horse of the Year with the older Dedicate. More versatile than Nashua, he was champion sprinter as a four-year-old. Bold Ruler entered stud in 1959 at Claiborne, then owned by Arthur B. "Bull" Hancock Jr., who had engineered the importation of Nasrullah on behalf of a syndicate.

According to Hancock, who purchased Nasrullah for $340,000 after a couple of unsuccessful attempts: "I picked him out because he was the best two-year-old of his year; he was third in the (Epsom) Derby; and got one and a quarter miles very well."

Nasrullah had more than his race record going for him. Bred in Great Britain by the Aga Khan, Nasrullah was by Federico Tesio's great unbeaten champion Nearco and traced in female family to foundation mare Lady Josephine. Nasrullah's half sister, Sun Princess, later produced Royal Charger (also by Nearco), who was imported to North America during his stallion career and whose offspring included Turn-to.

Bold Ruler came to be Nasrullah's greatest son at stud and carved a sire line all his own. He led the general sire list eight times, and seven of his male-line descendants won the Kentucky Derby in the 1970s, including Triple Crown winners Secretariat and Seattle Slew, plus Spectacular

Nasrullah (opposite, on his arrival day at Claiborne Farm in 1950, and at left) sired the great Nashua (below) in his first U.S.-based crop

Bid. Seattle Slew later led the general sire list.

Although Bold Ruler was Nasrullah's best son at stud, plenty of others excelled. Nashua sired seventy-seven stakes winners, including the filly Shuvee, who also won consecutive runnings of the Jockey Club Gold Cup. Never Bend sired sixty-one stakes winners, including European Horse of the Year Mill Reef and classic winner Riverman, both top sires.

Nasrullah's son Nantallah also proved successful as a stallion. Nantallah's daughter, Moccasin, was 1965 co-Horse of the Year as a two-year-old. Three years earlier Nantallah's son Ridan and Nasrullah's son Jaipur engaged in one of the great races of the century. The two ran as a pair the entire length of the 1962 Travers Stakes at Saratoga, with Jaipur getting the nod.

Other successful stallions tracing to Nasrullah in male line include T. V. Lark (1974 leading sire), Blushing Groom (sire of Arazi), Caro, and Fleet Nasrullah.

Plenty has been made about Nasrullah's blood mixed with fellow Claiborne stallion Princequillo. After all, Secretariat and Mill Reef were both by Nasrullah's sons out of Princequillo mares.

But not even that combination was deserving of a rhyme like the one below.

Match Nasrullah through a son,
And Nasrullah through a daughter,
To make it really blister
Match Nasrullah with his sister.

Nasrullah, whose total of ninety-eight stakes winners worked out to 23 percent from foals, died in 1959 at Claiborne. *DS*

24

Sir Gallahad III Is Imported

A.B. HANCOCK SR. epitomized a horseman's horseman. The master of Claiborne Farm appreciated a good horse, but far more importantly could discern a good horse, even from a photograph. So it was with Sir Gallahad III, whose importation introduced stallion syndication to the United States.

Hancock first became interested in Sir Gallahad III when the horse won the Lincolnshire Handicap in England. Photographs of the race in a British publication impressed him, for he saw in the stretched out, driving winner what one British Turf writer described, "When he (Sir Gallahad III) gets into action he bids us look at him a second and yet a third time, for he strides along in effortless style." One look at a photograph of Sir Gallahad III, showing a big, robust colt of regal mien, convinced him that this was exactly the type of horse Claiborne needed.

To Hancock, every facet of Sir Gallahad III gleamed with sire potential. The colt possessed considerable racing ability. Blessed with a brilliant turn of foot, he had notched a requisite for

attracting the right mares, a classic victory — the Poule d'Essai des Poulains over a mile. Yet, he had also exhibited enough stamina to finish a close third in the Prix du Jockey-Club (French Derby).

Physically, the handsome bay stallion with a medium-sized star and a large snip on his muzzle displayed the breed's most desirable traits: size and scope; a muscular, well-built body; intelligent eyes; a kind expression; and a quiet manner. His docile behavior belied the nature of a stallion. He liked nothing better than to have his tongue pulled and to receive an affectionate pat. So gentle, in fact, was his temperament that it prompted Hancock, a man who had been around countless numbers of horses, to extol, "Gallahad has given me more pleasure than any other horse I ever was connected with."

Sir Gallahad III also had a sterling pedigree. He was by Teddy, a horse who never realized his potential as World War I interrupted racing in France during his racing years (although he won a pair of classics in Spain), and out of Plucky

in 1976 and had won his first three starts of the year carrying progressively higher weight: 126 pounds in a May 20 allowance at Belmont, 130 in the Metropolitan Handicap a mere eleven days later, 132 in the June 13 Nassau County Handicap. Assigned 134 pounds for the July 5 Suburban Handicap, he could not overcome the nine-pound weight difference he gave former juvenile champion and 1975 Kentucky Derby winner Foolish Pleasure and lost by a nose.

Bouncing back in the July 24 Brooklyn Handicap, also under 134 pounds, he avenged his loss to Foolish Pleasure while still giving him eight pounds. (Foolish Pleasure finished third behind second-place Lord Rebeau, who was carrying a featherweight 114.) The 136 pounds assigned in the Haskell at Monmouth proved too burdensome as Forego finished third, beaten just a little more than a length by horses receiving twenty-four and seventeen pounds, respectively. The loss earned little relief, one lone pound to be exact.

Carrying 135, Forego next started in the September 18 Woodward at Belmont, and under Bill Shoemaker, who would ride him for the rest of the grand old warrior's career, he defeated a strong field of nine other handicap horses by a length and a quarter. With four wins in six starts with 130 or more pounds, it came as no surprise that for the important Marlboro Cup Forego would carry the heaviest impost of his career to date, 137 pounds.

And then came the rains. Forego never much liked the mud, and an October rain soaked the Belmont surface, jeopardizing his starting in the Marlboro Cup. However, because a firm foundation lay underneath the slick, soupy surface, Forego lined up against ten others who were all receiving weight from the champion.

A natural rite of passage is for youth to test its mettle against age. Among Forego's most formidable rivals was the three-year-old Honest Pleasure, whose juvenile year had ended in a rolling boil with five straight stakes victories leading to a juvenile championship. He had begun his sophomore year with the same heat, but unsuccessful attempts at the Kentucky Derby and Preakness had taken him off the boil. He had simmered back to life with a win in the Travers Stakes and had dead-heated to be third in Forego's Woodward Handicap, carrying 121 pounds. For the Marlboro Cup he was given the least amount of weight from the six-year-old leader of the handicap ranks, eighteen pounds; Enchumao, the light-weight in the field, got twenty-eight pounds from Forego.

The more than 31,000 fans that braved the rain witnessed a race for the ages, a race that did not start until it was nearly over.

Honest Pleasure had led throughout the mile and a quarter race. At the top of the stretch, Craig Perret had the son of What a Pleasure comfortably in control while Forego languished in fifth.

Shoemaker moved Forego to the middle of the track and let the big horse find his footing. With ever-lengthening strides, Forego took flight, devouring each opponent between him and the leader. The wire loomed, but Honest Pleasure still led.

Perhaps it was the roar of the crowd. Perhaps it was just the undaunted will to win, but it seemed as if Forego could not gobble up the ground fast enough. Little separated them; then less; then nothing. The photo finish showed that Forego had, almost impossibly, prevailed, and by the luxurious margin of a head.

Forego would be named Horse of the Year for a third consecutive time (only the mighty Kelso had more — five) and return in 1977 to defend his title. But that was the year of Seattle Slew's Triple Crown. Even though Forego won three of the six races in which he carried more than 130 pounds (he carried up to 138), Seattle Slew was named Horse of the Year while Forego earned a fourth championship as handicap horse.

We shall not look upon his like again. *TH*

Under the tremendous impost of 137 pounds, Forego catches Honest Pleasure at the wire

27 Tom Fool's Pimlico Special

THE GREENTREE STABLE of John Hay Whitney and his sister, Joan Whitney Payson, was one of the pre-eminent racing and breeding establishments in America following World War II.

Like so many other top stables of its day, Greentree bred to race, so it was a departure from the norm when the stable's trainer, John Gaver, in 1950 bought a well-bred colt from central Kentucky breeder Duval A. Headley. Eventually named Tom Fool, the colt was sired by Menow and was out of the Bull Dog mare Gaga, whose first foal, Aunt Jinny, would end up being crowned that year's champion two-year-old filly.

At the time of Tom Fool's birth, Headley was still training racehorses while he was developing his Manchester Farm. Lacking the time to have a consignment of sales yearlings in 1950, Headley approached Gaver about purchasing the colt for Greentree, which had secured 1949 Horse of the Year honors with Capot, another son of Menow. Though Tom Fool had a gash in his leg from a paddock accident, Greentree nevertheless acquired the colt for a sum variously reported as between $20,000 and $25,000.

And the rest is history — very rich racing history. A champion at age two, Tom Fool was one of the early favorites for the 1952 Kentucky Derby, a reputation solidified after he began the season with an allowance victory and a runner-up effort in the Wood Memorial. A Derby start did not materialize, however, after Tom Fool missed several weeks of training due to a cough and fever. Tom Fool had a commendable record that year, with six wins, five seconds, and one third from thirteen starts, but it paled in comparison with his championship campaign the year

Tom Fool wins the Pimlico Special (opposite); trainer John Gaver (left) and owners Joan Whitney Payson and John Hay Whitney with the champion

before, which had included victories in the Sanford Stakes and the Futurity.

It was in 1953, however, that Tom Fool showed the dominance over older horses that earned him the distinction of ranking eleventh in *The Blood-Horse*'s list of the top one hundred racehorses of the twentieth century. The American public will probably remember the 1953 racing season more for the way in which the then-new medium of television chronicled the feats of the charismatic gray colt Native Dancer, who won two legs of the Triple Crown. But sharing equal billing among racing fans was Tom Fool's undefeated campaign in which the Greentree colt won all ten starts. Displaying his versatility, Tom Fool won at distances ranging from five and a half furlongs to one and a quarter miles. He successfully carried from 126 pounds to 136, hefting the latter to victory in the Brooklyn Handicap as he completed a sweep of the coveted New York Handicap Triple Crown, which also included the Metropolitan and Suburban handicaps.

The colt was so impressive in winning his first six outings of the year that he faced only token competition in his final four starts, all betless exhibitions. In the Wilson Stakes, Tom Fool rolled by eight lengths over his only competitor, and he likewise faced only one other horse in an easy victory in the Whitney. In the Sysonby, Tom Fool went unchallenged by Alerted and Grecian Queen, the only other starters, and he took his

spotless season record into the one and three-sixteenths-mile Pimlico Special on October 24, 1953.

The Special lived up to its name as it truly was special for the champion. Facing token opposition from Navy Page and Alerted, Tom Fool posted an eight-length win in track-record time of 1:55 4/5 under jockey Ted Atkinson. "Tom Fool rapidly established a commanding lead while under restraint, galloped along in front without being challenged and appeared to have considerable speed in reserve," the *Daily Racing Form* chart noted.

The Pimlico Special brought Tom Fool's career to a close. Ridden by Atkinson in all thirty starts, Tom Fool retired with twenty-one wins, seven seconds, and one third. He earned $570,165.

Despite the publicity surrounding Native Dancer's campaign, Tom Fool edged the three-year-old for Horse of the Year honors. Tom Fool entered stud at Greentree in 1954 and was quickly determined to be a "shy breeder," which limited his first foal crop. He went on to sire the earners of more than $8 million, with his thirty-six stakes winners including Horse of the Year and eventual top sire Buckpasser, champion Tim Tam, and foundation broodmare Dinner Partner.

Voted "Horse of the Decade" by the National Turf Writers Association, Tom Fool was inducted into the National Museum of Racing's Hall of Fame in 1960. He died August 20, 1976, and was buried in Greentree's cemetery. *RM*

ON A COLD WINTER DAY in February 1965, a small bay stallion was led into the indoor arena at E.P. Taylor's National Stud Farm, in Oshawa, Ontario. His name was Northern Dancer, and he was about to breed — or try to breed — his first mare.

The colt had proven the best three-year-old in North America in 1964, winning the Kentucky Derby, the Preakness Stakes, and the Queen's Plate. But his entry into stallion service was viewed with much the same mixture of skepticism and grudging respect that had accompanied him throughout his racing career, and for the same reason — he was just too small (about 15.1 hands) for many people to take him seriously.

For that matter, he was too small even to make

Northern Dancer Enters Stud

a successful cover of his first mate, 1962 Queen's Plate winner Flaming Page. She was a worthy partner in terms of racing ability, but she was a hand taller than Northern Dancer and therein lay the problem. Finally, fed up with the stallion's unrewarding attempts to mount her, Flaming Page let fly with her heels and caught Northern Dancer squarely in the ribs, ending the attempted mating.

Human ingenuity solved the problem: a shallow pit was dug in the floor of the breeding arena, and when the stallion and mare were brought in again a day or two later, Flaming Page was led into the depression. Standing on the main floor, Northern Dancer now had enough of a height advantage to mate successfully with the mare.

The mating, alas, would result in a dead foal. But from this inauspicious beginning, the greatest stud career of modern times would arise. Twenty-one sons and daughters of Northern Dancer were born in 1966, and ten eventually became stakes winners, including 1968 Canadian Horse of the Year Viceregal. The Dancer's second crop contained two even more remarkable horses: Fanfreluche, also a Canadian Horse of the Year and later an excellent broodmare, and the great Nijinsky II, winner of the 1970 English Triple Crown. Nijinsky II was out of Flaming Page and so validated the judgment that had made her the Dancer's first mate, even if the results were a year late in coming.

Nijinsky II foreshadowed several aspects of Northern Dancer's stud career. First, the majority of his best runners would make their reputations in Europe, not North America — to such an extent that Northern Dancer, while physically based in Canada and later Maryland, led the English general sire list four times but the American general sire list only once. Second, many of those same runners would pass through the sales ring (just as Nijinsky II himself had — he sold for $84,000 at the 1968 Canadian Thoroughbred Horse Society yearling sale), sparking bidding wars between European and Arab interests and helping to fuel an unprecedented boom in the yearling sales market through the early 1980s. And third, many of Northern Dancer's sons would themselves prove great sires.

Nijinsky II was not quite enough to resolve the

doubts about Northern Dancer's ability to get top horses; after all, he strongly resembled his dam. But as the years rolled on, the Dancers kept coming: Lyphard, The Minstrel, Try My Best, Storm Bird, Nureyev, Shareef Dancer, El Gran Senor, Secreto, Sadler's Wells, Ajdal. For those breeders who bought shares at $75,000 when owner E.P. Taylor syndicated the Dancer in 1970, the stallion was proving a wonderful investment. The Northern Dancers came in all shapes and sizes: some small and stocky, some larger and more elegant. But virtually all were marked with their sire's superb balance and fiery spirit, and they could run.

So, too, could the Dancer's grandchildren. By the time Northern Dancer himself died on November 16, 1990, his sons Lyphard, Nijinsky II, and Nureyev had collectively won seven sire championships in North America, England, and France, and Nijinsky II's son Caerleon had reigned as England's champion sire for 1988 (a title he would repeat in 1991). Sadler's Wells was on his way to the first of his fourteen English sire championships, and in 1991, Danzig would begin a run of three consecutive sire championships in the United States. Since then, other descendants of Northern Dancer have carried his blood around the world, making the little Canadian colt the head of the premier sire line of modern times. Without him, there would be no Deputy Minister, no Storm Cat, no Danehill, no Montjeu … the list goes on and on.

The Dancer may be gone, but his legacy dances on. *AH*

Northern Dancer stretching his legs in his paddock at Windfields Farm, the Maryland farm where he stood later in his career, and (opposite) with trainer Horatio Luro

29 Man o' War's Upset

THE HORSE VOTED THE BEST of the twentieth century tasted defeat only once, and Man o' War's upset to the improbably named Upset remains one of the Turf's most enduring curiosities. Defeat came in the 1919 Sanford Memorial at Saratoga Racecourse, where the infamous event helped give rise to the track's reputation as the "graveyard of champions."

Man o' War's legend already had taken root when Samuel D. Riddle's strapping chestnut colt took on six rivals in the six-furlong Sanford. He had reeled off six victories in the course of six weeks, barely drawing a breath as he manhandled lesser rivals. He was already being described as

"great" and a "veritable giant" in the nascence of his career.

Bred by industrialist and horseman August Belmont II and raised at Nursery Farm near Lexington, Kentucky, Man o' War would have raced in the colors of his breeder but for World War I. Belmont's service with the Quartermaster Corps in Spain kept Belmont from home longer than expected, prompting him to sell most of his yearlings. Man o' War was among twenty-one Belmont yearlings offered at the Saratoga sale of 1918, where he brought five thousand dollars, a good but not spectacular price. *(See No. 18.)*

The son of the temperamental Fair Play came

to hand readily enough for trainer Louis Feustel and made his first start June 6, 1919, at Belmont Park. He won the five-furlong test by six lengths. Feustel wheeled him back in three days, and Man o' War "drew away," according to the chart, to win the Keene Memorial. The Youthful Stakes at Jamaica fell just twelve days later, but Man o' War's brief respite proved no hindrance — he galloped to win by two and a half lengths. Two days later Big Red was back, making short work of the Hudson Stakes at Aqueduct. The Tremont and U.S. Hotel stakes followed, and Man o' War was "never extended" in winning both while carrying a remarkable 130 pounds. In the U.S. Hotel, Henry Payne Whitney's Upset was among the field chasing him home.

Man o' War in his famous upset (opposite) and as a two-year-old with (starting third from left) John Loftus, Samuel D. Riddle, and Louis Feustel; (below) Upset's rider, Willie Knapp

What really occurred in the Sanford has been obscured by the passage of time, exaggerated, perhaps, and revised to fit the myth of Man o' War. What is known is this: A substitute starter, C.H. Pettingill, had trouble lining up the field, so much so that Golden Broom broke through the barrier prematurely three times. Man o' War, who had drawn next to the outside, broke poorly. Some accounts report that he was turned sideways at the start; others, that he was facing the wrong way. Accounts also vary as to the quality of the ride given by John Loftus, Man o' War's then-regular rider. The jockey either cunningly saved ground by moving to the inside or got the colt boxed in with no recourse but to look for room on the outside and lose lengths. Interestingly, both Loftus and Willie Knapp, Upset's rider, were denied licenses the following year by The Jockey Club with no explanation.

Whether chicanery, bad racing luck, or a combination of both played a role, no one disputed Man o' War's courage in the Sanford.

"He stood a drive such as no other colt has been asked to do

in the last twenty years without flinching," wrote Kent Hollingsworth in *The Great Ones*. "Never again will his courage be questioned henceforth. It was an unknown quality, for he had never before been put to the test. When the test came, he was not found wanting ..."

Golden Broom made the early lead, according to the charts, with Upset in close pursuit. Man o' War had gained fourth by the quarter-mile of the six-furlong contest.

Golden Broom weakened in the stretch; Upset overtook him; and Man o' War, swung wide by Loftus, bore down. At the wire, though, Upset had a half-length advantage, completing the distance in 1:11 1/5.

Man o' War and Upset met again ten days later in the Grand Union Hotel Stakes, with the Riddle colt the odds-on favorite under 130 pounds. Upset shot to the lead, but Man o' War soon overtook the pacesetter and at one point had three lengths to the good until Loftus eased him in the final strides.

Man o' War completed his two-year-old campaign in the Futurity Stakes at Belmont, then returned for an undefeated sophomore season of incredible records and weight-carrying feats. *JD*

JOHN HENRY'S HAIRSBREADTH victory over The Bart in the inaugural Arlington Million was hailed as an immediate classic by the media and racing fans alike. The image of a gritty John Henry flying low over the soft turf, ever so slowly gaining on The Bart as the wire neared is forever etched in racing's collective memory.

But America's first million-dollar race was more than just another exciting finish; it put Arlington Park back on the horse racing map and changed racing's landscape.

From the 1930s to the 1950s, Arlington Park, located just outside Chicago, rivaled New York as a top racing spot. Owners such as Calumet Farm, C.V. Whitney, and Alfred Vanderbilt raced there, and Equipoise, Busher, Citation, and Round Table were among the greats who won major stakes there. Then in the 1960s, after longtime owner Ben Lindheimer died and management changed, Arlington Park experienced a downturn in its for-

tunes — both financial and political — and conditions at the track deteriorated as did the racing quality.

In the early 1970s Arlington Park came under the ownership of Madison Square Garden Corporation and in 1976 Joseph Joyce Jr. was named track president. Under the leadership of Joyce and Madison Square Garden Corp. president Sonny Werblin and executive vice president Jack Krumpe, Arlington began a comeback, aided by favorable racing legislation in Illinois, that allowed the track to raise purses, thus luring better horses. In 1979 Joyce began developing the idea for the Arlington Million. Arlington Park already had a top-quality turf course, but the track needed a signature event to reach the highest echelons of the sport.

Arlington officials worked with the International Racing Bureau to gauge international interest. Results were favorable, and race details began to

30 John Henry Wins Inaugural Arlington Million

be ironed out. The distance of one and a quarter miles was arrived at because the IRB was concerned that a mile and a half would make the race too similar to Europe's main event, the Prix de l'Arc de Triomphe. The August 30 date was chosen because it did not conflict with the dates of any classic races around the world. As for the million-dollar purse, which gave the race its name, "Sonny, Jack, and I knew that if we were going to insist our race was the greatest in the world, then we'd have to come up with the richest of any Thoroughbred purse in the world," Joyce told *Daily Racing Form* in 1981. Most of the purse came from nomination, eligibility, and starting fees, meaning the track ended up having to pay only $113,500 for the first running.

Arlington Park also underwent $2 million in improvements, including an expanded paddock, infield land-scaping, and redecorated clubhouse, grandstand, and jockeys' quarters. In addition, a twenty-stall "Arlington Million" barn was constructed to house stakes horses for major events.

Joyce and Werblin went about promoting the race, which NBC would telecast internationally. The Million became part of a ten-day "equestrian festival" that featured show jumping, polo match-es, and a parade of horses, as well as the Arlington-Washington Futurity for two-year-olds and an infield steeplechase, the first held at the track since 1957.

On Sunday, August 30, 1981, a crowd of 30,367 fans watched as twelve horses lined up at the post for the inaugural Million. Among the standouts were the six-year-old gelding John Henry, who was having the best year of his career to that point with victories in the Santa Anita Handicap, San Luis Rey, and Hollywood Invitational; Rossi Gold, the local hero who had won the Washington Park Stakes; and Key to Content, who had won the United Nations Handicap on firm turf at Atlantic City in his last start. Of the international contingent, the French star

John Henry defeats The Bart in the inaugural Arlington Million (opposite); with trainer Ron McAnally

Argument, who had won the 1980 Washington, D.C., International, and Prix de Diane winner Madam Gay were the main hopes. There also was a five-year-old horse named The Bart, who had placed that year in several major turf stakes in California.

When John Henry and The Bart hit the wire together, viewers both at home and at the track were hard-pressed to know who won. In fact, NBC at first reported The Bart as the winner. But the photo showed otherwise, and the first Arlington Million became a part of racing's lore (a statue of the race finish stands at the top of Arlington's paddock). John Henry went on to cap-ture Horse of the Year honors for 1981, and he returned twice more to the race he helped launch, winning again in 1984 at the age of nine. In 2005 the Million was still going strong, having survived fire, regime changes, a track shutdown, and the addition of other million-dollar (and more) races to the calendar. Perhaps a million-dollar race was inevitable, but Arlington Park can always say it got there first. *JM*

31 Belmont Park Opens

GRANDEUR WAS RECOGNIZED as a requirement for the Turf in New York by the time Belmont Park was being planned. Since the Civil War, racing in the North had eclipsed that in the South, and by the Gilded Age, the idea of what a racetrack should be was comparable to what was meant by a "cottage" in Newport.

Jerome Park and then Morris Park had been the showcase structures in New York while Monmouth Park in New Jersey staked that state's claim to equal grandeur.

By 1903, when various aspects growing from the proliferation of racetracks and other matters condemned Morris Park to history, the leaders of the Westchester Racing Association had no doubt that its successor should be cast in its own heroic mold. The *Illustrated Sporting News* looked forward boldly to the "grandest race course in the history of the world." The publication was banking on the financial strength and personal tastes of the likes of William Collins Whitney, J.P. Morgan, W.K. Vanderbilt, James R. Keene, and Turfman extraordinaire August Belmont II. There would be no disappointment.

Belmont Park, wrote racing official and historian Walter Vosburgh, was "a revelation. People were in ecstasies over it. It was by far the most extensive property that has been opened."

All appointments had to be the best: The saddling paddock "was the most beautiful seen anywhere in this country," and the huge oval track itself had enough adjoining and nearby chutes that it offered the variety of racing distances and directions reminiscent of the grandest racecourses in England. The layout covered 650 acres.

The handsome stands, detached club, and spacious green grounds opened on May 4, 1905.

The name it all was given, Belmont, was already deep in the traditions of New York and American racing. The Belmont Stakes, named for August Belmont I, had been run since 1867, and W.C. Whitney pressed for the new track to be named for that sporting gentleman and financial giant as well.

Opening day was highlighted by the Metropolitan Handicap, first run at Morris Park in 1891. It was one of many established prizes transferred to the new track, abetting Belmont's eventual status as "Headquarters of the Turf." The Metropolitan field included Belmont's grand filly Beldame, who later lent her name to an important race but who ran a poor race that day and finished ninth. The race resulted in a dead heat between another champion of the time, Sysonby, and the longshot Race King.

The Keene stable's Sysonby, a great horse who won fourteen of fifteen races, was co-favorite with Beldame at 3-1, according to the bookmaker odds recognized in the official race chart. He was a three-year-old under 107 pounds.

Belmont Park celebrated its centennial in 2005. The glamorous plant had been buffeted by the whims of the interceding century and had been rebuilt more than once. Anti-gambling sentiment halted racing for two years, 1911–12, but when it was reinstated, the crowds flocked back to the young queen of the sport. In 1917 arsonists destroyed the huge stand, and racing was conducted for two years in front of a makeshift viewing structure. Major renovations were completed by 1921, at which time the length of the stand had been increased to 950 feet. That year, the racing was changed from clockwise to counterclockwise, which had become the familiar pattern in the United States.

From 1963 through 1967, Belmont was idle, although the backstretch was still the base of many stables. Structural flaws and wear and tear required reconstruction of the stands. This was accomplished in time for Belmont to welcome back the Belmont Stakes, which had been run for several years at nearby Aqueduct. The year was 1968, and the Belmont had its hundredth running that day.

Over the years many great horses helped secure their places in history at Belmont Park, and many of the top races in the country are still run there. The eleven Triple Crown winners completed their heroic trilogies at the track, while Belmont's Suburban Handicap anchored the older horses' counterpart series (Metropolitan, Suburban, and Brooklyn handicaps). The likes of Man o' War, Citation, Native Dancer, and Nashua won the

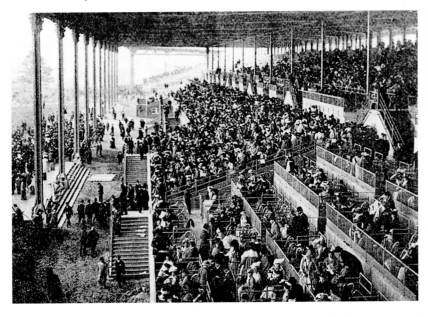

(Opposite) Sysonby (on rail) and Race King dead heat in the Metropolitan Handicap, centerpiece of Belmont Park's opening day

Futurity, while Top Flight, Twilight Tear, and Ruffian were among many who distinguished the history of the Coaching Club American Oaks.

In more recent years the purposely transient Breeders' Cup is the autumn climax of an American racing season. Belmont Park has hosted four of them, and while one was tainted by the death of Go for Wand, it was at Belmont, too, that Cigar concluded his perfect-ten season in 1995.

The handsome arched and brick solidity of the present Belmont Park carries on the feel of the past, and the glories of many of today's champions are gathered on the very grounds of history incarnate. *ELB*

32 Calumet Farm Purchases Bull Lea

SOMETIMES BEING RICH, savvy, and daring is just not enough. Sometimes what's important is being in the right place at the right time, and in that respect Warren Wright was indeed a very lucky man.

In the 1930s there was no Keeneland yearling sale in the heart of the Bluegrass, and all roads led to Saratoga. There, racing's elite gathered to see, be seen, and pluck the plum Thoroughbred yearlings from the consignments railed in from different sections of horse country.

On a fateful Friday night in August 1936, the owner of Calumet Farm, a fledgling

Thoroughbred enterprise, was seated next to his trainer, Frank Kearns, as he had been the eight other nights yearlings paraded through the ring to the cadence of the auctioneer's spiel. Wright was there, but Ethel Mars of Milky Way Farm was not.

Like Calumet, Milky Way Farm was a relatively new entry into the world of Thoroughbred racing, and, like Calumet, the stable had its origins in the big business crucible of Chicago. Founded by Frank Mars, who had turned a cottage candy business into the multi-million dollar Mars Inc., the farm used the Saratoga venue to supply runners for its racing stable.

Wright, of baking powder fame, and Mars were businessmen cut from the same bolt of cloth: Neither let the cost stop him from purchasing what he thought to be the best, especially a new horse for his racing stable. Although Mars died before he could see his dreams come to fruition, his widow, using this same philosophy, carried on in his stead.

As in previous years, Mrs. Mars had been a vocal presence; throughout the first week of the 1936 sale she bought with abandon. Bankrolled with a sweet fortune from her late husband, she took on the stalwarts of racing's elite, outbidding Isabel Dodge Sloane for a Man o' War colt at $18,000; outlasting Joseph Widener for a Sir Gallahad III colt at $18,000; outstaying Alfred Vanderbilt for a Royal Minstrel colt at $14,000. With dogged determination, she bid without bounds on anything that struck her fancy, failing on one occasion to get a Gallant Fox colt (that went to Sanford Stud) only because, being slightly deaf, she mistakenly thought the final bid hers.

On another occasion she had even gone head to head with Wright and come out on the winning end, snatching from him a Blue Larkspur—Risk colt (later named Sky Larking) for $13,500. But fate intervened at a most opportune time for Wright. Mrs. Mars caught a cold, became quite sick, and missed most of the second week. Alas, her trainer, Robert McGarvey, who represented her, was a bit more conservative with purse strings that weren't his.

What Wright and Kearns saw on that Friday night was a splendid colt that entered the Saratoga sales ring the property of Coldstream Stud, a farm just a little way across Fayette County from Wright's property. The bay son of Bull Dog out of the Ballot mare Rose Leaves certainly pleased the eye: strong, beautifully made, alert, confident. There was just something about him: Perhaps it was the splendid head, so unlike the usual Bull Dog type but more reminiscent of the colt's maternal grandsire; the well-sloped shoulder, the strong forearm leading into wide knees and short, flat cannon bones; or the strong, good-sized feet.

Mrs. Mars had also dog-eared her catalog for this handsome colt to sport the chocolate, orange, and white Milky Way silks, but, unfortunately, she was not there.

A spirited bidding fray dwindled to three: Isabel Dodge Sloane, Mrs. Mars' representative, and Wright, who went home with the colt after dropping $14,000, not a small sum in Great Depression dollars (considering that at the local Great Atlantic and Pacific Tea Company, three Milky Way candy bars could be purchased for a dime; today a single Milky Way costs seventy-five cents).

Although Mrs. Mars and Milky Way Farm would beat Calumet to the leading owner's title (1936) and to the winner's circle at the Kentucky Derby (Gallahadion, 1940), Wright's purchase would have lasting implications, for that bay colt named Bull Lea would be the main thread used to spin a legend, the most successful breeding establishment Thoroughbred racing has ever known.

A better than average racehorse, Bull Lea transcended all expectations at stud. From a mere $750 his first year, his stud fee had risen to $5,000 by the end of his career, a fee rivaling only that of Man o' War. And it was not without cause, for Bull Lea sired fifty-seven stakes winners (twenty-seven of which earned more than $100,000); was leading sire five times and leading broodmare sire four times; and sired the leading money winner and first millionaire (Triple Crown winner Citation), the leading money-winning gelding (Armed), the leading money-winning filly (Bewitch), three Kentucky Derby winners (Citation, Hill Gail, and Iron Liege), ten champions, and runners that earned more than $13.5 million. *TH*

Bull Lea as a racehorse (opposite) and as a stallion

113

33 Count Fleet's Belmont

COUNT FLEET'S DISDAINFUL trouncing of his Kentucky Derby and Preakness rivals scared off the competition and captivated the public. "Beat him?" Ed Christmas, trainer of Preakness challenger Vincentive, asked rhetorically. "They haven't even caught him yet."

Such was The Count's virtuosity that only two dared face him in the 1943 Belmont Stakes. He might as well have run by himself.

With John Longden never letting him fully extend, Count Fleet streaked to a twenty-five-length victory with only the dust from the ill-groomed Belmont Park surface at his heels. The 19,000 or so who watched the coronation of the sixth Triple Crown winner did so amid sirens on the marker poles and a sign advising "In Case of Air Raid Keep Calm." As World War II continued to impose hardships on Americans, Count Fleet, wrote *Daily Racing Form*'s Charles Hatton, "provides a sports-loving populace a sure-fire antidote."

Count Fleet raced in the yellow-and-black colors of his breeder, John D. Hertz, an American success story much admired in his day. The Austrian immigrant went to work while still a

schoolboy and parlayed his business acumen into ownership of Yellow Cab Company and later a rent-a-car empire bearing his name.

Hertz had purchased Count Fleet's sire, Reigh Count, as a two-year-old, impressed by the colt's biting a rival during a race. Reigh Count won the 1928 Kentucky Derby, then went to stud first at Hertz' farm in Illinois, then to Claiborne Farm near Paris, Kentucky. Hertz purchased his own farm near Claiborne, named it Stoner Creek Stud, and moved Reigh Count there. From the stallion's first Stoner Creek crop came Count Fleet, who made such a poor impression that Hertz tried to sell the future Triple Crown winner.

No one wanted to pay the sale price of $4,500, so Hertz sent the skinny, feminine-looking youngster to trainer Don Cameron. In his first spin aboard the colt, John Longden reportedly declared him a lunatic. But somehow the champion jockey agreed to partner Count Fleet, who raced in the name of Mrs. John D. Hertz, and would ride him in all his starts.

Count Fleet always had some trouble breaking from the gate, and this difficulty cost him his first

"Longden's task ... is to keep his amazing mount from running too fast, once he has killed off his field, rather than seeing how fast he can induce Reigh Count's son to run," Hatton wrote.

Count Fleet added the Withers to his skein, then tuned up for the Belmont in a June 1 mile work around two turns in an extraordinary 1:36 3/5.

Fairy Manhurst and Deseronto bravely went postward with the champion but provided only token competition. War-time restrictions prevented regular watering of the Belmont surface, leaving it dusty, slow, and uneven in places. Count Fleet appeared to skim the surface, but he wrenched an ankle during the race. He nevertheless recorded the largest margin of victory in that classic, one that would stand until Secretariat's thirty-one-length tour de force in 1973.

Legendary jockey John Longden aboard Count Fleet

few starts. He put it together in time for the Champagne Stakes, which he won in world-record time for a two-year-old. He equaled the track record in the Pimlico Futurity and won the Walden Stakes at the same track by thirty lengths.

"He runs with a high head, his stride is slashing, he rises high off the ground in air-flight, has strong finishing capacity and goes at his work with utmost resolution," wrote John Hervey in *American Race Horses* of 1942.

For the colt's juvenile feats, racing secretary John B. Campbell assigned Count Fleet a then-record 132 pounds on the Experimental Free Handicap.

Count Fleet tuned up for the Triple Crown with a romp in the Wood Memorial and, as the favorite, took the Derby and Preakness, then held a week apart, wire to wire. He didn't set any records but was impressive nonetheless.

Unfortunately, Count Fleet's finest hour was his last as a racehorse, for the injury failed to heal properly, and the Hertzes decided to retire their star. In twenty-one starts, Count Fleet had sixteen wins, four seconds, and one third and earnings of $250,300. As a stallion, he sired 1951 Kentucky Derby winner Count Turf, and his daughters produced such champions as Kelso and Lamb Chop. He is buried at Stoner Creek. *JD*

34 Barbara Jo Rubin's Historic Riding Victory

WHEN BARBARA JO RUBIN crossed the finish line first the night of February 22, 1969, she won more than just her riding fee. The nineteen-year-old won a place in the record books as the first female jockey to win a pari-mutuel Thoroughbred race at a recognized track in the United States.

But no one made it easy.

In her determined quest to ride races, Rubin endured a boycott by male riders, jeers, and rocks hurled through the windows of her living quarters. Press reports at the time described Rubin — a talented rider who had put in years on the back of a horse — as a jockette, a pigtailed girl, and a pert brunette.

Rubin's victory at Charles Town Races in West Virginia that winter night helped validate the cause of other female jockeys,

among them Kathy Kusner, Diane Crump, and Mary Bacon. Rubin and other aspiring female jockeys had to go to court to win the right to ride, their cause embraced by the American Civil Liberties Union.

Kusner applied for a license to ride in Maryland in 1967 but was turned down by state racing regulators. A year later a judge ordered the Maryland Racing Commission to issue her a license, ruling that she had been denied because of sex discrimination. A broken leg delayed Kusner's debut, and Crump became the first woman to ride in a pari-mutuel race in the United States, this milestone occurring at Hialeah on February 7, 1969. Collectively, these female riders broke down the doors of a once-impenetrable fraternity, leading the way for latter-day phenomena such as Julie Krone and Donna Barton.

"All I wanted was a chance," Rubin said after she was boycotted at Tropical Park near Miami.

Determination marked Rubin from her earliest days. At age six, after spending months in the hospital fighting polio, she took up riding to strengthen her withered legs. She had a natural affinity with horses and by age twelve she was riding horses on the bush circuit in Florida.

After a brief stint in college, Rubin decided to pursue a career in racing. She worked as a hot walker, exercise rider, and pony rider before getting her license as an apprentice jockey.

Unable to get a jockey's license in Florida, Rubin moved to New England, where she worked for trainer Dave Harper at Suffolk Downs. There she became known for her knack with problem horses.

Rubin later moved to Maryland to work for trainer Bryan Webb, who supported her effort to become a jockey. The young rider was eventually licensed in Florida and set to make her debut at Tropical Park in January 1969, but male jockeys boycotted. Rubin then went to Nassau's Hobby Horse Hall, where she piloted Fly Away to victory.

On February 22, Rubin exercised horses at Pimlico in the morning then napped while Webb drove her to Charles Town Races. Though the

Barbara Jo Rubin walks shoulder to shoulder with her male peers; (opposite) Rubin goes to the track with trainer Bryan Webb (center)

Charles Town jockey colony initially balked at the prospect of racing against Rubin, track management persuaded riders not to boycott. Nevertheless, Rubin had to dress in the track's first aid room and state troopers flanked her on the way to the paddock.

Fans pushed through the turnstiles, eager to see history be made.

Rubin rode Cohesian in the Washington Purse, a six and a half-furlong event. She was part of the Bryan Webb entry that evening with Larry Kunitake aboard Reely Beeg. Press accounts from that time suggest that Kunitake eased up on his mount to allow Rubin the neck victory. Cohesian completed the distance in 1:20 1/5.

Rubin's victory and the attendant publicity made her a popular draw, and she soon became the first woman to ride in New York and New Jersey. She made appearances at numerous tracks, which were eager to capitalize on the novelty of a female jockey.

Injuries and difficulty maintaining her weight, however, shortened Rubin's career, and she retired in 1970 with twenty-eight wins from ninety-eight mounts.

Rubin remains involved with horses today. She lives in her native Illinois, competing in various disciplines and giving riding lessons. *JD*

35 The New York Racing Association Is Created

THE NEW YORK RACING ASSOCIATION was created in something of a crisis. Nearly fifty years had passed since the last racetrack in the metropolis had been built, and deteriorating grandstands, competition from other states, and desultory customer service threatened New York's status as the nation's leading racing circuit.

The state had attained that status after the Civil War, when most of the South fell on troubled economic times. Although Kentucky maintained its ranking as the premier breeding state, New York rose to the fore in the racing sector.

By the latter decades of the nineteenth century, New York was the scene of handsome, glamorous racetracks such as Morris Park and Jerome Park, while upstate, Saratoga offered racing with a unique charm and flair. And in 1905 the grandest of the grand tracks, Belmont Park, opened. Wealthy racehorse owners ran the racetracks, so

John Hanes

there was little "us versus them" conflicts between tracks and owners.

As the twentieth century advanced, other states threatened New York's status as a leader by becoming active and aggressive in the sport. New Jersey, where handsome Monmouth Park revived racing in the middle 1940s, got into the action, while to the west, Chicago built upon its own long tradition of major racing.

Though New York racing had been feeling the pressure, things came to a head in 1953. That year Alfred Vanderbilt's champion Native Dancer earned $18,850 for winning the revered old Travers Stakes at Saratoga compared to the $97,725 and $66,500, respectively, he had earned for his trips to win Chicago's Arlington Classic and American Derby. Moreover, Eugene Mori had moved boldly to make his upcoming stakes for two-year-olds, the Garden State Stakes at neighboring New Jersey's Garden State Park, the richest stakes in the world.

The great New York races such as the Belmont Stakes, Futurity, and Suburban Handicap retained their cachet, but this status was not guaranteed in perpetuity. Meanwhile — although it might seem difficult to imagine now — racing men lived in the fear that their beloved playground called Saratoga would be shut down for political expedience because at the time it generated less state tax revenue than would a comparable meeting downstate.

In August that year, at a dinner at the Reading Rooms in Saratoga, Ashley Trimble Cole, the chairman of the New York Racing Commission, decried the state of decay and decline in New York racing. He put attending sportsmen on notice that if racing was unable to reverse this trend, the state was prepared to step in and take matters into its own hands.

Ogden Phipps, vice chairman of The Jockey Club, took quick action. Phipps named three sportsmen with great industrial/business backgrounds as a committee to devise a plan to uplift New York racing: John W. Hanes, Captain Harry F. Guggenheim, and Christopher T. Chenery. (Somewhat ironically, it was Guggenheim who won more than $150,000 a few months later by sending his colt Turn-to to New Jersey's Garden State Stakes.)

The three captains of industry and sport met frequently and by the next January had an outline for the formation of the New York Racing Association. Following the routines of an average fan, Hanes took a train to the races and found it difficult to bet, buy a hot dog, or even see the races. He was all the more convinced that better treatment of the public not only was essential to maintain the sport's popularity but was consistent with good business — and would increase state revenue.

In brief, the plan was to buy the stock at New York State's existing racetracks — Belmont Park, Jamaica, Aqueduct, and Empire City in the Metropolitan area and Saratoga upstate.

Aqueduct, already on a train line, would be demolished and replaced. The plan called for Jamaica and Empire City to be closed and Saratoga to undergo extensive renovations.

To accomplish all this, a corporation would be formed to raise some $45 million and would be run by racing men receiving no dividends. In order to secure financing from banks, the corporation requested a twenty-five-year franchise to operate the racetracks.

By the time of the legislation that created the New York Racing Association, the governor was W. Averell Harriman, who as a young man had owned a powerful racing stable prior to launching his career in government. The bill was duly signed, and the rescue effort began.

Although they needed government's blessings, Guggenheim, Hanes, and Chenery knew to be wary of politicians — those in office and those who would follow. Guggenheim's papers include a letter to Hanes, in which he wrote, "The objective I have in mind is not only to solve the immediate problem of a new race track for New York but to attempt to close the door to political control ... for a very long time to come."

Aqueduct was ready for its grand opening in the summer of 1959 and was quickly dubbed "The Big A" as crowds of up to 70,000 began to pour through the gates. Belmont Park had to be closed late in 1962 because of structural problems and it too was rebuilt, opening in 1968 in time to host the hundredth running of the Belmont Stakes.

At the time of The Big A's debut, W.C. Heinz wrote in *Reader's Digest*: "There's been a revolution in New York State that should interest taxpayers, legislators, horse lovers, and horse racing fans throughout the United States. All the profit in Thoroughbred racing in New York now goes to the state or to improvement of the tracks, thanks to a concept unique in American legislation, big business, and sport ... Thanks to the hard work of a group of public-minded citizens we have a way of returning all (racing's) profits to taxpayers."

As recounted in a retrospective in *The Blood-Horse* in 2005, through the 1960s New York racing experienced a boom: "Attendance soared, (race tracks) often seeing more patrons than major league baseball games in the city. For the state, too, the money was rolling in from NYRA."

The changing landscape of racing, politics, and competing interests eventually would challenge this new structure, but for the time being New York racing's course had been righted. The sport, the public, and the state had been well served. *ELB*

Racing Comes to Television

NATIVE DANCER WAS THE FIRST television star of racing, arriving on the scene in 1953, the dawn of the fascinating new medium.

With his distinctive color and the splashy diamond silks of owner Alfred G. Vanderbilt, the dominant colt known as the Gray Ghost was easy to follow on the small black-and-white screen. Millions of Americans watched the colt win and win. And when he suffered his loss by a head for the Kentucky Derby, viewers were crushed.

This was the sort of reaction racing and television executives hoped for when they planned how racing should appear on the networks. At a press conference on March 25, 1953, racing officials and A. Craig Smith, vice president of the Gillette Safety Razor Company, announced that Belmont Park, Aqueduct, Jamaica Race Track, and Delaware Park had contracted with NBC to televise their Saturday feature races during the spring of 1953. ABC would handle the radio broadcasts.

As befitted the complex new medium of television, the productions included many ingredients, including some alluring promotions and even a telethon aspect. Part of Gillette's responsibility as the races' commercial sponsor was to donate a Hackney pony, from the Ward Acres Farm in New Rochelle, New York, each week to auction off among viewers and listeners. The money, in turn, went to the Damon Runyon Memorial Fund for Cancer Research. The first pony used for this promotion was a two-year-old named Stonehenge Surprise. He was paddocked inside New York's Ambassador Hotel during the press conference, posing for photographs and refusing to be blanketed.

But more excitement than bidding for a pony awaited racing fans. The races to be televised included the Wood Memorial, the Withers Stakes, the Suburban Handicap, the Metropolitan

Handicap, and the Coaching Club American Oaks. The first race in the series was the $30,000-added Gotham Stakes for three-year-olds. The as-yet-unbeaten Native Dancer was taking on eight others, and the Gray Ghost delighted racing's first television audiences by romping to a two-length win.

The television triumphs of Native Dancer and other stars of the fifties, including the great handicap horse Tom Fool, helped bring racing a new heyday. In 1953 Stanley Levey wrote in the *New York Times* that "Horse racing, which used to be called the sport of kings, is threatening to become the king of sports." On the Brooklyn Dodgers' opening day in 1953, more people went to the races at Jamaica than to the ball game. It was because racing had planned its television coverage so well, Levey argued, that more people went to the track, where they could see all the races on a card rather than only those on television. Televising racing was designed to entice viewers to learn more about the sport and head for the races. In comparison, baseball oversaturated its audience with constant games on screen.

Televising horse racing helped legitimize the sport and garner a larger audience. In *The Blood-Horse*'s "Thoroughbred Round Table" feature on October 24, 1953, one panelist supported televising the races because "a lot of people who have never been to a racetrack think it's some back alley with a bookmaker in a derby hat, or something …"

Even with all this success, after Native Dancer retired fewer people watched racing on television. Match races, however, continued to draw viewers. When Kentucky Derby winner Swaps took on Preakness and Belmont stakes winner Nashua at Chicago's Washington Park in 1955, CBS broadcast Nashua's victory nationwide.

In the early 1970s, racing underwent another surge in popularity as people turned on their televisions to see Secretariat, whose bright chestnut coat stood out on the new color sets. Like Native Dancer, Secretariat was a television star who brought new fans to racing. Millions tuned in on July 6, 1975, for a match race between Kentucky Derby winner Foolish Pleasure and the undefeated filly Ruffian. Sadly, that day became tragic when Ruffian broke down.

Today millions of Americans watch the Triple Crown and Breeders' Cup races each year on network television. With the myriad options available through cable and satellite television, there are even channels devoted solely to providing horse racing coverage around the clock, something unimaginable in 1953, when audiences watched from home as Native Dancer thundered across the finish line time and again that spring. *EMG*

Today's camera crews get close to the action; (opposite) owner Alfred Vanderbilt with Native Dancer, the first equine TV star, who won the Wood Memorial (opposite bottom) and other televised races

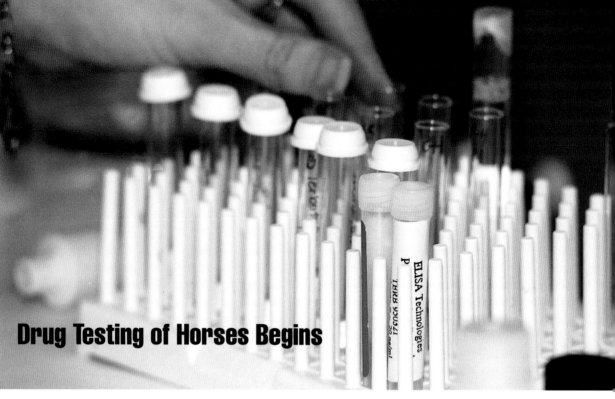

37 Drug Testing of Horses Begins

THOUGH MARIJUANA WAS his primary target, Harry Anslinger broadened his scope and went after horse racing stimulants in his assault on drugs in the 1930s. As head of the Federal Bureau of Narcotics, this mini-version of J. Edgar Hoover wielded plenty of power. He crusaded against the prevalent use of stimulants in horse racing and demanded that racing leaders take action against the scourge. He went so far as to conduct highly publicized raids at racetracks across the country, arresting a series of people found giving horses drugs, primarily caffeine, to make them run faster.

Racing leaders were well aware that doping had become a formidable problem, and the raids had brought it to the forefront. In an August 5, 1933, editorial following the arrests, *The Blood-Horse* wrote: "It now is definitely up to owners, trainers, jockeys to see to it that no horses are drugged, just as it has all along been the duty of the officials to stop the practice, the inauguration of which they should never have permitted. A house is just as clean as its occupants make it. Why live in filth?"

Florida was one of the first states to try and get its house in order, and Hialeah Park at its winter meet of 1934 was one of the first racetracks to initiate drug screening. The track imported saliva testing from France, where it had been used for a couple of decades. In fact, Joseph E. Widener, the track's president and a leader in the racing affairs of America and France, claimed he and his associates had prompted the government to investigate the use of stimulants in American racing in the first place.

As part of instituting the saliva test, the Florida Racing Commission made trainers responsible for any positive test results. Stewards would choose horses by lot before each race, and no indication would be given until the horse was ordered to the testing box. As part of its enforcement efforts, the commission also hired guards to watch the stables an hour before the horses were sent to the paddock.

The horsemen took issue with the procedure, claiming the guards were incompetent and the Florida Racing Commission lacked any racing expertise. Their complaints increased in number and intensity as the meet progressed.

Two drug positives in particular, both in the second week of March, riled the trainers. On March 9, 1934, John Partridge observed his horse acting strange, withdrew him from the race, and requested a saliva test. The test came back positive for caffeine. On March 13, 1934, H.C. Trotter reported after a race that he thought someone had given his horse a stimulant. Trotter asked for a saliva test for his horse, and it also came back positive for caffeine.

These cases went before the racing commission on the morning of Friday, March 16, one day before the meet concluded with the much-anticipated Florida Derby. One hundred horsemen attended the meeting and demanded the horses be more carefully guarded against stimulation, and any penalties for stimulation should be imposed against the guards, not the trainers.

The commission disagreed with the horsemen, and though it did find trainer Partridge blameless, it suspended trainer Trotter for the remainder of the Florida season. According to the commission, Trotter should have reported his suspicions before the race. Though the Trotter penalty was much less severe than the typical punishment — banishment from racing — it still was lengthy.

The angry horsemen vowed to strike and not enter Saturday's races. They met with Widener to try and resolve the matter. Widener then met with the racing commission, which refused to change its procedures. Despite Widener asking them not to strike on Florida Derby day, the horsemen con-

tinued their boycott. Widener vowed to race even if only one horse were entered in each race. He kept entries open until seven that night, but other than the two stakes races, the other five races on the card did not fill.

Saturday morning the racetrack and the racing commission took action to end the strike. They ruled four strike leaders off the track for inciting disorder. Once these four agitators were removed, the races all filled quickly, with a total of sixty-six horses.

The Blood-Horse correspondent found the Florida Derby Day crowd "probably was the largest attendance ever assembled at Hialeah Park for racing." He also wrote, "Never have I seen a greater outpouring of the true sporting spirit, nor such a tribute to the probity of good Turf management."

More than seven decades after its introduction, drug testing remains a volatile issue. While testing has become increasingly sophisticated, so has the illegal doping of horses, with racing chemists widely acknowledged to be playing catch up with cheaters. Developing super tests for so-called designer drugs and seeking uniform medication laws look to occupy regulators as the new century unfolds much as those issues did in the old. *RB*

A horse leaves the detention barn after post-race testing, which is standard procedure today

38 The Jersey Act Is Rescinded

ALTHOUGH THE NAME sounds most official, the Jersey Act was not an act of the British government. It was no Stamp Act that led to bloody revolution. Rather, it was nothing more than a policy set forth by the English Jockey Club in 1913 to keep the blood of the English Thoroughbred pure. Under the urging of Lord Villiers, the seventh earl of Jersey (his ancestor had bred Glencoe, one of the most important stallions imported to the United States), the *General Stud Book*, the official registry of English Thoroughbreds, was amended to read thusly: "No horse or mare can, after this date, be considered eligible for admission, unless it can be traced without flaw on both sire's and dam's side of its pedigree to horses and mares themselves already accepted in the earlier volumes of this book."

For the most part the American Thoroughbred had its genesis in the blood of the English Thoroughbred. However, an official registry for the American Thoroughbred did not appear until 1873, almost a century later than the English *Stud Book*. Thus, record keeping was not always accurate. Records had also been destroyed, especially during the Civil War when fighting occurred in regions that were hotbeds of the Thoroughbred industry. So for a horse in the early 1900s to trace its ancestry back "without flaw" might be most difficult. In effect, the Jersey Act relegated most American-bred horses to the status of "half-breds."

Anglo pride compounded the problem. The American Thoroughbred was good and could compete on a par with its more pure-bred English cousins; therefore, English horsemen treated any horse from the colonies with hostility.

Many rich Americans had begun sending their horses to be tested in the kiln of English racing, and in 1881 Iroquois, an American-bred son of Leamington—Maggie B. B., dared win the most venerated of all classics, the Epsom Derby. Other horses followed, and when the historic prizes of the English Turf fell to the invaders, rumblings began among the racing gentry, but they generally amounted to nothing palpable; rather, they just festered beneath the surface of proper decorum.

The outlawing of gambling in many important racing jurisdictions in the United States in the early twentieth century escalated the problem further. American breeders and owners sought other outlets, and Europe became a prime market. J.B. Haggin, a leading American breeder, shipped huge consignments to England for sale there. As rich sportsmen such as August Belmont, H.P. Whitney, and Joseph Widener moved their centers of racing to England and France, the situation came to a head.

When the Jersey Act was adopted in 1913, the U.S. Thoroughbred industry was in such disarray that American breeders put up no protest. And the English *Stud Book* became the standard by which Thoroughbreds in all other countries were judged. Even though English Thoroughbreds had already been contaminated by impure blood, the escape clause "unless it can be traced without flaw on both sire's and dam's side of its pedigree to horses and mares themselves already accepted in the earlier volumes of this book" secured their inclusion. The English breeding industry was once more an island of purity.

Among those horses made ineligible for the registry were such great names as the legendary Man o' War, Triple Crown winner Gallant Fox, and any descendant of the great American sire Lexington, who dominated the American sire list sixteen times. Although his offspring could race in England, they could not be accepted into the *General Stud Book*, effectively eliminating their sale as breeding stock.

Leading American sire Lexington (opposite), whose descendants, like English classic winner My Babu (left), were ineligible for inclusion in the English *Stud Book*

As racing in the United States thrived during the 1930s and reached its zenith in the 1940s, more and more American breeders took umbrage with the Jersey Act and began overtures to have it amended. Among the most influential of these was William Woodward Sr., a long-time patriarch of racing on both sides of the Atlantic. Woodward campaigned the leading English three-year-old in 1948, Black Tarquin. An American-bred, the great-grandson of Man o' War on his female side had won the classic St. Leger Stakes but was not eligible under the Jersey Act for inclusion in the *General Stud Book*. My Babu, winner of the 1948 Two Thousand Guineas, also illustrated this point. An honorary member of England's Jockey Club, Woodward had long advocated the repeal of the Jersey Act.

By June 1949, thought had shifted, and quietly the Jersey Act was abolished. New language directed that "any animal claiming admission from now on must be able to prove satisfactorily some eight or nine crosses of pure blood, to trace back for at least a century, and to show such performances of its immediate family on the turf as to warrant the belief in the purity of its blood."

The new ruling had little effect on the American Thoroughbred, which had already established its dominance in the world of racing. What it did do for American breeders was salve their pride, which had been wounded for thirty-six years. *TH*

39 The 1967 Woodward Stakes

BUCKPASSER! Damascus! Dr. Fager! That's all the New York Racing Association needed to stir the nation's interest in the 1967 Woodward Stakes. There was no need for giveaways or any other gimmicks; just three powerhouse names that had commanded the sports pages all year with one spectacular feat after another.

Not only was the Woodward going to determine Horse of the Year, it was being called by some the "Race of the Decade" and by others the "Race of the Century."

Despite the enormity of the event, no one could appreciate the true magnitude of the showdown. History would go on to record the 1967 Woodward as a meeting of three Horses of the Year and Hall of Fame members who among them captured thirteen championships, equaled or broke nine track records and set two world records, and won carrying 130 pounds or higher eighteen times. In eighty-five combined starts they won sixty-four races (fifty-four of them stakes) and finished out of the money only three times — Dr. Fager on a controversial disqualifica-

tion, Damascus due to a bowed tendon that ended his career, and Buckpasser in his first career start when he finished fourth, beaten one and a quarter lengths.

Damascus, who possessed one of the most electrifying moves on the far turn ever witnessed on an American racetrack, was the dominant three-year-old, having already captured nine major stakes that year, including the Preakness and Belmont; the Travers, in a track record-equaling twenty-two-length romp; and the American Derby, in a track record-breaking seven-length effort.

The brilliantly fast Dr. Fager, who had defeated Damascus by a half-length in the one-mile Gotham Stakes in their only meeting, won the Withers Stakes in its fastest running in the history of New York racing by a three-year-old and scored easy wins in the Arlington Classic and New Hampshire Sweepstakes, breaking the track record for a mile and a quarter in the latter.

Buckpasser, whose strength was a powerful late surge, was the defending Horse of the Year who had won thirteen of his fourteen starts as a three-year-old, setting a world record for the mile in the Arlington Classic. In 1967 he had won the Metropolitan Handicap under 130 pounds and the Suburban Handicap carrying 133 pounds.

Also in the Woodward field were the speedy Handsome Boy, who had handed Buckpasser an eight-length beating in the Brooklyn Handicap, and Damascus' stablemate Hedevar and Buckpasser's stablemate Great Power, who were entered as rabbits to kill off Dr. Fager.

In addition to being televised by WPIX in New York (there was no national TV coverage of racing back then other than the Triple Crown races), special arrangement was made for the race to be shown on closed circuit at Atlantic City Race Course and to stations in Philadelphia, Miami, and Ocala. The race, which drew more than 55,000, was also broadcast around the world via Armed Forces Radio.

With Dr. Fager losing his regular rider, Braulio Baeza, who was committed to ride Buckpasser, trainer John Nerud named Bill Boland to replace him. Bill Shoemaker, as usual, was aboard Damascus.

The story of the 1967 Woodward can be told simply. What started as Buckpasser, Damascus, and Dr. Fager, ended as Damascus. The rabbits did their job early, as both Bobby Ussery on Great Power and Ron Turcotte on Hedevar broke from the gate screaming and whipping their horses in order to get Dr. Fager stirred up. Great Power dropped out of it quickly, but Hedevar, himself a former world-record holder for the mile, stayed

The "Race of the Century" pitted three of racing's greatest stars: Damascus (opposite), Dr. Fager (below), and Buckpasser (left)

with the Good Doctor for over five furlongs, pushing him through suicidal fractions of :22 2/5 and :45 1/5. By the time Dr. Fager finally shook off Hedevar and opened a clear lead, he had run the six furlongs in a scorching 1:09 1/5.

Damascus and Buckpasser were biding their time, more than a dozen lengths off the pace. As they rounded the far turn, the two closers began chopping into Dr. Fager's lead. Buckpasser was being pushed along but couldn't keep up with the quicker Damascus, who liked to pounce on horses like a cat on its prey. By the quarter pole, the result was already obvious. Damascus surged past a leg-weary Dr. Fager and quickly turned the "Race of the Century" into a procession, winning by ten lengths in 2:00 3/5, an excellent time over a drying-out track. Buckpasser just got up to beat out Dr. Fager for second.

Two days after the Woodward, Buckpasser was retired. Dr. Fager would go on to record perhaps the greatest season ever the following year, winning an unprecedented four championships, while carrying staggering weights all year and breaking Buckpasser's world record for the mile.

Damascus, who had easily clinched Horse of the Year in the Woodward, had an excellent four-year-old campaign, winning five major stakes, also carrying high weights. After losing the Suburban to Dr. Fager, he defeated his arch rival in the Brooklyn, in which he broke the track record for a mile and a quarter. Damascus was forced to give up his crown to Dr. Fager, but history will show that on September 30, 1967, he stood among the mighty and towered over them all. *SH*

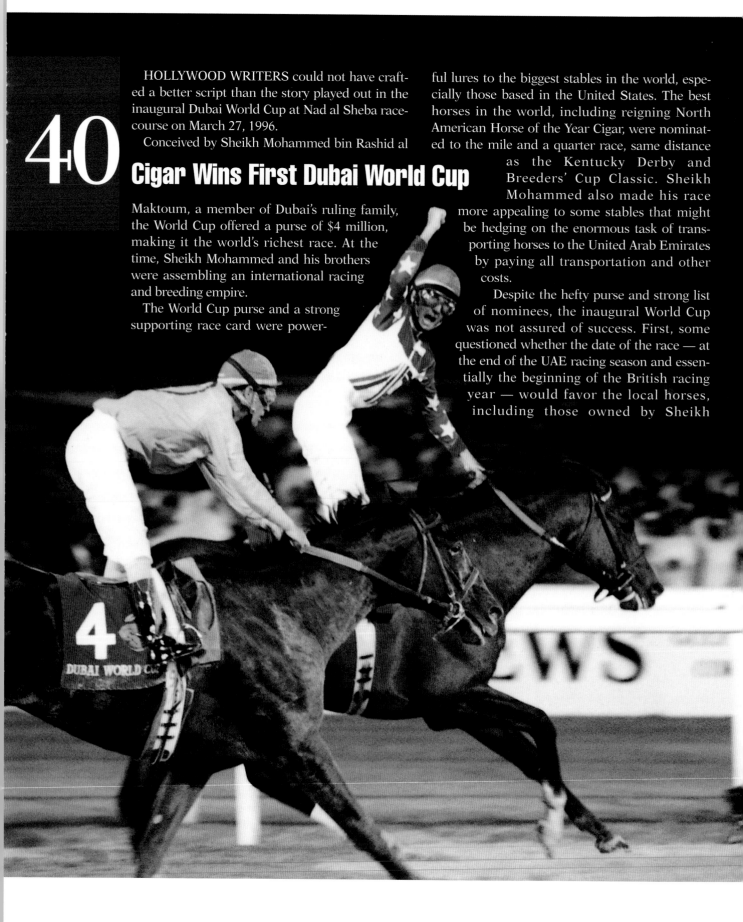

40

Cigar Wins First Dubai World Cup

HOLLYWOOD WRITERS could not have crafted a better script than the story played out in the inaugural Dubai World Cup at Nad al Sheba racecourse on March 27, 1996.

Conceived by Sheikh Mohammed bin Rashid al Maktoum, a member of Dubai's ruling family, the World Cup offered a purse of $4 million, making it the world's richest race. At the time, Sheikh Mohammed and his brothers were assembling an international racing and breeding empire.

The World Cup purse and a strong supporting race card were power-ful lures to the biggest stables in the world, especially those based in the United States. The best horses in the world, including reigning North American Horse of the Year Cigar, were nominated to the mile and a quarter race, same distance as the Kentucky Derby and Breeders' Cup Classic. Sheikh Mohammed also made his race more appealing to some stables that might be hedging on the enormous task of transporting horses to the United Arab Emirates by paying all transportation and other costs.

Despite the hefty purse and strong list of nominees, the inaugural World Cup was not assured of success. First, some questioned whether the date of the race — at the end of the UAE racing season and essentially the beginning of the British racing year — would favor the local horses, including those owned by Sheikh

Mohammed and his family. Also of concern were the nearly fourteen inches of rain that had fallen in Dubai (where the yearly average is two inches) and a forecast for more rain, and its effect on the racing surface. Other concerns, especially for the American-based runners, included the banning of raceday medication, having to race under the lights at night, and racing over a primarily sand-based surface. Finally, even after Cigar's arrival, his status for the race remained in doubt due to a bruised foot that had knocked him out of the Santa Anita Handicap earlier in the month.

But any trepidation was more than offset by the show put on by the oil-rich host country for its international guests. Consistent with his vision for the World Cup to become the pre-eminent race in the world, Sheikh Mohammed also scheduled a week of festive events and an equine symposium to precede World Cup day. Cigar's owners, Allen and Madeleine Paulson, soaked up the atmosphere and their equine star was the center of attention every time he went to the track.

When the gates for the World Cup opened, the race lived up to expectations for the more than 20,000 in attendance. The rain did not materialize and trainer Bill Mott's aggressive treatment of Cigar's bruise enabled the horse to reach the starting gate.

Ridden by Jerry Bailey, Cigar settled into a stalking position just behind the first group of leaders. When the field rounded the turn into the stretch, Cigar was eager to run and his jockey obliged. With a quarter of a mile left, the son of Palace Music had a clear lead before being challenged by fellow American runner Soul of the Matter. After Soul of the Matter poked his head in front, Cigar responded to the challenge, winning the stretch duel for a half-length victory in final time of 2:03.84. Soul of the Matter held second

and L'Carriere, who had been the early leader, was another eight lengths back in third, for a 1-2-3 finish by U.S.-based horses.

Having already taken the previous year's Breeders' Cup Classic for his twelfth consecutive win, Cigar was crowned the unofficial "Horse of the World" by virtue of his victory at Nad al Sheba. The winner's purse of $2.4 million pushed Cigar past Alysheba as the all-time leading North American earner with $7,669,015.

Of course, Cigar continued his winning ways, eventually tying Citation's modern-day record of sixteen consecutive wins. After securing his second Horse of the Year title, Cigar was retired with

(Opposite) Cigar's historic victory in the desert; Sheikh Mohammed with Allen and Madeleine Paulson

a record of nineteen wins from thirty-three starts and earnings of $9,999,815. Despite a lucrative deal for Cigar to stand at Ashford Stud, the horse was unable to match in the breeding shed the superior performance he exhibited on the racetrack. The horse proved sterile and after prolonged negotiations, he was relocated in 1999 to the Hall of Champions at the Kentucky Horse Park.

Meanwhile, the Dubai World Cup had cemented its place on the annual international racing calendar. By 2005 the purse had been increased to $6 million and American horses had won five of the first ten runnings.

Cigar's inaugural victory in the darkening desert remains the benchmark against which all future World Cups will be judged, however, for he brought enough of the magic and glamour to satisfy Sheikh Mohammed's loftiest goals. *RM*

41 Bold Ruler Leads Sire List a Record Eight Times

BOLD RULER HAD been dead two years when his greatest son, Secretariat, ended a twenty-five-year drought in Triple Crown winners with a flourish difficult to imagine. Secretariat's remarkable prowess that year, 1973, returned his deceased sire to a domain Bold Ruler had dominated in life. Posthumously, the stallion added to his twentieth-century record by leading the American sire list an eighth time. No other horse had held the title so often since Lexington led the list sixteen times during a nineteenth-century reign over a sport far smaller and quite different from the Bold Ruler era.

A son of Nasrullah—Miss Disco, Bold Ruler exemplified the highest hopes and aspirations of the Thoroughbred breeder. He was bred to be a good one, and he turned out to be a great one.

Nasrullah had been imported to Claiborne Farm in 1950, and among the mares farm owner A.B. (Bull) Hancock Jr. had been eyeing to breed to him was the stakes winner Miss Disco, by Discovery. After several tries he had been able to purchase the mare. At the same time, however, he was looking for a mare to purchase for one of his loyal clients, Mrs. Henry Carnegie Phipps of Wheatley Stable. It made sense to offer Mrs. Phipps the option of buying Miss Disco, which she did. In April 1954, Miss Disco foaled Bold Ruler for Mrs. Phipps.

Bold Ruler was not a perfect specimen. He had a hernia as a young foal, and later Hancock recalled he never had been completely happy with the youngster's condition while the colt was at Claiborne. By the time Wheatley's trainer of long standing, Sunny Jim Fitzsimmons, unleashed the colt onto the racing scene, though, he had grown into a sprightly young athlete with impressive qualities.

Bold Ruler was widely seen as the best two-year-old of 1956, although a couple of late-season losses denied him the championship. At three he had as much brilliance as a horse is likely to possess, but his distance limitations also came into play. He failed in the Kentucky Derby and Belmont Stakes but at year's end did win a major race at one and a quarter miles. That day he ran away from top-class colts Gallant Man and Round Table in the Trenton Handicap. Bold Ruler also won the Flamingo Stakes, Wood Memorial, Preakness, and a slate of lesser races, and he shared Horse of the race and winning by five and a half lengths. He also, however, came out of the race sore in his left foreleg. An osselet in the ankle was diagnosed. Jones, who later in published reports blamed the racetrack condition for the ailment, had the ankle pinfired, but it didn't improve. Citation was rested for all of 1949.

When Citation returned to racing, he was still a great racehorse but lacked the brilliance he had shown as a three-year-old. He won two races out of nine starts, which included setting a world record of 1:33 3/5 in the Golden Gate Mile Handicap on June 3, 1950. Citation's other win, however, had come in an allowance race at Santa Anita Park in January. The colt, considered two years earlier to be the equal of Man o' War, was now being called racing's "biggest disappointment."

Wright kept him in training, determined to make Citation racing's first millionaire. The master of Calumet, however, would not live to see the day. Wright died on December 28, 1950. His widow, Lucille, and Jones continued the quest with equal determination.

Citation progressed toward that goal with a second in the Argonaut Handicap on May 30, 1951. He went on to win a $15,000 handicap at Hollywood Park on June 14 and the American Handicap on the Fourth of July. That victory made the six-year-old the richest Thoroughbred in history with $985,760 in earnings and put him only $14,240 shy of the million-dollar goal.

Jones set his sights on the $100,000 Hollywood Gold Cup for Citation's next start. Ten horses entered the race including two Calumet stablemates: Bewitch, who with at least a second-place finish was poised to become the richest Thoroughbred mare, and All Blue. The two horses were described at the time by Associated Press reporter Bob Myers as "a com-

bination of policeman and fireman." All Blue was the policeman to ensure an honest pace, and Bewitch was there to rescue the race for Calumet in case Citation ran into trouble and faltered. Other challengers were top West Coast handicap runners Be Fleet, who had beaten Citation by three lengths in the Argonaut, and Sturdy One, who had been only a neck back in third in the same race.

All Blue did his job by taking the early lead in the mile and a quarter Gold Cup, and Bewitch, who did not need to save the race, finished second to get her record.

Be Fleet went with All Blue but didn't press the pace, allowing Citation's jockey, Steve Brooks, to settle his mount in third through the clubhouse

(Opposite) Citation gallops to victory in the Hollywood Gold Cup; (left) Citation, with owner Lucille Wright, makes his final public appearance at Hollywood a week after his Gold Cup

turn and down the backstretch. The pace wasn't changing, so Brooks let Citation make his move early. Nearing the half-mile pole, Citation took the lead and kept on rolling. The crowd of more than 50,000 roared as Citation crossed the wire. In the winner's circle he was draped with a bright gold blanket bearing the inscription "Citation: First Thoroughbred Millionaire."

"It was the greatest thrill of my life," said Jimmy Jones. *EM*

135

44 The "Fighting Finish" Derby

THE 1933 KENTUCKY DERBY, run during the bleakest days of the Great Depression, seemed perfectly scripted for the times. Known for eternity as the "Fighting Finish" Derby, it showcased a conflict as desperate as that played out on American streets.

The race's rivals were both bred to win. Head Play was sired by My Play, a full brother to Man o' War. Brokers Tip, like 1924 Kentucky Derby hero Black Gold, was sired by Black Toney, a top sire owned by prominent Kentucky breeder E.R. Bradley. Bradley, who also owned Brokers Tip, had already won three Kentucky Derbies with Behave Yourself in 1921, Bubbling Over in 1926, and Burgoo King in 1932.

But few watching the 1933 Derby would remember the horses. Instead, they would recollect how two young jockeys — Herb Fisher, on Head Play, and Don Meade, on Brokers Tip — made history by racing down the stretch, locked in battle.

Making the turn for home, Brokers Tip traveled a length behind Head Play, who had the lead. As Fisher brought Head Play into the straightaway, they veered out, pushing a horse named Charley O. wide. Now, three horses — Head Play, Charley O., and Brokers Tip — raced on together.

Meade brought Brokers Tip up along the rail. Charley O. lagged, as Head Play and Brokers Tip surged on. "Then," *The Blood-Horse* reported, "ensued one of the most regrettable incidents in the history of the Kentucky Derby ... Through the last three-sixteenths of a mile the contest was not a horse race so much as a hand-to-hand combat between the jockeys."

Because the race took place before recording tools such as multiple-angle cameras existed, the exact order of events remains muddy. But by the time the horses crossed the finish line, Fisher had Head Play's head yanked toward the right because he was holding Brokers Tip's saddlecloth on the left. Fisher hit Meade with his whip at least once as they crossed the line.

Fisher kept Head Play galloping until he got to the judges' stand to lodge a claim of foul. Meade had started everything, he said. Although the judges listened to Fisher's complaints, the official sign went up that Brokers Tip had won.

Fisher next attacked Meade in the jockeys' room. Meade mostly tried to shield himself from the blows, and a valet and a reporter eventually managed to pull Fisher away from Meade. "He beat me out of it; he beat me out of it," Fisher cried.

Photographer Wallace Lowry snapped the now-famous photograph showing Meade's right hand hanging onto Fisher's shoulder. The Associated Press photograph had not captured Meade's right arm, so it was difficult to see what was happening in any picture besides Lowry's. Even in Lowry's

Don Meade (left) and Herb Fisher battle it out aboard Brokers Tip and Head Play

photograph, it is not easy to tell which horse is the winner.

The image shows Fisher's left hand grabbing Brokers Tip's saddlecloth, and each jockey canting toward the other.

A newsreel was needed to prove Fisher had been the first offender by grabbing Brokers Tip's saddlecloth just as Meade put his horse on the rail. Brokers Tip tried twice to move off, but both times Fisher grabbed the pad. That was the moment when Meade fought back, grabbing Fisher's shoulder. The stewards suspended both Meade and Fisher for thirty days, with Fisher getting five extra days for starting the fight in the jockeys' room.

Lost in the furor over the Fisher-Meade battle was the racing history made as Bradley won his fourth Derby. But it turned out that despite the loss in the Derby, Head Play was the more successful racehorse. He went on to win the Preakness, the San Juan Capistrano Handicap, and the Suburban Handicap while Brokers Tip finished last in the 1933 Preakness, never winning another race.

Meade once said: "It was the survival of the fittest. I couldn't sit there and let him rough me around and not do nothing about it ... I'm not blaming him for trying to do what he did because in those days that's what you did. If you didn't do it, you wasn't a race rider." *EMG*

45 The Caliente Safety Helmet Is Introduced

JOHN ALESSIO, the executive director of Caliente racetrack, couldn't help but be saddened by the horrible accident at his track in December 1955, when the promising young jockey LeRoy Nelson was trampled in a spill. The rider died from his injuries, which included severe head trauma. Alessio decided something

had to be done to protect jockeys better during a race.

At the time, jockeys wore only a light plastic skullcap under a silk cap, which offered little protection from flying hooves and hard ground. Alessio began investigating different styles of riding helmets. Working with Hawthorne, California-based designers Fred Welch and John McMurry, Alessio soon developed a model and provided much of the financial backing for the project. The new safety helmet was similar to ones worn by motorcycle riders and automobile and speedboat racers. Made of laminated fiberglass, it was contoured to provide as much cranial protection as possible while still being lightweight. The helmet's shell was designed to withstand eighteen hundred pounds of pressure per square inch — as the *Los Angeles Times* reported in 1956, a hammer could punch a hole in the old skullcap but merely bounced off the new safety helmet. The new helmet also came with "sweat-resistant nylon" bands and "undyed non-allergy orthopedic leather" padding.

Alessio debuted the new "Caliente" safety helmet at the Tijuana, Mexico, racetrack, on Sunday, April 7, 1956. He had made the helmet mandatory equipment for riders at Caliente, and the helmet quickly received approval from industry officials, especially from the Jockeys' Guild, the organization that provides a central voice in racing for jockeys at all levels. Bert Thompson, then western representative of the Jockeys' Guild, was an enthusiastic supporter, telling *The Blood-Horse* that he was "completely sold" on the helmet and planned to show samples to racing officials at other western tracks.

In August 1956 Del Mar racetrack in Southern California became the first U.S. track to adopt the Caliente safety helmet as required gear. It didn't take long for the helmet to prove its worth. According to the book *The Agua Caliente Story*, jockey Alex Maese witnessed a bad riding accident at Caliente during the summer of 1956 in which two riders were struck in the head, but because they wore safety helmets, they both came out of the spill with minor scratches. Maese quickly began wearing the helmet and credited it with saving his life when just a few months later he was tossed over the outside rail by his mount and landed on concrete. The helmet cracked but Maese was okay.

On April 1, 1957, the safety helmet became mandatory for jockeys at New York tracks, and a year later the New York State Racing Commission amended its rule to include exercise riders. Before long, most major racing jurisdictions had adopted the Caliente safety helmet.

But not all jockeys were pleased with the new equipment. Some said the helmet was too cumbersome and bulky; others said the straps bothered their vision. And the macho factor came into play, as well — that whoever wore the helmet showed a lack of courage. But that opinion gradually changed as more big-name riders began wearing it.

According to an October 1956 story in the San Francisco *Examiner*, Ted Atkinson, best known as Tom Fool's jockey, was skeptical about wearing the Caliente helmet until Thompson informed him that Ralph Neves, another top-class rider, wore one.

" 'You mean to tell me, Bert,' Atkinson said, 'that a guy with the guts of Neves wears a helmet all the time?' Assured by Thompson that such was the case, Atkinson snapped this order at Thompson: 'Get me one immediately.' "

Another supporter was legendary rider John Longden, who, while riding at Golden Gate Fields in 1956, told the *Examiner* that "you get used to it and don't even know that you are wearing it." Nine years later, in a *Blood-Horse* article, Longden commented on the Caliente helmet: "It is so wonderful. It is impossible to put a value on it."

In September 1957 the Jockeys' Guild honored Alessio as the organization's Man of the Year for his role in creating the safety helmet. As *Daily Racing Form* reported that August, in just the year and a half since the helmet had been introduced, not one jockey fatality resulting from a head injury had been reported.

Since the Caliente helmet's inception, designers and manufacturers have improved on safety helmets' designs to provide even greater protection. In addition, jockeys and exercise riders now wear flak jackets to protect their bodies further. But those advancements wouldn't have been possible without John Alessio and his desire to protect other jockeys from LeRoy Nelson's fate. *JM*

The Caliente helmet (opposite) championed by Caliente track president John Alessio (opposite bottom, with jockeys); today's helmet as worn by Jerry Bailey

46 Carl Nafzger's Famous Derby "Call"

"HE WON IT, MRS. GENTER! He won it! You've won the Kentucky Derby! ... Oh, Mrs. Genter, I love you!"

Plenty of sports broadcasts are more famous or perhaps more gripping. But for sheer unabashed emotion, it's hard to top trainer Carl Nafzger's impromptu stretch call of the 1990 Kentucky Derby to ninety-two-year-old Frances Genter, who sat in her box, unable to see over the crowd, her eyes wide and face filled with excitement as Nafzger shouted out the finish for her.

The Derby winner was Unbridled, a handsome bay colt who was Mrs. Genter's first starter in the Run for the Roses.

Mrs. Genter began racing horses in the 1940s with her husband, Harold. The Genters' first stakes winner was Swiv, whom they had purchased as a yearling at Saratoga for $3,600 in 1941. Another early stakes winner was the first Unbridled, a son of Unbreakable (grandsire of Native Dancer). Until Harold Genter's death in 1981, the couple raced nineteen stakes winners, including 1959 champion juvenile filly My Dear Girl; 1951 Santa Anita Derby winner Rough'n Tumble (later the sire of Dr. Fager), and In Reality, who won the 1968 Manhattan Handicap and 1967 Florida Derby among his ten stakes wins. Afterward, Mrs. Genter raced thirty-five stakes winners under the banner of Frances A. Genter Stable, including 1986 champion sprinter Smile (a homebred).

When her husband took ill, she enlisted the help of son-in-law Bentley Smith to help run the racing and breeding operation. They developed a plan to build up the stable's broodmare band and breed the mares to In Reality, acquire interests in outside stallions, and find new bloodlines through mare and weanling purchases.

One of those weanling purchases was the second Unbridled. Mrs. Genter paid $70,000 for the son of Fappiano at the Tartan Farms/John A. Nerud dispersal at the 1987 Fasig-Tipton Kentucky November mixed sale. Unbridled had been a last-minute purchase. "When he was shagging around in the ring at a reasonable price, I thought, 'Gee, I think we can buy him.' He didn't sell for as much as he should have," recalled Bentley Smith after Unbridled's Derby. The stable also bought Unbridled's dam, the Le Fabuleux mare Gana Facil (in foal to Fappiano), for $275,000 from the Tartan dispersal.

The young Unbridled was sent to trainer Carl Nafzger, who had about ten other Genter Stable runners in his barn. A former professional bull rider from Texas, Nafzger turned to training Thoroughbreds in the early 1970s and by 1990 had saddled thirty-seven stakes winners, including graded winners Coolawin and Home At Last.

Under Nafzger's care, Unbridled made six starts at two, breaking his maiden by ten and a half lengths at six furlongs in his first start. In his final start at two, the colt captured the mile and one-sixteenth What a Pleasure Stakes at Calder Race Course by five lengths. In between he had placed in four stakes, including the In Reality division of the Florida Stallion Stakes.

At three Unbridled needed a couple of races to find his best form, which he showed off in a four-length victory in the Florida Derby at Gulfstream Park. After a promising third-place finish in Summer Squall's Blue Grass Stakes, Unbridled seemed primed for a big effort on Derby Day.

Fifteen horses were entered in the 116th Kentucky Derby with the top contenders being Summer Squall, the unbeaten Mister Frisky, and Gotham and Wood Memorial winner Thirty Six Red.

Mister Frisky, who had raced in Puerto Rico at two and in his three-year-old debut before being shipped to California where he won the Santa Anita Derby and two other preps, was made the favorite. Unbridled went off at nearly 11-1.

At the break Unbridled was sandwiched briefly before settling into stride. Jockey Craig Perret sat patiently as the duo went into the first turn. Mister Frisky dueled on the lead, while Summer Squall bided his time back in sixth place. As the field headed out of the backstretch and into the final turn, Summer Squall began moving up — and so did Unbridled. But Summer Squall seemed to lose his concentration as he and jockey Pat Day turned for home, and Unbridled went by. The speed horses, including Mister Frisky, were backing up, and closers such as Pleasant Tap and Video Ranger weren't closing in time to catch Mrs. Genter's colt.

Unbridled pulled away to a strong three and a half-length victory, as Carl Nafzger gave Mrs. Genter and a worldwide television audience a special moment they would not soon forget. *JM*

Carl Nafzger, with Unbridled; (opposite) Unbridled on his way to Derby victory for Frances Genter (inset)

CHANGE IN THE THOROUGHBRED industry comes so reluctantly that it required World War II and the resulting gas rationing until a gavel could be heard dropping in Kentucky. Prior to the war the country's best-bred yearlings were sold by Fasig-Tipton in a summer sale at Saratoga Springs in upstate New York. Kentucky breeders had to ship their horses by train, and they dreaded the risk and discomfort of the trip, which ended with a six-to-seven-block walk from the train station to the Fasig-Tipton sales pavilion. The perception at the time, however, was that New York was the only place to sell top-shelf yearlings because the premier Saratoga race meet was a magnet for well-heeled owners and buyers.

Everything changed beginning in late 1942 when the federal government began rationing gasoline and limiting travel to what was considered necessary. Shipping sale yearlings more than 650 miles did not fall in that category, so Fasig-Tipton decided to transplant the August yearling sale to Lexington, Kentucky. The makeshift auction was held on the grounds of Keeneland Race Course beneath a tent to shield the crowd from the blazing Bluegrass sun. Kentucky breeders

liked the change so much that a consortium formed the Breeders' Sales Company to keep the auction alive after Fasig-Tipton decided not to return to Keeneland the following year. The idea of holding sales at Keeneland was not a radical concept. The racing company's prospectus nearly ten years earlier included plans to hold sales.

"There was some trepidation (in forming a new sales company), not only because of the wartime economy, but also that they were striking out on new ground," said James E. "Ted" Bassett III, who served as president of the Keeneland Association from 1970 to 1986.

The Kentucky sale seemed blessed from the beginning. A son of Sir Gallahad III caught the eye of a novice Thoroughbred owner and successful Florida road contractor named Fred W. Hooper. Hooper paid $10,200 for the colt, his first Thoroughbred ever bought at auction, and named him Hoop, Jr. Two years later Hoop, Jr. won the 1945 Kentucky Derby for Hooper.

The sale was turning out to be exactly what its founders had hoped: an opportunity to buy and sell quality yearlings in a location convenient to Kentucky breeders. "It was an important decision

4·7 Keeneland Conducts First Summer Yearling Sale

that this wasn't to be an overall sale for everyone to present and disperse their yearlings," said Bassett.

The Breeders' Sales Company and Keeneland solidified their commitment to one another in 1948 when the auction company built a sales pavilion on the racetrack grounds and helped finance the construction of six barns that would also be used to house horses during the race meets. The sale's reputation as a national hub for quality Thoroughbred stock grew steadily. In 1961 a colt named Swapson, a son of Kentucky Derby winner Swaps, became the first yearling to bring a six-figure price, selling for $130,000 at the Keeneland July sale. Six years later Majestic Prince sold for a record $250,000, and Spendthrift Farm's Leslie Combs II became the first commercial breeder to gross more than $1 million at a sale. Majestic Prince went on to win the 1969 Kentucky Derby and Preakness.

Combs' success and the rich price of Majestic Prince were important milestones, but their effect on shaping Keeneland's status pales in comparison to the transformation sparked by a $42,000 colt named Sir Ivor and his European trainer, Vincent O'Brien. After O'Brien won the 1968 Epsom Derby with Sir Ivor, he quickly became a regular at Keeneland's summer yearling sale.

"O'Brien had the foresight, wisdom, and courage to select North American-bred horses in the belief he could adapt them to European training methods and have them successfully compete against European counterparts," Bassett said. And compete he did, enjoying phenomenal success in Europe's major classics with Nijinsky II, The Minstrel, Roberto, and Alleged. Keeneland in the 1970s morphed from an important national sale into a true international marketplace. Sale company officials quickly got wise in the ways of international banking, currency exchange, and credit evaluations. During this time the Breeders' Sales Company was folded quietly into the Keeneland Association, and a permanent sales staff was hired, including a sales director.

O'Brien's success brought a European invasion and more growth. In 1976 Keeneland sold the first million-dollar yearling, a son of Triple Crown winner Secretariat later named Canadian Bound. And yet even more dramatic changes were still to come. In the 1980s the Maktoums, the ruling

Hoop, Jr., the 1945 Kentucky Derby winner, came from the first Keeneland sale, conducted under tents

family of Dubai, became major players in Thoroughbred breeding and racing and made their presence felt at the Keeneland July sale. Oil money pouring into their country fueled their passion for the sport, and the objects of their affections were mostly the progeny of Northern Dancer. In 1983 Sheikh Mohammed bin Rashid al Maktoum rocked the Thoroughbred world when he paid $10.2 million for Northern Dancer's son Snaafi Dancer. The record price couldn't even be displayed on the electronic bid board because the board only had seven digits. The previous record had been $4.25 million, set the year before. The world record fell again two short years later when B.B.A. England spent $13.1 million for a son of Nijinsky II named Seattle Dancer. It's a record that still holds.

A severe market correction caused the bottom to fall out of the commercial market through the late 1980s and early '90s. When the market had recovered fully by 1996, the Keeneland summer sale quickly regained its status. From 1996 through 2000, the Keeneland July sale was the leading North American yearling auction by average price and by the percentage of graduates that became stakes winners, graded/group winners, and graded/group I winners. Despite all its success, however, the July sale was not immune to market pressures. Escalating prices for horses sold through the Keeneland September yearling sale's select sessions and a shift among leading buyers to pay more attention to conformation than pedigree forced Keeneland to put the July sale on hiatus in 2003. The sale has not been held since, though sale company officials have said they still believe the market will support a premier summer sale. *EM*

48 Calumet Farm Files for Bankruptcy

WITH ITS EIGHT KENTUCKY DERBY winners and unrivaled skein of champions, Calumet Farm reigned for decades as America's most famous racing and breeding operation. Encompassing 847 jewel-like acres on the outskirts of Lexington, Kentucky, Calumet has always embodied the pinnacle of the sport of kings. Through the 1940s until the early '60s, Calumet's distinctive devil's red-and-blue silks adorned a parade of legendary horses: Whirlaway, Twilight Tear, Armed, Bewitch, Citation, Real Delight, Tim Tam, and others.

So few events in horse racing have been as shocking as Calumet's 1991 plunge into bankruptcy. Crippled by $127 million in debt, the farm's collapse was the largest such failure in racing history. Repercussions of the bankruptcy forced its sale, sent one of the farm's principals to prison, and raised still unanswered questions about the death of leading stallion Alydar. (*See No. 73.*) From its lofty supremacy to its inglorious crash, Calumet Farm told a uniquely American saga of empire-building, sportsmanship, and wasteful excess.

Its roots were founded on entrepreneurship. William Monroe Wright, reaping the success of his Chicago-based Calumet Baking Soda Company, purchased land west of downtown Lexington in 1924 for his nascent Standardbred farm. In 1931, son Warren Wright inherited the farm upon the death of his father. With no interest in harness racing, he transformed Calumet into a Thoroughbred farm. Wright's pivotal purchase of future foundation sire Bull Lea in 1936 put Calumet on the road to unparalleled success. (*See No. 32.*) So did the hiring of Ben and Jimmy Jones, the father-and-son training team, in 1939.

Calumet homebreds Whirlaway and Citation won the Triple Crown in 1941 and 1948, respectively, and the latter became racing's first millionaire. (*See No. 43.*) Pensive, Ponder, Hill Gail, Iron Liege, Tim Tam, and Forward Pass also claimed the roses for Calumet. Calumet's dominance from the 1940s to the early '60s has been likened to the New York Yankees' virtual lock on the American League pennant during a similar period.

Wright died in 1950 and his widow, Lucille, took over the farm's operation. She later married Admiral Gene Markey. Though Calumet did not enjoy the same level of success in later decades, the 1970s produced champions Our Mims and Davona Dale and the gritty colt Alydar, who ran second to Affirmed in the 1978 Triple Crown.

Lucille Parker Markey, who died in 1982, had expressed fear about Calumet's future under the management of her eventual heirs. Yet Markey refused to consider selling the farm. Management was turned over to J.T. Lundy, a rough-hewn Kentuckian who had married Markey's grand-daughter, Cindy. Change occurred quickly. Key people who had overseen Calumet for decades left, as did John Veitch, the young trainer who had helped return Calumet to the winner's circle

Calumet Farm flourished under Warren and Lucille Wright (opposite), plunged into bankruptcy under J.T. Lundy (near left), and was revived by Henryk de Kwiatkowski (left)

after a prolonged dry stretch.

Lundy's tenure coincided with Alydar's ascent as a great stallion whose champion offspring included Easy Goer, Alysheba, Althea, and Turkoman. Lundy capitalized on Alydar's success by expanding the stallion's book to upwards of one hundred mares a year. He also pre-sold breeding rights and permitted Alydar to be bred to Quarter Horse mares. (Ironically, Calumet bred 1991 Kentucky Derby winner Strike the Gold, but the son of Alydar raced for different owners.) During the 1980s Calumet invested heavily in other stallions as well as outside businesses.

Though Mrs. Markey had left the farm debt-free, Calumet's financial burdens escalated and creditors eventually forced the farm into bankruptcy. The farm's demise became the basis for Ann Hagedorn Auerbach's well-regarded book, *A Wild Ride: The Rise and Tragic Fall of Calumet Farm, Inc., America's Premier Racing Dynasty*.

Bankruptcy proceedings dragged on for months until a judge ordered the property sold at auction. Henryk de Kwiatkowski, who campaigned champion Conquistador Cielo, flew to Lexington on March 26, 1992, from his home in the Bahamas and purchased Calumet. The Polish-born de Kwiatkowski became a hero, and under his aegis Calumet recaptured much of its luster. De Kwiatkowski died in 2003 and his children continue to maintain this Lexington landmark.

Lundy served nearly four years in federal prison on bank fraud and other charges and returned to Lexington upon his release. *JD*

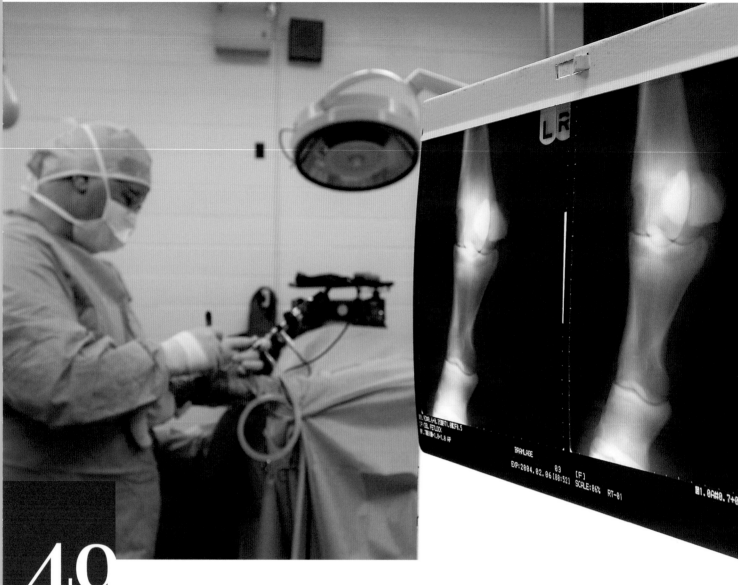

49 The Advent of Arthroscopic Surgery

ARTHROSCOPIC SURGERY, the ability to peer inside joints to diagnose and repair fractures using only tiny incisions, has revolutionized orthopedic surgery in the horse. Not only has this less invasive surgery helped talented horses stay on the racetrack, but many times it also has saved horses' lives.

An arthroscope is a flexible instrument inserted into a joint space through a tiny incision. It allows the surgeon to visualize a damaged joint with magnification. Like many advances in vet-

erinary medicine that have benefited equine athletes, arthroscopic surgery evolved out of human medicine.

"Although generally considered a modern surgical procedure, the technique took considerable time to develop," explains Dr. Wayne McIlwraith, professor of surgery and director of the Orthopaedic Research Center at Colorado State University's College of Veterinary Medicine, in his text, *Diagnostic and Surgical Arthroscopy in the Horse.* In 1933 a Japanese scientist reported in the medical literature that in 1918 he had used arthroscopy to visualize the inside of human knee joints. Beginning in 1930, U.S. researchers described arthroscopic techniques in human medicine. Another Japanese researcher developed a practical arthroscope and described basic principles of its use in the knee; a Canadian researcher brought the techniques to North America in 1965.

By the mid-1970s scientists worldwide realized they could operate on human joints using the arthroscope to monitor their surgical progress. Since then they've progressed dramatically — arthroscopic surgeries are now commonplace in the human shoulder, elbow, wrist, digits, ankle, hip, and jaw.

Equine arthroscopy followed a similar path. German scientists first reported using large-animal arthroscopy in 1973. American scientists followed in 1974, using arthroscopy to visualize and diagnose problems in the equine carpus (knee), although McIlwraith and Dr. J.F. Fessler described the technique more extensively in 1978. Surgeons used diagnostic arthroscopy in other joints, and by 1982 it was being used in the stifle.

In the early 1980s Dr. Willard D. Ommert wrote about the first arthroscopic carpal surgery in the horse. Other scientists followed, describing surgery on other joints.

The Blood-Horse of March 19, 1983, gave the Thoroughbred industry a chance to follow an arthroscopic surgery. "The very nature of arthroscopic surgery — small incisions rather than a large cut exposing the joint — makes infection less of a risk than in conventional surgery," said the article. "The procedure is a test of hand-eye coordination for the surgeon, who must approach the lesion from below with his instruments while watching the procedure from above, magnified 10 times." In the photographs, the surgeon has his eye up to the scope. The use of a video camera in arthroscopic surgery has since become standard, and surgeons watch their work on a screen in the surgery suite.

By 1984 McIlwraith reported he used arthroscopic surgery "as the routine method of joint surgery for virtually all conditions." By 1990 the procedure had gone from being used by a select few surgeons for diagnosis to being the accepted way of performing joint surgery. All the years of using arthroscopy for diagnosis, though, had taught the surgeons about the many things that can go wrong in a joint.

Over the past fifteen years, surgeons have documented success rates in using arthroscopy for surgeries to remove many types of bone chips, to repair a variety of fractures, and to treat joint disease in potential athletes. They also have been able to learn more about how lesions in tendons and ligaments can contribute to joint disease.

Arthroscopic surgery in the 1980s (below) and today (opposite)

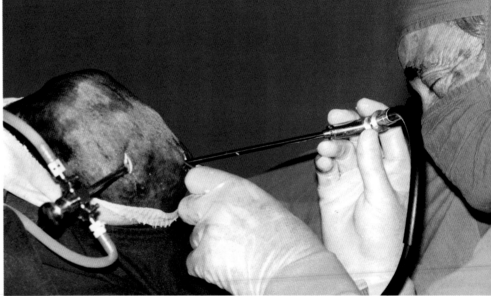

Large equine hospitals that once saw a thousand horses come through their doors each year for any type of surgery are now seeing as many as thirteen hundred arthroscopic surgery cases alone per year. It's not unusual for an orthopedic surgeon to scrub in for more than ten arthroscopic cases in an average surgical day. Each operation provides an opportunity to improve the future of a crooked foal, remove a bone chip to relieve an athlete's pain and return him to the track, or save the life of a horse with a fracture that could have once sentenced the horse to euthanasia. *SLC*

50 The First Network Radio Derby Broadcast

THE 1925 KENTUCKY DERBY promised to be thrilling. Racing fans were eager to see the black colt Flying Ebony paired with the great jockey Earl Sande. The colt had won all four of his races at age two and his first start at age three, making him the Derby favorite. Could Sande propel Flying Ebony to victory the way he had the famous Zev in 1923?

Attendance for the Derby was at an all-time high, with 75,000 spectators in the stands. Up to ten thousand cars with out-of-state plates thronged the parking area, crowding it to the point that Churchill Downs officials considered parking vehicles by state so people could find their cars more easily after the race. Many of the finest automobiles belonged to horsemen who the previous day had descended upon the late August Belmont II's Nursery Stud outside Lexington for a dispersal of the country's finest stock.

Not only did the race promise excitement for those at Churchill Downs, but, for the first time, faraway listeners could hear the whole contest unfold over the radio. WHAS, the station owned by the *Louisville Times* and *Courier-Journal*, would broadcast the race call. And WHT out of Chicago would pick up WHAS' signal and rebroadcast it.

Other races had been on the radio before, but never the Derby. For example, on June 24, 1922, the $50,000 Kentucky Special was broadcast from Latonia racetrack in northern Kentucky. The broadcast was something of a novelty, as the *New York Times* reported: "One of the most ambitious radio undertakings attempted since the wide vogue of the wireless telephone was the broadcasting of the running of the big race." For the Special, transmission equipment was installed in the press balcony of the grandstand, and the track's form chart compiler called the race as it was run. Radio fans listened in and instantly learned which horse had won — in this case, Harry Payne Whitney's Whiskaway.

The first commercial radio station, Pittsburgh's KDKA, had been established in 1920, and by 1925 most families owned a radio and were becoming accustomed to gathering around their radios for real-time news and sports.

Audiences had heard President Calvin Coolidge's inauguration speech, one of the first nationwide broadcasts, on March 24, 1925. Radio station programming was still very general. A sample of a schedule for a California station called KPO on the same day shows that after the inauguration, other programming included a physical fitness show; the market report on eggs, butter, cheese, and poultry; a scripture reading; and a performance by Rudy Seiger's Fairmont Hotel Orchestra.

So racing fans were ready to hear one of the biggest races of the year unfold before their ears. At Churchill Downs, engineers tried to decide where to set up. WHAS employees carried their heavy equip-ment up five flights of stairs to one of the Twin Spires, but about an hour before the race, high winds began whistling fiercely. Hail and then sheets of rain fell on the track. The announcer, Credo Fitch Harris, barely made it down in time to broadcast the Derby from the safety of the ground.

In later years the famous voice of the Kentucky Derby was that of Clem McCarthy. McCarthy, whose sandy voice narrated many races and fights on national radio, had worked as a handicapper for the *Daily Racing Form* and called races over loudspeakers at Bowie Park and Arlington Park in Chicago. McCarthy narrated the Kentucky Derby from 1928 until 1950.

But in 1925, no one cared who was behind the microphone. They just huddled in and listened as Flying Ebony won the race over Captain Hal by a length and a half. The on-track crowd gave Sande a standing ovation, and then plowed onto the track to see him. "Fences and police barriers were nothing to that great crowd, which surged on to the track," reported the *New York Times*.

An estimated six million people heard the race over the radio. The racetrack crowd made one kind of history, setting an attendance record, while those clustered around their radios, holding their breath as Harris narrated each step, made another. *EMG*

(Opposite) NBC broadcasts the trophy presentation for Burgoo King's 1932 Derby; (left) announcer Clem McCarthy becomes known as the voice of the Derby

51 John Longden's Derby Double

IT WAS MID-JUNE IN 1956 and Johnny Longden was driving for the wire in a relatively tight finish at Hollywood Park in California. Suddenly, his horse, Tribal Chief, ducked in toward the rail and hit it. The horse's legs buckled and Tribal Chief went out from underneath Longden. The jockey barely managed to grab onto a handful of mane before his leg hit the aluminum rail, and he bounced back up into the saddle as if he had planned it. The rail had also righted Tribal Chief, and the pair went on to finish the race in company.

More than a year earlier, also at Hollywood Park, Longden was on Amblingorix, vying for the finish. Suddenly, a patrol judge gulped over the intercom system, "Longden's going down between horses!" Almost before the words were out, jockey George Taniguchi, on the inside, grabbed Longden by the left arm and hauled him back into the saddle as Rogelio Trejos, on the outside, helped steady Longden until the almost unseated jockey got his stirrups back. Longden nodded his thanks and went on to win the race.

What are the odds? But then again, what are the odds that this same man who had won the Derby on Count Fleet in 1943 (not to mention the Triple Crown) would go on twenty-six years later as a trainer to saddle Majestic Prince and win the 1969 Run for the Roses (and the Preakness)?

At four-foot-eleven Longden was short even for a jockey. His hands and arms, though, were powerful from working as a teenager in the coal mines to help support his family. He had been born in England in 1907, but he and his mother emigrated twelve years later to the tiny town of Taber in western Canada. (Some accounts say Longden left England in 1912 but almost did not make it. Because a train taking them to Southampton on the British coast was late, Longden and his mother missed their scheduled trip on the *Titanic*.)

Growing up in Taber, Longden found his claim to fame riding Roman races, in which each contestant stood straddled on the backs of two galloping horses.

Longden's official racing career began at seventeen, with a grand total of sixteen mounts at the fairgrounds in Salt Lake City, Utah. Notes show that earlier in his career Longden rode seventy-eight winners on the Canadian Fair Circuit for

Despite all of Afleet Alex's accomplishments, including victories in the Hopeful, Arkansas Derby, and Belmont Stakes, the one race that will define him is the Preakness, in which he somehow managed to pull himself up off the ground and go on to score a resounding four and three-quarters-length victory.

Earlier that spring Alex, as he was called by most people, returned from a lung infection that derailed him in the Rebel Stakes to romp by eight lengths in the Arkansas Derby before finishing a solid third in the Kentucky Derby, beaten only a length.

In the Preakness he was sent off as the 3-1 favorite in the fourteen-horse field, which included Kentucky Derby winner Giacomo, Derby runner-up Closing Argument, and the previous year's Breeders' Cup Juvenile winner, Wilko.

Jockey Jeremy Rose was able to compensate for the disadvantageous twelve-post by steering Alex to the inside to avoid being hung wide on the first turn. After dropping back to tenth, Rose moved Alex up along the inside before angling him off the rail midway around the far turn.

By now, Scrappy T, winner of the Withers Stakes, had shaken free from his closest pursuers and opened a clear lead approaching the head of the stretch. When Rose asked Alex for his run, the colt exploded and blew by High Limit as if he had been put in reverse. Alex then swung to the outside of Scrappy T and was moving so swiftly that the only question at this point was how far he was going to win by.

Just then, Ramon Dominguez, on Scrappy T, reached back and gave his horse a roundhouse left-handed crack of the whip that sent Scrappy T veering sharply to the outside, directly in the path of Afleet Alex. There was no time for Rose to react. Alex clipped Scrappy T's heels and stumbled so badly that his nose virtually grazed the ground.

A collective gasp could be heard from the crowd, as everyone braced for a potentially catastrophic spill. Rose could do nothing but grab a chunk of Alex's mane and pray. In one of the most amazing recoveries ever seen in any sport, Alex,

his front legs spread-eagled, lifted himself and Rose out of the abyss. Not only did Alex recover, averting certain disaster, he took it one step further. He immediately regained his composure, cut to the inside of Scrappy T, changed to his right lead in a matter of two strides, and drew off to win by daylight.

When the stunned crowd realized what it had just witnessed, it proceeded to give Alex a thunderous ovation upon his return. With every wave from Rose, the cheers grew louder. Once the

Afleet Alex nearly goes down (opposite) then rebounds to win the 2005 Preakness

Preakness was over, people again had a chance to reflect on what had happened. Words such as "amazing," "incredible," and "unbelievable" could be heard throughout Pimlico. Veteran jockeys and trainers said they'd never seen anything like it in all their years in the sport. NBC showed the incident over and over, from different angles and at different speeds. Photographers frantically searched their disks to see if they had captured a piece of history.

The morning after the race, NBC gathered the Cash is King Stable partners, trainer Tim Ritchey, Rose, and Liz Scott, mother of Alex Scott, and set up a group interview outside the barn for the Sunday *Today* show.

No one knows how history will treat Afleet Alex, who never raced again after the Belmont due to a foot injury. But his place in racing lore is secure, thanks to a single incident that was over in a heartbeat but defined the athleticism and courage of the Thoroughbred. *SH*

JULIE KRONE EXPERIENCED MORE than her share of "firsts" in horse racing, so it was only fitting that the first lady of racing become the first female jockey to win a Triple Crown race. Krone did just that with her victory aboard Colonial Affair in the 1993 Belmont Stakes.

Krone rode Colonial Affair for Hall of Fame trainer Scotty Schulhofer and owner Centennial Farms. Schulhofer had helped Krone move her tack from New Jersey, where she started her rise to stardom, to the tough New York circuit. After the Belmont he said of the highly competitive Krone: "If she develops much more, I don't know what we'll do. The boys may have to quit."

But Julie Krone didn't start race-riding to be the number one female rider; she just wanted to be the number one rider, period. Krone won her first race in 1981 at Tampa Bay Downs and soon made the transition to New Jersey, where she won multiple riding titles at Atlantic City, Meadowlands, and Monmouth Park in the late 1980s.

Once in New York, Krone didn't let up. By 1989 she was already the all-time leading female rider, and the following year she reached a career milestone of two thousand wins.

Then came the 1993 Belmont. Krone had ridden Colonial Affair, a handsome bay son of Pleasant Colony, twice during the colt's two-year-old season, then became his regular rider in late spring 1993. They won back-to-back allowance races, the first at Aqueduct and the other at

55 Julie Krone Wins the Belmont Stakes

Belmont Park four days after Sea Hero's Kentucky Derby. Next came a runner-up finish to Virginia Rapids in the nine-furlong Peter Pan Stakes at Belmont, setting up Colonial Affair and Krone perfectly for the big race.

However, the big colt, who was new to the Triple Crown scene, was not one of the favorites in the thirteen-horse field. Preakness winner Prairie Bayou and Kentucky Derby winner Sea Hero, who were meeting for a supposed rubber match, were the first two choices, then came Preakness runner-up Cherokee Run and Virginia Rapids, both at 4-1. Colonial Affair was nearly 14-1, but with his 17-hand stature, he was expected to enjoy the wide turns and long stretch at Belmont Park.

Rain just an hour before the Belmont Stakes caused the track to be listed as "good," even though riders were saying the going was more "slippery." Sadly, as the field entered the backstretch, Prairie Bayou broke down. Colonial Affair, however, was unaffected, being farther up in the pack, and with a confident ride from Krone he pulled away in the stretch to win by two and a quarter lengths. For Krone it was the fulfillment of a childhood dream.

"I couldn't stop crying when I pulled him up," she said after the race. "I was so happy."

For her accomplishment Krone was named the 1993 Female Athlete of the Year by ESPN's American Sports Awards, and *Glamour* magazine named her one of its ten Women of the Year.

Two years later Krone came out with her autobiography, *Riding for My Life*, written with Nancy Ann Richardson. She also hit the three-thousand-win mark in 1995, but a series of serious racing injuries hampered her career, and in 1999 Krone announced her retirement from riding.

The next year Krone experienced yet another

first. She became the first woman to be inducted in to the National Museum of Racing's Hall of Fame. In 2002 she returned to riding, this time in Southern California, after a stint as a racing analyst on TVG. It was like she had never left, and she added two more "firsts" to her tally. In winning the 2003 Pacific Classic with Candy Ride, Krone became the first female jockey to win a million-dollar race in the United States, and later that year she became the first woman jockey to win a Breeders' Cup event other than the steeplechase when she rode Halfbridled to victory in the Juvenile Fillies at Santa Anita. Injuries once again forced her retirement, but she went out with 3,704 wins (17 percent) from 21,411 mounts and $90,122,764 in earnings, having ridden some of racing's top horses over the years, including Da Hoss, Rubiano, Clear Mandate, Classy Mirage, Peaks and Valleys, and, of course, Colonial Affair.

When asked in 2000 what the most important thing she took with her from the track was, Krone responded: "Knowing that I was able to do something I loved so much, especially with my attachment to the horse. I was passionate about it." *JM*

Centennial Farms' Don Little joins the winner's circle celebration after Julie Krone pilots Colonial Affair to a historic Belmont victory

159

56 Jim Dandy Upsets Gallant Fox

THE BILLING FOR THE 1930 Travers Stakes promised a sensational showdown between Triple Crown winner Gallant Fox and the formidable Whichone, the previous year's champion colt. The two had met just twice before, each one claiming a victory over the other. The Travers, Saratoga's classic contest for three-year-olds, would settle the question of supremacy.

Instead, the lamentably overmatched Jim Dandy upset them both, speeding to an eight-length victory at odds of 100-1. It was the most shocking upset since Upset defeated Man o' War in the 1919 Sanford Memorial Stakes at Saratoga.

Jim Dandy's improbable feat is recognized today in the Jim Dandy Stakes, run at Saratoga

every August. His upset also cemented Saratoga's reputation as the "graveyard of champions."

Whichone had earned division honors in 1929, winning the Saratoga Special, Futurity, and Champagne stakes. Harry Payne Whitney's colt had defeated Gallant Fox in the Futurity in their only meeting as juveniles. Gallant Fox, a Belair Stud homebred, had been lightly raced at two, owner William Woodward Sr. preferring not to tax his young horses. The son of Sir Gallahad III had won just twice from seven starts in 1929.

Jim Dandy, meanwhile, won the 1929 Grand Union Hotel Stakes at Saratoga as the longest shot in the field. Bred and initially owned by W.S. Dudley, Jim Dandy captured the attention of trainer John B. McKee after the colt broke his maiden at Churchill Downs. McKee wrote a check for $25,000 on behalf of his young client, Californian Chaffee Earl. After Jim Dandy's victory at Saratoga, the colt went west, racing without distinction at Agua Caliente in Mexico and in California.

Gallant Fox reappeared at age three in the Wood Memorial with a new partner, the legendary Earl Sande, in the irons. The Fox of Belair won impressively, then overcame a rough trip to win the Preakness Stakes, held that year before the Kentucky Derby. The colt added the Derby and the Belmont Stakes to his resume, defeating Whichone in the latter. Victories in the Dwyer Stakes and Arlington Classic followed before trainer Sunny Jim Fitzsimmons gave his star a break.

Gallant Fox had captured public fancy with his sleek bay coat, white-ringed eye, and temperamental attitude. His Triple Crown triumph provided an exciting diversion during the early throes of the Great Depression.

While Gallant Fox rested, Whichone easily took Saratoga's Whitney Stakes over older foes, stamping him as a worthy foe for the Travers. Despite Jim Dandy's mediocre record, trainer McKee shipped the colt by rail to Saratoga, where he finished last in an overnight handicap eight days before the big race.

A deluge the night before the Travers changed Jim Dandy's fortunes. His previous Saratoga upset had occurred over a muddy track, and the surface softened to a rich ooze — a balm to Jim Dandy's tender feet.

Fans, though, dismissed him at 100-1 while installing Gallant Fox as the 1-2 favorite and Whichone the second choice at 8-5. Sun Falcon rounded out the field.

By post time the weather had changed for the better, and the famed racetrack beckoned the crowds.

"How big was the 1930 Travers Stakes?" Bill Heller writes in his book, *Graveyard of Champions: Saratoga's Fallen Favorites*. "Well, national radio covered it live, one of the first live national broadcasts of a horse race, with famed broadcaster Clem McCarthy doing the honors. New York Governor Franklin Delano Roosevelt and his wife, Eleanor, attended. Gene Tunney, the great boxer, made it. So did as many as 50,000 others, an estimate made by the New York *Herald-Tribune*."

Though other newspapers estimated a smaller crowd, automobiles were reported to be abandoned two miles from the track and the concessionaire ran out of clam chowder.

Gallant Fox and Whichone battled from the start, neither relenting until the far turn, when Whichone carried the favorite wide and began to tire. Through the hole on the rail shot Jim Dandy, and he soon had lengths on his rivals. He won by eight, with Gallant Fox six lengths ahead of Whichone, who bowed a tendon.

Sande lamented the loss when he spoke to reporters: "I'm sorry, more than you can imagine, for it hurts to lose on such a great horse."

Gallant Fox and Sande never lost again, with the colt taking the Saratoga Cup, the Lawrence Realization, and the Jockey Club Gold Cup, and earning the three-year-old championship and Horse of the Year title. Jim Dandy ran for eight more seasons, picking up a few minor wins, but if not for his two upsets at Saratoga, the hard-luck colt's name would be long forgotten. *JD*

Jim Dandy delivers a shocker in the Travers Stakes, leaving Gallant Fox (opposite) lengths behind

HIALEAH PARK LAST HELD a race meet in 2001 and remains in limbo as the owner and government officials debate its fate, but behind the padlocked gate lies a racetrack that was once known as one of the most beautiful ever built.

The track, which sits in the heart of the South Florida city for which it is named, opened in 1925 as the creation of Jimmy Bright and Joseph Smoot during the Florida land boom of the 1920s. Bright provided the land, and Smoot the money.

Joseph E. Widener, a leading breeder-owner and a member of The Jockey Club, was the man behind the push for elegance, splendor, and major-league racing at the track. Widener had been the driving force behind the earlier beautification of Belmont Park after taking charge following the death in 1924 of track president August Belmont II. So beautiful were Belmont Park and Hialeah that Belmont was called the "Hialeah of the North," and Hialeah the "Belmont of the South."

Starting in the early 1930s, Widener transformed Hialeah from a struggling track to a major winter destination for the wealthy. In 1929

Widener became a member of the Miami Jockey Club that operated Hialeah, and it wasn't long before he went into action to improve the track's purses and image.

With financial backing from prominent breeder-owner E.R. Bradley and the legalization of pari-mutuel betting, Widener embarked on an ambitious program to modernize and beautify the track. He hired a young architect, Lester Geisler, to design a new facility. Geisler, a protégé of society architect Addison Mizner, worked in Palm Beach, Florida. Widener, who was partial to French architecture, sent Geisler to France to get a feel for architecture and landscaping. The architect also visited several racetracks, including the Parisian track Longchamp. Following his return, Geisler traveled to Belmont and Saratoga to study racetrack design.

Geisler's ability to supervise the construction was put to a stern test. The construction period lasted only from June 1931, when the meeting ended, to the following January, when the new meeting began.

Landscaping played an integral part in Hialeah's beauty. The majority of plants that pro-

57 Hialeah Park Popularizes Winter Racing

Mr. Prospector certainly possessed the raw genetics to be a top sire.

His sire, Raise a Native, was undefeated at two and was co-champion two-year-old colt of 1963 (with Hurry to Market). He also proved to be a sire of sires, through sons Alydar, Exclusive Native, and Majestic Prince. Gold Digger, Mr. Prospector's dam, was a multiple stakes winner of $127,255. Her female family traces back to the champion sprinter Myrtlewood — the same tail-female family that produced Seattle Slew.

Savin was shopping as much for a stallion as a racehorse when he paid a sale-topping $220,000 for Mr. Prospector at the 1971 Keeneland July select yearling sale.

"You nickel-and-dime it around and you'll never do any good," he told *The Blood-Horse* after the purchase. "I find the horse business just like the contracting business; if you see something you like that's good, go ahead and spend some money on it."

Mr. Prospector was certainly worth the price. Though he did not race at two because of shin problems, he launched into his three-year-old campaign with fire and determination. Mr. Prospector won his first three starts and set a Gulfstream Park record of 1:07 4/5 for six furlongs in his third race, which happened to be on the Florida Derby undercard. The Florida Derby that year was won by Savin's Royal and Regal. Jimmy Croll trained both horses. Mr. Prospector finished second in the Derby Trial but was injured during the race and stayed off the racetrack until his four-year-old year. Once healthy, he set another six-furlong track record of 1:08 3/5 at Garden State Park in the Whirlaway Handicap and later won the Gravesend Handicap. Mr. Prospector's racing career ended after he fractured a sesamoid while training over a heavy track at Monmouth Park. His injury occurred three days before his full brother, Kentucky Gold, sold for $625,000, then a world record, at the Keeneland July yearling sale.

Initially, it was reported that Mr.

Prospector would go to stud in Kentucky, but he wound up at Savin's Aisco Farm. No matter. The young stallion got off to a fast start with his first crop, which included 1978 co-champion juvenile filly It's in the Air and the Sorority Stakes runner-up Fine Prospect. Mr. Prospector was the leading freshman sire by progeny earnings in 1978. He had eight winners, one stakes winner, and three stakes-placed horses out of fourteen runners that earned $309,201.

With such quick success it didn't take long for syndicate members to begin questioning whether Florida was the right place for Mr. Prospector. Leading the push for relocation was Brant, who believed the Florida market too small to make the most of Mr. Prospector's potential. Over time Brant convinced Savin that Mr. Prospector would do better if bred to higher-quality, classic-type mares that could add stamina to the stallion's progeny. Brant ended up buying ten or eleven shares from Savin, of which he added two to the shares he already owned and sold the rest to Claiborne Farm.

Mr. Prospector died in 1999 at age twenty-nine and is buried at Claiborne Farm. *EM*

Mr. Prospector in the auction ring at Keeneland as a yearling

60 Dancer's Image's Derby Disqualification

SINCE ITS FIRST RUNNING in 1875, the Kentucky Derby has had its share of controversial outcomes, impossibly close finishes, and improbable victories. But only one horse has been disqualified.

Dancer's Image basked in Derby glory for thirty-six hours until a positive drug test stripped him of the roses and cast him in infamy. Calumet Farm's Forward Pass, the runner-up and 2-1 favorite for the 1968 renewal, was declared the victor.

Dancer's Image's alleged doping and the subsequent chain of events are a tangled tale that time has not unraveled. Ironically, the drug allegedly given to Dancer's Image — the anti-inflammatory

phenylbutazone — had been legal until 1962 and became a permitted raceday medication once again just six years after the disqualification debacle. Today, Bute is so commonly used it is no longer noted in racing programs next to starters' names.

Businessman Peter Fuller's homebred Dancer's Image inherited his sire's looks and also his troublesome ankles. The great Native Dancer had captivated a nascent television audience when his gray form ranged across screens in the early 1950s *(See No. 36)*. His lone defeat came in the 1953 Kentucky Derby *(See No. 21)*, and he remained otherwise invincible in spite of tender ankles.

Trainer Lou Cavalaris Jr. urged Fuller to sell

Dancer's Image and the deed nearly came to pass. But as the colt stood in the auction ring at Hialeah, Joan Fuller entreated her husband not to let the colt go. Fuller complied, buying Dancer's Image back for $26,000 and turning him over to Cavalaris to train.

Dancer's Image won eight of fifteen starts at two and the Canadian juvenile championship. Early in the colt's three-year-old season, Fuller began to contemplate the Kentucky Derby for his prized buy-back. The colt's victory in April in the Governor's Gold Cup at Bowie racetrack was especially meaningful. Not only did Dancer's Image stamp himself a legitimate classic contender, his victory gave Fuller a way to honor the Reverend Martin Luther King, whose murder two days before the race had deeply grieved the sportsman. Fuller pledged a portion of the Governor's Gold Cup prize money to King's widow and presented her with the gift in a private ceremony. When news of Fuller's gift later was made public, the gesture drew criticism from some quarters in this racially divided era; Fuller got his share of hate mail.

Dancer's Image next won the Wood Memorial at Aqueduct in fine style, prompting an offer for $2 million — double an offer Fuller previously had turned down. It was on to the Derby for Dancer's Image.

When Derby week dawned, so did an inflamed right ankle for Dancer's Image. Louisville veterinarian Alex Harthill immediately was enlisted to care for the colt as he had for so many other Derby starters over the years.

In a 2000 interview with John McEvoy, author of *Great Horse Racing Mysteries*, Harthill said a friend had asked him to tend to Dancer's Image though the veterinarian knew nothing about the colt and did not meet Fuller until the day before the Derby. After examining the colt, Harthill and Cavalaris agreed that four grams of Bute would be the best treatment. At that time Bute was permitted for training but not racing. Harthill testified later he believed the drug, administered the Sunday before the Derby, would clear the colt's system in plenty of time for no trace to appear in a post-race test.

Fuller told McEvoy: "As far as I know, the only Bute my horse got in Kentucky was given to him that Sunday morning of Derby week."

Dancer's Image responded quickly to the treatment, and his Derby preparations continued. Though reports vary on Dancer's Image's soundness at posttime, he crossed the finish line first on May 4 in the good time of 2:02 1/5.

A urine sample taken from Dancer's Image after the race, identified only as number 3956, was sent to Louisville Testing Laboratory for analysis. It came back positive. To corroborate the finding, lab officials sent some of the sample to the highly regarded chemist Lewis Harris in Lincoln, Nebraska. Harris declared that sample negative.

Meanwhile, Churchill Downs stewards, alerted to the initial positive, informed the Kentucky Racing Commission, which in turn notified trainer Cavalaris. After three days of hearings, stewards disqualified Dancer's Image and suspended Cavalaris and assistant trainer Robert Barnard.

Fuller appealed the ruling and the case dragged on for many years. Hearings revealed bizarre schemes to clear names and smoke out possible culprits. But whether Dancer's Image received additional Bute or whether the positive test

Owner Peter Fuller leads in Dancer's Image (opposite) after the colt's short-lived Derby victory (below)

reflected the presence of Azium, a drug with similar properties to Bute, remains unknown.

Dancer's Image ran third in the Preakness but was disqualified to eighth. A flare-up of ankle problems forced the colt's retirement before the Belmont Stakes. Dancer's Image stood at stud in Maryland, Ireland, and France, and then in Japan, where he died in 1992. *JD*

61

Laura Hillenbrand's Best-Seller Sparks Seabiscuit Mania

WHEN LAURA HILLENBRAND'S BOOK *Seabiscuit: An American Legend* was published in 2001, there was no expectation from its publisher that it would become the runaway best-seller of the year, nor did its writer imagine that her four-hundred-page biography would launch a second nationwide frenzy of Seabiscuit mania. Indeed, Hillenbrand said she would be happy if she were able to sell five thousand copies of the book from the trunk of her car. But her engaging story of the knobby-kneed 1938 Horse of the Year quickly became a publishing phenomenon, selling more than three million copies and going back to press more than eighteen times. On its heels came a popular exhibition, tourism, staggering sales of kitsch and memorabilia, a blockbuster movie, an award-winning documentary, and the raised hopes of the racing industry for a wider audience.

Shortly after *Seabiscuit: An American Legend* was published, the National Museum of Racing and Hall of Fame in Saratoga Springs, New York, opened a major Seabiscuit exhibit. Hillenbrand loaned the museum many items that chronicled the first wave of Seabiscuit mania in the 1930s including original newspapers, advertisements, and Seabiscuit games. The exhibit drew overflow crowds throughout the summer Saratoga racing season.

Seabiscuit fans were also drawn to central Mendocino County, in northern California. Here Charles and Marcella Howard, Seabiscuit's owners, had their Ridgewood Ranch near the small town of Willits. Seabiscuit retired to the ranch, and when he died in 1947, Howard buried him on the property at a secret location. Hillenbrand's book reawakened the area's claim to fame.

Willits Chamber of Commerce was besieged by phone calls. In September 2002 the chamber of commerce together with the Seabiscuit Heritage Foundation, the Mendocino County Museum, and the ranch's current owners offered the first series of walking tours, which were quickly sold out. Guests were treated to old movie footage of Seabiscuit and ranch life and a tour of the original buildings, including the Howards' craftsman-style home.

In October 2002 San Mateo's Bay Meadows racetrack held Seabiscuit Day at the Races, giving away Seabiscuit bobbleheads to paid-admission patrons, who snapped up all 8,500 of the plastic horses before the first race. A few months later Santa Anita Park produced similar bobbleheads

67 Citation's Sixteen-Race Win Streak

CITATION CEMENTED HIS REPUTATION as one of racing's all-time greatest horses on January 11, 1950, when after more than a year away he came back to win his sixteenth straight race. The winning streak, a North American record in modern times, has only been matched by Cigar in 1996 and Hallowed Dreams in 2000.

A son of Bull Lea and Hydroplane II, Citation was born at famed Calumet Farm on April 11, 1945. He was a dark bay who at maturity stood 16 hands and had a twenty-five-foot stride. Owner Warren Wright sent him as a yearling to the Florida stable of father-and-son trainers Ben and Jimmy Jones to learn his early lessons. From there, it was on to Maryland with Jimmy Jones to begin the colt's racing career.

In his first two years racing, Citation amassed twenty-seven wins in twenty-nine starts, his two defeats resulting in runner-up efforts under questionable circumstances. "My horse could beat anything with hair on it," Jimmy Jones used to say. Citation's sixteen-race streak commenced with a victory in the 1948 Chesapeake Stakes at old Havre de Grace racetrack in Maryland.

Citation's next victory in the Derby Trial Stakes the week of the Kentucky Derby guaranteed his status as favorite in the Run for the Roses. He did not disappoint, winning with ease over a sloppy track. Jockey Eddie Arcaro wrote in his autobiography that during the race, he heard the voice of Ben Jones saying, "the horse that Citation could not run down had not yet been born." That day Jones' voice was right. Citation next won the Preakness and Belmont Stakes (adding a Jersey Stakes victory in between) to become the eighth horse to win the Triple Crown. He started nine more times that year, winning them all, including the Jockey Club Gold Cup, the Pimlico Special (in a walkover), and, in his final start that season, the Tanforan Handicap — his fifteenth consecutive victory.

But after his shining three-year-old season, in which he won a record $709,470 and was named

Pollard had been aboard Seabiscuit for his first three starts of 1940 and badly wanted to ride him in the Santa Anita Handicap. The jockey's leg had never healed from his earlier spill and had worn down to the circumference of a broomstick, and he was blind in his right eye, but he also was flat broke, newly married, and expecting a child. His fervor to win the prize and to take care of his family outweighed any limitations his body imposed.

Seabiscuit himself was not the model Thoroughbred. Writers often described him as bad-legged, and racing journalist David Alexander quoted Pollard as saying he and his favorite mount had "four good legs between them." One day as Seabiscuit had limped to post, a friend told "Silent" Tom Smith, the horse's trainer, "Tom, that horse of yours can't walk."

"Runs, though," Smith told the man.

And, he wasn't exaggerating. Seabiscuit worked hard for a living, having raced eighty-eight times before the Santa Anita Handicap, winning thirty-two of those races, finishing second fifteen times, and coming in third thirteen times. He had started his career in the claiming ranks, so unimpressive that his first trainer, Sunny Jim Fitzsimmons, agreed to sell him for $7,500 when Charles Howard, owner of the largest Buick dealership in the nation, came along looking for a nice allowance horse.

Under Howard's colors and Smith's tutelage, Seabiscuit launched a spectacular career. His blue-collar, workaday style, and ensuing success under heavy weight made him the sentimental favorite on his home turf, the West Coast. On the East Coast he hadn't been taken seriously until Howard barnstormed him cross-country in 1937, garnering wins in ten stakes races. In 1938 he capped his achievements by defeating Triple Crown winner and Horse of the Year rival War Admiral in a much-anticipated match race (*See No. 2*).

When Seabiscuit emerged from stud to race again in 1940, his fans were thrilled to see him reunited with Pollard. In his first two attempts to comeback, Seabiscuit showed little, but a brilliant victory in the San Antonio Handicap in track record-equaling time set in Howard's sights the opportunity for his horse to become the world's leading money winner. Sun Beau had earned the title in 1931 with earnings

of $376,744. As Seabiscuit headed into the $100,000 Santa Anita Handicap, he lagged $35,897 behind the record holder.

Ironically, Seabiscuit had twice raced in the Santa Anita Handicap and had twice been beaten after gaining the lead in the stretch. In preparation for his third try at the race he had sustained the tendon injury that had sent him to stud duty.

Now he was back at a high weight of 130, with his hard-luck jockey aboard, and the crowd wanting nothing less than a fairy-tale ending on that day, March 2, 1940. Out of the gate Whichcee sprinted to the lead. Pollard urged Seabiscuit, who had broken from the outside, ahead of the fray going into the first turn and dropped him in behind Whichcee. Down the backstretch he slowly gained on the leader. At the eighth pole, Seabiscuit got a head in front, drawing a huge cheer from the stands. The only horse to challenge the two leaders was *Kayak II, who moved into third as his stablemate, Seabiscuit, took the lead. Whichcee lost ground as Seabiscuit swept past him under Pollard's drive. The son of Hard Tack crossed the finish line a half-length in front of *Kayak II, who had overtaken Whichcee by a length.

After the race, Whichcee's jockey, Basil James, claimed foul, saying Seabiscuit had cut in on him at the sixteenth pole. As race officials reviewed the claim, the crowd anxiously waited.

"You know," Pollard told writer Alexander years later, "not a single one of those 80,000 people was making a sound."

When Seabiscuit was declared the winner, the cheers cut the silence like a sonic boom. The country had a new hero, a track record, and the world's leading earner. It also had its fairy-tale ending. *RB*

66 Seabiscuit and Red Pollard Make Their Comeback

IT'S NO WONDER THE STORY of Seabiscuit has been turned into both books and movies. Fiction writers could not have crafted a comeback so eloquent that it led a crowd of 80,000 to stone silence as it awaited the official word whether its hero would be taken down.

The year was 1940, and the race was the mile and a quarter Santa Anita Handicap, then the richest race in the world. The question was not which of the thirteen horses in the field would win the race but whether Seabiscuit would win it.

A tendon injury had sent the beloved West Coast runner to stud a year earlier. Now, at seven, he was back for his fourth try that year at regaining his former glory. On board was his former jockey, Red Pollard, a sinewy matchstick of a man who had ridden Seabiscuit in twenty-six consecutive starts before a spill on another horse in early 1938 sidelined him in the prime of his career and Seabiscuit's. With Pollard out of commission, his close buddy George Woolf had ridden Seabiscuit to Horse of the Year honors.

umph because he had two horses in the Turf. In one of the most dramatic finishes of the day, Mandella-trained Johar charged from the back of the field under jockey Alex Solis to catch defending champion High Chaparral at the wire. Following an agonizing thirteen-minute wait for racing officials to review the photo, the race was declared a dead heat, with both horses credited with the victory. For Mandella, his third win of the day tied the record then held by D. Wayne Lukas. As if to underscore the kind of day he was having, Mandella also trained the fourth-place finisher in the Turf, The Tin Man.

The best was yet to come.

With Solis aboard again for Mandella in the Classic, Pleasantly Perfect gradually gained ground throughout the mile and a quarter race and wore down Medaglia d'Oro for a one and a half-length triumph at 14-1 odds. Mandella's fourth winner of the day and the second for Solis was the first Breeders' Cup winner for owner Gerald Ford's Diamond A Racing Stable. Topped by Pleasantly Perfect's $2-million winner's purse, Mandella's stable earnings for the day stood at $4,564,040.

Mandella was at a loss for words after his Classic victory. "I never thought lightning would strike twice, but it struck harder," Mandella said of his record day. "I don't know how to describe it."

While rewarding for Mandella, his owners, the jockeys, and everyone associated with the stable, the timing of Mandella's record day could not have come at a better time for filmmakers Bill Yahraus and Robin Rosenthal. For the previous fifteen months, Yahraus and Rosenthal had followed Mandella on a daily basis for *On the Muscle*, a three-hour, three-chapter documentary.

They were thrilled to film the celebration surrounding Halfbridled's victory, but by the end of the day, Yahraus and Rosenthal had much more than they came for.

"It (film) was good before then and it's just unthinkably good now," Rosenthal said.

All because of Richard Mandella's unthinkably good day on October 25, 2003. For the record-setting trainer, a day at the races couldn't get any better. *RM*

From the top, Mandella's winners: Halfbridled, Action This Day, Johar, and Pleasantly Perfect

Horse of the Year, Citation was diagnosed with an osselet, a bony growth in the fetlock joint. Throughout 1949 Calumet had to rely upon the talented Coaltown to captivate fans while his famous stablemate healed.

To recover from his injury, Citation was on stall rest alternated with very light exercise. The osselet kept flaring up so it wasn't until the end of 1949 that he resumed regular work. He came back to racing as a five-year-old on January 11, 1950, thirteen months after he had last been to the post. The race, called the Belmont Purse, was a five-thousand-dollar allowance at six furlongs at Santa Anita Park, and the field had just three horses besides Citation: Bold Gallant, Roman In, and Chutney.

Race day was chilly and rainy, so miserable for those used to sunny California that, despite the champion's return, the crowd was the smallest of the season with only 13,000 in the stands. Also, Jimmy Jones had warned that if the track was muddy, Citation would not run. The weather and the possibility of Citation's being scratched discouraged more people from coming out to see the return of the champion. To make things even less auspicious, an earthquake rocked the track just before the first race.

In the end Jones decided even the soaked track and shaken earth should not prevent Citation's return. His horse looked like a winner before the race started. Citation gave a couple of frisky bucks as he was saddled and was in good flesh — some onlookers even thought the horse seemed fat.

Jockey Steve Brooks broke last on Citation. Brooks said the colt had kept one foot up while in the gate, an old habit. Citation remained in third until he hit the stretch, and Brooks kept him out in the center of the track, with Roman In on the rail and Bold Gallant in between.

Brooks went to the whip briefly at the quarter-pole. In the middle of the stretch, Bold Gallant collided briefly with Citation. Brooks urged Citation on by waving his whip in front of his mount's right eye, and the horse took the lead to win by a length and a half over Bold Gallant in 1:11 2/5.

After such a long layoff, the taste of victory was sweet but unfortunately short-lived, for Citation won only one other race during the 1950 season. However, he did finish second four times to Noor, that year's champion older horse, including in the Santa Anita Handicap and San Juan Capistrano Invitational.

But Citation had already long proven his pre-eminence. "These gentleman deserve some credit for their sportsmanship," *The Blood-Horse* wrote of the competition's owners the day of the Belmont Purse, "for they knew when they entered they were filling a race for Citation." *EMG*

(Above) Citation records the fifteenth of his sixteen straight in the Tanforan Handicap; (opposite) in the familiar hands of trainer Jimmy Jones and jockey Eddie Arcaro

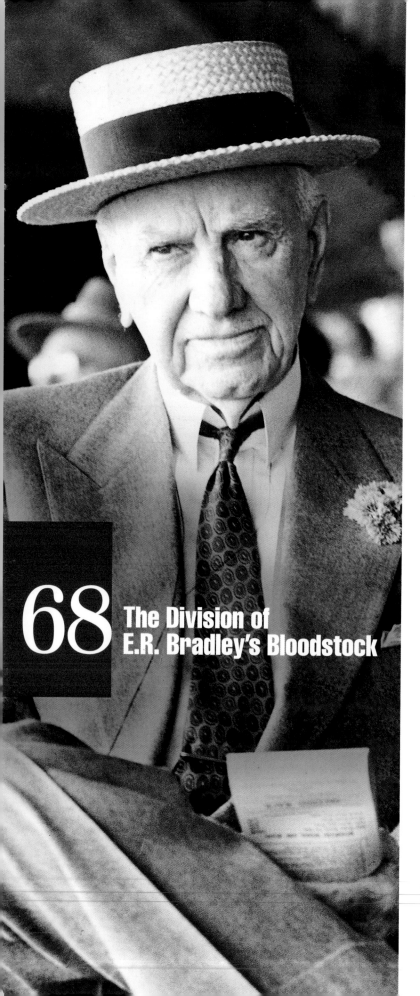

THE DEATH OF EDWARD RILEY BRADLEY on August 15, 1946, ended an important era. No more horses carrying the storied white silks with green hoops would find a familiar spot in the winner's circle. Bradley's Idle Hour Farm, home of four Kentucky Derby winners, would cease operation — its racing colors retired, the land sold, and the farm's powerful racing and breeding stock dispersed.

However, like wind-borne seeds, some of these sons and daughters from generations of Bradley bloodstock fell on fertile soil — the breeding programs of three of racing's greatest sportsmen: Robert Kleberg Jr., Ogden Phipps, and John Hay "Jock" Whitney.

The race meet at Saratoga provided the stage for the opening scene. Every August the pillars of the racing industry made a pilgrimage to the small town in upstate New York. Robert Kleberg, owner of King Ranch in Texas, was no exception.

As usual, the Whitneys had opened their Saratoga house for the season, and Jock had invited the Phippses to be houseguests. As a guest of the Whitneys at the expansive Greentree estate (which included stables and a private one-mile training track for the Whitney horses adjacent to the historic track), Phipps enjoyed his fellow social lion's hospitality: good food, good wine, good conversation with a variety of interesting guests.

But on this one occasion being Ogden Phipps' host had more perks than being Jock Whitney's guest.

News of Bradley's death must have spread quickly through the hotels, bars, restaurants, stables — any place horsemen gathered. Kleberg, who had learned that the Bradley land and bloodstock might be purchased in a package deal, contacted Phipps and offered him a chance to participate. Phipps, being the houseguest of Whitney, asked that the offer extend to his host as well.

Through Major Louie Beard, the racing manager for the Whitney stable, this triumvirate of power and wealth negotiated with the Bradley executors. At stake were the fully equipped farm (1,292 acres), two stallions (Bimelech and Blue Larkspur), a select group of proven broodmares (Bradley bred 128 stakes winners and fifteen champions), along with blue-blooded yearlings, weanlings, and horses of racing age. On

November 7 the final deal was struck for the option price of $2,681,545. At the time, it was the largest private sale of a farm and horses in history.

After each of the three men had selected horses for himself, the syndicate lost little time in recouping some of its investment as it immediately sold part of the acreage and a group of horses to Edward S. Moore and his wife, Evelyn, who operated nearby Circle M Farm. A draft of horses in training was conveyed to Charles S. Howard, owner of the stalwart Seabiscuit. A single lot, a weanling colt by Triple Crown winner War Admiral—Baby League, by Bubbling Over (a full brother to future Horse of the Year Busher) went to Elizabeth Arden Graham's Maine Chance Farm. Named Mr. Busher, the chestnut colt won the rich Arlington Futurity before becoming a useful sire.

Bradley's Irish luck quickly smiled its blessing upon each recipient.

Kleberg retained part of Idle Hour for the Kentucky division of King Ranch, and among his bloodstock choices was a two-year-old daughter of Blue Larkspur named But Why Not. She would be a champion at three and at four. He also

Kleberg   **Phipps**   **Whitney**

picked a yearling colt by Bimelech—Bee Mac, by War Admiral. This colt, who was named Better Self, won many important stakes and nearly $400,000. He went on to sire numerous stakes winners for Kleberg and others as did Beau Max, the Bull Lea foal Bee Mac (War Admiral—Baba Kenny, by Black Servant) was carrying at the time of the sale.

Whitney, too, gleaned benefits from the Bradley legacy. Among the mares transferred to Greentree Farm in Kentucky were the grande dame La Troienne, who was in the twilight of her produc-

ing years; Blade of Time (Sickle—Bar Nothing, by Blue Larkspur), who produced three stakes winners; Big Event (Blue Larkspur—La Troienne, by Teddy), who was the second dam of Greentree's useful stallion The Axe II; and, perhaps best of all, the stakes-winning Bimlette (Bimelech—Bloodroot, by Blue Larkspur), the dam of three stakes winners, including Wood Memorial winner and useful sire No Robbery.

But the Phipps selection proved to be most valuable. The weanling full brother to But Why Not became the champion steeplechaser Oedipus, who raced for Mrs. Ogden Phipps. A yearling filly (Challedon—Bird Flower, by Blue Larkspur) named Flitabout produced three stakes winners including Broadway, the dam of champion two-year-old filly Queen of the Stage.

Two of the mares relegated to the Phipps fold came bearing gifts from War Admiral. Baby League (Bubbling Over—La Troienne, by Teddy) carried the filly Striking, who became a stakes winner for Phipps and ancestress of champions Numbered Account and Rhythm. Businesslike (Blue Larkspur—La Troienne, by Teddy) also produced a 1947 filly. Named Busanda, she proved an excellent racehorse. Among her stakes wins were the historic Alabama Stakes and the Suburban Stakes, in which she beat males. As a broodmare, she foaled the great champion Buckpasser, who as a leading broodmare sire would pass genes engineered by Bradley to future generations.

E.R. Bradley has been dead for sixty years, but the genes he masterminded through his astute study of pedigrees continue to flourish in the twenty-first century. *TH*

Seattle Slew Sells for $17,500

IN RETROSPECT, it was probably the most lopsided transaction since the Dutch gave Native Americans twenty-four dollars worth of beads and trinkets for the island of Manhattan.

For a final hammer price of $17,500 in the summer of 1975, Karen and Mickey Taylor, along with their associates, Jim and Sally Hill, purchased an eventual Triple Crown winner, a successful stallion, and a legend: Seattle Slew.

Relative newcomers to Thoroughbred racing, the Taylors had traveled from their home in south central Washington state to Lexington for Fasig-Tipton's second annual Kentucky July yearling sale in 1975. There, they teamed with the Hills to

purchase a couple of horses, one of which was a dark bay or brown colt by Bold Reasoning out of the Poker mare My Charmer.

Bred in Kentucky by Ben Castleman, the colt didn't make the cut for the Keeneland July yearling sale but had enough quality for the Fasig-Tipton venue. Horseman Ted Bates, assessing yearlings for Fasig-Tipton, scored Seattle Slew as "above average in size — shoulder developed well — good angle and strong back — good through the middle, with good spring of rib — nice hind leg, but passes close at hocks — quick appearance — turns out moderately right front from knee down."

Jim Hill, a veterinarian, assessed him a little

186

until Alydar was derailed with a fractured wing of the coffin bone in his left front foot that sidelined him for the year. Seattle Slew was headed postward with a new rider, Angel Cordero Jr., after Slew's regular rider, Jean Cruguet, was dismissed for criticizing the champ's training and raising doubts that the horse was as good as he had been the previous year. Cordero had been aboard Dr. Patches in the Paterson.

And then there was racing secretary Tommy Trotter's weights for the Marlboro. He assigned Seattle Slew 128 pounds, two pounds over the scale weight of 126 pounds for a top older horse at that time of year. Affirmed was assigned 124 pounds, three pounds over the traditional scale of 121 pounds for a three-year-old while facing older horses. In essence, Affirmed would be "spotting," or carrying one more pound, than Seattle Slew.

Affirmed's trainer, Laz Barrera, was concerned about the pace and did not want young jockey Steve Cauthen to let Cordero steal away to an easy lead. That proved to be paramount, for at the break of the great race Seattle Slew went to the front and was allowed to cruise through early fractions of :24 and :47 as Affirmed tracked him, two lengths back.

"You just don't go in :24 and :47," Barrera said afterward. "Impossible. I told him (Cauthen) to stay one length away at most off that horse — the only one he had to beat. On a straightaway course, :24 and :47, you can't do that."

Affirmed didn't, but he surely made Slew work

hard for it, pushing the older horse through quicker fractions as the race went on. Seattle Slew's advantage after a mile in 1:33 3/5 was three lengths, and it was the same margin at the finish in 1:45 4/5. The final five-eighths of the race had been run in a sensational :58 4/5. In the inaugural Marlboro Cup in 1973, when Secretariat set a world record of 1:45 2/5 for the distance, he ran the final five furlongs in :59 2/5.

The two great warriors met again October 14 in the Jockey Club Gold Cup. While the race probably is best remembered for Seattle Slew's bravest effort while losing by a nose to Exceller (*See No. 78*), Affirmed's participation was diminished in the annals of history as his saddle slipped as the field ran down the backstretch, and he faded to finish fifth of six.

Slew polished off his racing career November 11 with an easy farewell victory in the Stuyvesant Handicap at Aqueduct. Affirmed rebounded and had a terrific four-year-old campaign in 1979. He ended his racing career with a score in the Woodward Stakes and a dramatic victory over Spectacular Bid in a second try at the Jockey Club Gold Cup. *EH*

Seattle Slew wears the victor's blanket after defeating Affirmed (below) in the Marlboro Cup (opposite)

73 Alydar's Death

NO THOROUGHBRED'S DEATH has been scrutinized or debated with as much intensity or fervor as Alydar's, the Calumet Farm racing star of the 1970s and leading American sire of the 1980s, who died after a mysterious accident in his stall in November 1990.

Some people, including a federal prosecutor in Houston, Texas, believe Alydar was purposely killed so Calumet — which was struggling under a huge debt load and headed for bankruptcy — could stay afloat with a $36.5-million mortality insurance settlement. Others discounted the theory, claiming Alydar was worth more to Calumet alive than dead.

The prevalent theory in Central Kentucky horse industry circles was that one of the shady characters with whom Calumet president J.T. Lundy did business may have hired a "hit man" to kill the horse to get back at Lundy for a deal gone awry.

Nothing, however, was ever substantiated to support that dubious suggestion.

Lundy, along with key members of the farm's staff and attending veterinarians who tried to save Alydar's life, said the fifteen-year-old stallion's death was a freak accident — and nothing more.

At about ten o'clock the night of November 13, 1990, Alton Stone, a night watchman making rounds at the legendary Lexington, Kentucky, farm, found Alydar in distress in his stall. Stone immediately called for help, and within minutes Lundy, farm veterinarian Lynda Rhodes, insurance adjustor Tom Dixon, and others arrived on the scene.

What they found was a ghastly injury to the son of Raise a Native's right hind leg. The cannon bone, the large bone connecting the knee and ankle, was nearly severed, Alydar's leg virtually held together by soft tissue. Sedatives were administered to the stallion, and the renowned veterinary surgeon Larry Bramlage was summoned.

A decision was made to try and save Alydar, though this severe of an injury would routinely result in almost immediate euthanasia. The injured leg was temporarily stabilized with a makeshift splint, consisting of a pair of two-by-fours and a temporary cast; surgery was planned for the next morning.

Bramlage, along with Dr. William A Baker, was able to stabilize the fracture during a two-hour, forty-minute surgical procedure employing a bone graft, plate, pins, and a fiberglass cast. Following the surgery, a statement from the farm said the fracture was "adequately repaired," but that Alydar's prognosis remained guarded. Curiously, despite the severity of the injury, the statement added that in the absence of complications Alydar "should be able to stand the 1991 breeding season."

Alydar was placed in a sling in an effort to keep weight off the injured leg, a tactic that had worked well with another valuable stallion, Nureyev, a few years earlier when he suffered a serious leg injury while standing at Walmac-Warnerton Farm in Lexington. But while Nureyev had a calm demeanor and was able to adjust to being in a sling, Alydar became agitated, possibly from colic that may have been caused by the sedatives he was given.

The morning after the surgery it was clear the sling would not work, and Alydar was allowed to stand on his own. Calm at first, he tried moving about his stall but lost his balance and crashed to the ground, landing on his right hip. Baker was in the stall with Alydar but unable to stop the fall, which occurred with such force that it snapped the stallion's femur, the large bone in his upper leg.

Nothing could be done to save Alydar from such a severe injury. Within minutes, he was given a lethal injection of barbiturates.

At the time of Alydar's death, Calumet, the farm that had produced Triple Crown winners Whirlaway and Citation, was a financial house of cards ready to collapse. Lundy's questionable wheeling and dealing and high-roller lifestyle came at a time when the horse industry was going through a down cycle.

Alydar, whose gallant second-place finishes to Affirmed in the 1978 Triple Crown had brought glory back to Calumet after a lengthy slump, became the farm's largest source of revenue as his success at stud grew. But the millions of dollars in lifetime breeding rights to Alydar that Lundy had sold in the mid-1980s were gone by 1990. Cash flow became a serious problem as banks began to call in their loans. Even the $36.5-million insurance settlement could not keep Calumet out of bankruptcy. Officials filed for protection from creditors July 11, 1991, and Calumet was sold in a court-ordered auction the following year (*See No. 48*).

Lundy's financial trouble was the motive that led many to believe Alydar's original injury was caused by a human. Lundy, Bramlage, and others who diagnosed the injury postulated that Alydar broke his leg either by kicking a wall or somehow wedging his leg in a narrow gap between his stall door and a side wall. Bramlage insisted an intentional blow to the leg with a crowbar or similar instrument would have caused small pieces of broken bone in the fracture, something not evident during his diagnosis.

Alydar during the height of his stallion power (opposite) and memorialized at Calumet Farm

No charges involving the death of Alydar were ever filed against Lundy, though during the sentencing phase of a criminal trial for bank fraud against the former Calumet president and one of his associates, federal prosecutor Julia Tomala presented evidence suggesting Lundy should be held responsible for the stallion's death.

Though Lundy was found guilty of the bank fraud charges and served nearly four years in jail, U.S. District Court Judge Sim Lake said Lundy could not be held responsible for Alydar's death.

"Although there is some physical evidence and the circumstances surrounding the events were suspicious," Lake said, "I am not able to conclude by the preponderance of the evidence that Mr. Lundy is responsible." *RP*

Princequillo Moves to Claiborne Farm

"THE WRONG KIND OF HORSE in his racing record, backed by the wrong kind of pedigree," is how scholarly Thoroughbred breeder Abram S. Hewitt described Princequillo. Certainly, he had a point. Even today the American breeder would tend to sniff and look away if presented a stallion prospect with the following description: former claimer with an offbeat pedigree; matured late and needed longer distances to excel.

Well, there is also a counterpoint to fashion and logic, and that counterpoint is the sobering phrase that breeding racehorses is "an inexact science."

Princequillo began his stud career standing for $250, which even in 1945 was a badge of modesty. He was standing at Ellerslie Stud in Virginia. While Ellerslie bore the distinction as having been the original site of the Hancock family's Thoroughbred dynasty, by the mid-1940s it was recognized as the second tier of that family enterprise, whose star had risen at Claiborne Farm near Paris, Kentucky.

Princequillo would surely have earned his way to Claiborne via the prowess of his early foal crops, but he moved to Claiborne before even early results at the racetrack had been recorded. Determining that Claiborne would be not just the first team but the sole locus of the already historic family enterprise, A.B. Hancock Sr. sold Ellerslie to Robert Schlesinger in 1946.

Princequillo had stood two seasons at Ellerslie, and by late 1946 the Claiborne ads in *The Blood-Horse* listed him on the Kentucky farm's roster and already "booked full" for 1947.

Individuals intimately involved in the career of Princequillo left conflicting versions of how he came to be a Hancock stallion. Joe Hirsch quoted his trainer, Horatio Luro, in the book *The Grand Senor* to the effect that Luro had to overcome A.B. Hancock Sr.'s resistance to convince him to give the horse a chance. Luro recalled that Hancock felt that Claiborne had so many sources of stamina in its stud barn that adding Princequillo would represent an "over-balance" — a tactful shading on the concept of too much of a good thing.

Conversely, Hancock's son, A.B. "Bull" Hancock Jr., recalled for *The Blood-Horse* in 1971 that he had been keen to stand the horse. Mindful that Princequillo had won at six furlongs, when

Hancock saw the horse expand his credentials by winning the lengthy Saratoga Cup, he told his father, "This is one horse we've got to have."

Princequillo was bred by an American in Paris, one Laudy Lawrence, who was Metro-Goldwyn-Mayer's head man in France. The colt was foaled in Ireland but was sired by Belgium-bred Prince Rose. The latter was such a star at the races that the Belgian government for a time banned his exportation, but Belgium is hardly recognized as top level in international racing. The approach of World War II negated such stances of national pride, and Lawrence took the horse to France, where the stallion was killed by artillery fire. The dam of Princequillo was Cosquilla, whose sire, Papyrus, won the English Derby.

Imported to this country, Princequillo was demoted to $1,500 claiming company at one point. He was claimed for $2,500 by Luro for expatriate Russian Prince Dimitri Djordjadze and the prince's wife, the former Audrey Emory, a rich American.

Under Luro's astute handling, Princequillo developed into an effective stayer, winning such races as the Saratoga Handicap, Saratoga Cup, (one and three-quarters miles), and Jockey Club Gold Cup (two miles). He won twelve of thirty-three races and earned $96,550.

Ensconced for two breeding seasons at Ellerslie, Princequillo benefited from geography. Chris Chenery had a farm in Virginia and thus sent to Princequillo the mare Hildene. In his second crop Princequillo sired the champion Hill Prince from Hildene. Hancock patron William Woodward Sr. also sent a couple of mares and thus got Prince Simon, who came within a photo finish of fulfilling Woodward's long-held ambition of winning the English Derby.

With the sale of Ellerslie speeding what would surely have been his transfer to Claiborne on the

Princequillo's relocation to Claiborne enabled him to become one of America's most influential sires

basis of results, Princequillo continued similar success. He sired a total of sixty-five stakes winners (14 percent) and scrummed with fellow Claiborne stallion Nasrullah in a rivalry for premier status among American-based stallions. Nasrullah led the sire list five times, but Princequillo got in two years as leader, in 1957–58.

Princequillo's signature son was Round Table, Horse of the Year in 1958, three-time turf champion, and for a time the leading money earner in history. Round Table was one of his five American champions, being joined by Misty Morn, Hill Prince, Dedicate, and Quill. The Garden State Stakes winner Prince John was another distinguished son of Princequillo and was among contributors to his standing as a sire of sires. Prince John's sons included Stage Door Johnny.

Princequillo, who died in 1964, led the broodmare sire list eight times, and his daughters produced 170 stakes winners. His proximity to Nasrullah facilitated a confluence of their blood with each other's daughters. The ultimate combine was created by Nasrullah's son Bold Ruler and Princequillo's daughter Somethingroyal. In 1970 that combine produced a colt named Secretariat. *ELB*

75 The Triumvirate of Sangster, O'Brien, and Magnier

AN IMPORTANT MOMENT in the shaping of international sales, racing, and stallion operations was the arrival of a group from England and Ireland at the Keeneland summer sale of 1975. Vincent O'Brien, the soft-spoken Irish trainer of Epsom Derby and Grand National winners, was perhaps best known although English football pools magnate Robert Sangster was soon to be the most visible individual in the international arena. They were accompanied by the well-regarded bloodstock agent Tom Cooper and by an intense, quiet young man named John Magnier, who had impressed his elders by his skill in putting together stallion syndicates.

From this team would grow the establishment of Coolmore Stud, today renowned as one of the leading commercial stallion operations in the world, an enterprise whose array of important horses has included Sadler's Wells, the fourteen-time leader of the Irish-English stallion lists, and Danehill, sire of an unprecedented total of more than three hundred stakes winners

As would be expected, while the formation of this team — with various add-on partners from time to time — might be seen as a moment unto itself, it was in fact built upon other factors. O'Brien was a key figure. In 1968 he had won the Epsom Derby with the American-bred colt Sir Ivor (*See No. 89*), who had been sent to him by the sporting Raymond Guest, U.S. ambassador to Ireland.

In 1968 O'Brien attended the Canadian yearling sale at Woodbine racetrack, where his eye was taken by a tall, lengthy colt by Northern Dancer from the Windfields Farm consignment. Northern Dancer had won the 1964 Kentucky Derby and Preakness for E.P. Taylor's Windfields, fulfilling Taylor's devout wish to prove he could raise top-class horses in Canada. *(See No. 28.)* Northern Dancer was short and stocky, as many of his better runners would be, but the colt O'Brien liked was of a different stripe. Charles Engelhard bought the colt for $84,000, then a record for Canada, and sent him to O'Brien.

Under the name Nijinsky (the suffix II was added when he returned to North America), this strapping individual was a champion at two and then won England's first Triple Crown in thirty-five years. Europeans now had cause to be smitten with Northern Dancer.

John Magnier had a situation similar to that facing Seth Hancock of Claiborne Farm in the early 1970s. Both were in their early twenties when the death of their fathers hastened what would likely have been a more orderly path of succession. Both have stood the test of time.

Magnier's grandfather had stood the important National Hunt (steeplechase) stallions Cottage and

Fortina as owner of Castle Hyde and Grange Stud in Ireland. Magnier was only twenty-three when he put together the syndication of a nice colt named Green God, striking a deal with prominent owner David Robinson. The syndication's success showed his business acumen although the horse would not prove a major success.

The wheels turned quickly. Sangster and O'Brien acquired an interest in Coolmore Stud from Tim Vigors, and then invited the dynamic young Magnier into their company.

The first yearlings included The Minstrel, who won the English and Irish derbies (wearing Sangster's colors); Alleged, who won two runnings of the Prix de l'Arc de Triomphe, and the group-winning Northern Dancer colt Be My Guest.

The prestige of The Minstrel and Alleged was such that the economics of the time dictated they stand in America, and their syndications at $9 million and $16 million, respectively, greased the rails for further investment.

Although Alleged was of the Ribot sire line, Sangster and company decided to concentrate on Northern Dancer blood. As described in the *Racing Post*, "Magnier honed his skills in promotion and marketing and quickly demonstrated a knack for maximizing stallion income."

With age, O'Brien (whose daughter Susan had married Magnier) became less active, and Sangster concentrated much of his efforts on his own Swettenham Stud. Magnier became not only the owner of the Coolmore enterprise, but the key figure in the Irish bloodstock world. His efforts were abetted by a 1969 government decision to eliminate the taxes on stallion income, an enlightened bit of government leadership that was tied to the Irish love of the horse. (The tax break is set to be rescinded in 2006.)

Having been involved with National Hunt horses, Magnier applied to Thoroughbred stallions the steeplechase practice of breeding large books of mares. This practice was aided by the advance of veterinary procedures such as ultrasound, which made the matter of discerning just when a mare should be bred more a science than a matter of intuition.

Moreover, he began sending horses to stand a second season in the Southern Hemisphere, and Coolmore developed a stallion operation in Australia. For its Kentucky branch the Coolmore outfit had acquired Ashford Stud in 1984. Ashford covered 465 acres at the time and has since grown to 1,600 acres. Coolmore also acquired Sangster's Creekview Farm in Kentucky.

By 2005 what had seemed a revolutionary approach in breeding books of one hundred mares was no longer so novel. The leading four sires of 2005 in book size in North America were all Ashford stallions and each covered more than 200 mares.

Armed with the season-income potential of that management philosophy, Magnier has a heavy club when negotiating for any stallion prospect he might want. After the $4-million yearling Fusaichi Pegasus blossomed into the Kentucky Derby winner of 2000, Magnier acquired him based on an evaluation reported at $60 million.

Such economics also ended the era when virtually all the best-bred classic horses of Europe would be imported to stand in the United States. Sadler's Wells, another Northern Dancer stallion, was the mainstay at Coolmore in Ireland, while Danehill (by Northern Dancer's son Danzig) traveled between Ireland and Australia. The American syndicates were no longer in the driver's seat.

The pattern continues with the young Sadler's Wells stallions Montjeu and Epsom Derby winners Galileo and High Chaparral, all at Coolmore in Ireland. On the other hand, Magnier chose to stand Giant's Causeway at Ashford after the son of Storm Cat's gallant second in the 2000 Breeders' Cup Classic.

So, Magnier was central to more than one change of direction. The original pattern was (1) buy in America, (2) prove abroad, (3) sell high back to America. Now, he is breeding, buying, and selling on all fronts and has devised a stallion investment-management system that is virtually an international economy unto itself. *ELB*

The Minstrel was one of the early and successful purchases for (opposite, clockwise from left) O'Brien, Sangster, and Magnier

76 The Thoroughbred Retirement Foundation Is Created

IN 1982, WHEN THE THOROUGHBRED Retirement Foundation was founded, some 42,000 Thoroughbred foals were registered with The Jockey Club. The vast majority of those young horses never made it to the racetrack, much less won. Colts and fillies with nice pedigrees and the ability to win probably had futures as breeding animals; popular geldings probably had future retirement homes lined up. For example, the famed John Henry would retire to the Kentucky Horse Park in a few years and become a favorite tourist attraction.

But what about the many horses that languished on the racetrack, usually getting by in the lower claiming ranks and passing from one owner to another? English-born trainer Daphne Collings wanted to find a way to keep these hors-es from being ruined on the racetrack or to help them avoid the slaughterhouse and began a "horse haven foundation." She penned a newspaper article detailing the plight of many racehorses and her plans for a foundation to provide a home for ex-racehorses with nowhere else to go.

The article struck a chord with Monique Koehler, a New Jersey pharmaceutical representative. She wasn't a horse person and didn't know much about racing, but being an animal lover she sent a donation and letter of support to Collings. Several months later the two met for dinner, and Koehler soon found herself agreeing to become president of the newly christened Thoroughbred Retirement Foundation. Its mission was to provide lifetime care for retired racehorses, even those that couldn't be ridden because of injury or age.

Koehler set up numerous meetings with horse people, including Secretariat's owner, Penny Chenery, who was quick to lend her financial support and became a member of the TRF board of directors. In 1983 the Internal Revenue Service recognized the TRF as a tax-exempt organization, which aided in fund-raising. But the TRF's main obstacle was the issue of land. Where would the horses be housed?

The solution came from New York Senator Howard Nolan, an early TRF supporter who suggested using available land at the Wallkill Correctional Facility, located upstate. Koehler reached an agreement with the New York Department of Correctional Services to establish a vocational training program in equine management for the inmates in exchange for land use and labor.

On July 26, 1984, the first horse arrived at Wallkill. His name was Promised Road, and he had raced until the age of nine, winning nine of sixty-four starts and $39,547. (Promised Road died in 2005 at the age of thirty at the Wallkill facility and is buried there.)

Since that day, the TRF has taken in thousands of horses and expanded its operations to nine other facilities in various states, including other correctional facilities such as the Blackburn Correctional Complex in Lexington, Kentucky, and the Marion Correctional Institute in Ocala, Florida.

Teaching inmates to care for horses has benefited both humans and equines. "The prisoners found in themselves something they never had before — the capacity for love," Koehler told *The Blood-Horse* in 2004. "Respect for another living being. And the animals didn't care about what these people did before." Numerous former inmates have gone on to find successful jobs in the horse industry after serving their sentences.

Two of the TRF's facilities — the Secretariat Center at the Kentucky Horse Park and Exceller Farm in Poughquag, New York — help retrain Thoroughbreds for adoption and possible second careers. The twenty-two-acre Secretariat Center, which opened in spring 2004, has space for twenty retired Thoroughbreds and has an outdoor arena and several paddocks. At Exceller Farm, which opened in 2001 and was named for the top racehorse Exceller who died in a Swedish slaughterhouse in 1997 (*See No. 64*), ex-racehorses are rehabilitated and adopted out as pleasure and companion horses or even show horses. One Exceller adoptee became a member of a mounted police unit.

The TRF receives financial support from numerous high-profile members of the horse industry, as well as donations from concerned racing fans. While the TRF's ultimate goal — "saving all Thoroughbred racehorses from needless suffering or slaughter" — may never be realized, the organization has helped raise national awareness of the plight of retired racehorses and ensured that at least a small percentage of these horses find a better life. *JM*

A retiree enjoys the perks of the Secretariat Center (opposite); a former racehorse with a new career

Dahlia's International Achievement

CLASS IN A RACEHORSE is one of those intangible, inexplicable qualities: hard to define but easily recognized when it is present. As queen of the globe-trotting set during the early 1970s, Nelson Bunker Hunt's lovely chestnut Dahlia exuded class. Her form and determination on the racetrack propelled her to wins in major races in five countries, a feat unparalleled in the twentieth century (the great undefeated race mare Kincsem traveled the breadth of European racing in the nineteenth century).

Dahlia hailed from the first crop of Vaguely Noble, who had won the 1968 Prix de l'Arc de Triomphe in the light and dark green blocks of Hunt's racing colors. From the outset she exhibited the demeanor that would stand her in good stead on the world's racetracks. John Thornbury, who schooled her initially, remembered her as doing "everything just beautifully."

Having been sent to France and the barn of the famed Maurice Zilber, who trained Hunt's

European division, Dahlia must have warranted great expectations. Zilber chose a stakes race (restricted to first-time starters) as her initial test, the five-furlong Prix Yacowlef over the Deauville grass. She did not disappoint. This maiden victory launched Dahlia into a current of excellence. Over the next two years her accomplishments would rewrite the record books.

Zilber used a win in the 1973 Prix de la Grotte to prep Dahlia for the first classic of the French racing season, the Poule d'Essai des Pouliches. There, she collided with the previous year's champion two-year-old filly, Allez France. Dahlia finished third and regrouped with a victory in the Prix Saint-Alary. A second classic skirmish with Allez France, this time in the Prix de Diane, proved to be just as futile. In a crowded field of twenty-five three-year-old fillies, the Hunt filly was nearly taken to her knees coming into the final turn but still finished well to be second.

Not to be denied a classic victory, Dahlia made

her first foray outside France. In the Emerald Isle she contested the Irish Oaks, where she easily trounced eleven other fillies. By the next weekend she had had her passport stamped in England, where she lined up against many of the best older males in the King George VI and Queen Elizabeth Stakes at Ascot. After being last of twelve with four furlongs remaining, she doled out a six-length whipping to a field that included French and English champion Rheingold.

Following a brief vacation, Dahlia resumed her winning ways over males in the Prix Niel. She suffered a deep gash in a hock when struck by another filly and came back lame in the Prix Vermeille. Probably not fully recovered from this injury and compromised by an outside post position in a huge field of twenty-seven, Dahlia turned in her most dismal performance ever, finishing sixteenth (to the previously vanquished Rheingold) in the Prix de l'Arc de Triomphe.

With group I races in three countries on her resume, Dahlia assailed her native shores, having been invited to participate in the Washington, D.C., International at Laurel. A hoped-for meeting with Secretariat failed to materialize when the Triple Crown hero departed the racetrack for the breeding shed at Claiborne Farm. In the International, Hunt's all-time favorite filly booked her return flight to France with a decisive win.

Dahlia lagged in returning to form at four. By the time racing moved to historic Saint-Cloud, she had come to hand while adding muscle to her light frame. A neck victory in the 1974 Grand Prix de Saint-Cloud sparked a summer of successes. From her home base in France, she returned to England and duplicated her victory in the King George VI and Queen Elizabeth Stakes, becoming the first and only filly to win back-to-back runnings. The Benson & Hedges Gold Cup at York enticed her across the channel yet again for her third straight group I victory. Her earnings in this race garnered her the honor of being the first female to earn more than a million dollars.

North America's lucrative fall turf stakes beck-

oned Dahlia to the United States. But this journey was not without its problems.

After a long transatlantic flight, Dahlia was vanned to the quarantine facilities at Clifton, New Jersey, to spend some time in accommodations that ill befitted a queen of the Turf. When she arrived at Belmont Park, her physical condition was not completely up to par. Dahlia, however, had always been a good traveler and she rebounded to win the Man o' War.

The Canadian International summoned next. If Dahlia won in Canada, she would have major races in five major racing ports, a singular accomplishment in the twentieth century. She would not be denied.

Dahlia winning the Benson & Hedges Gold Cup; Nelson Bunker Hunt leads in his champion after the Man o' War

Dahlia would go on to race for two more years. Although she failed to sustain the brilliance she showed at three and four, she won important races in Europe and the United States. Retired from racing with multiple championships, she proved to be as valuable as a broodmare, foaling six stakes winners, four of them grade I winners. *TH*

78 Exceller and Seattle Slew's Jockey Club Gold Cup

MUCH HAS BEEN MADE of the courage of Seattle Slew in losing the 1978 Jockey Club Gold Cup to Exceller by a nose. Yet Exceller's effort in making up twenty-two lengths to overtake and then hold off the champion was no less courageous.

Seattle Slew's finest hour might have come in defeat, as some racing pundits maintain, but Exceller's victory confirmed his quality as a runner of the highest order. Many consider the son of Vaguely Noble to be one of the best horses never to win a championship. Yet on that dank day in October, Exceller was a champion in the eyes of owner Nelson Bunker Hunt and trainer Charlie Whittingham.

If the 1978 Gold Cup might best be remembered for Seattle Slew's loss, it also contained numerous fascinating subplots, including the ill-timed slipping of a saddle. Affirmed, the charismatic 1978 Triple Crown winner, lost all chance when his tack started creeping up his neck. Before that unfortunate development, the race had tantalizing possibilities.

"The 60th running of the famous race which has had so many notable renewals was one of the most exciting of the series. It had everything, starting with three million-dollar winners, the best 3-year-old, the best 4-year-old, and the best 5-year-old in America, two of them Triple Crown winners," *The Blood-Horse* reported.

In the Gold Cup, Seattle Slew, the 1977 Triple Crown winner, and Affirmed would meet for the second time. In the earlier Marlboro Cup, the first meeting of Triple Crown winners, the older colt got the best of Affirmed by three lengths (See No. 72). Seattle Slew also had defeated the five-year-old Exceller by four lengths in the Woodward Stakes that September. Slew's dominance was all the more impressive in that he had suffered a life-threatening viral ailment early in his four-year-old season.

Seattle Slew, a $17,500 yearling purchase (See No. 69), had remained unbeaten through his Triple Crown campaign of 1977. His young owners, Karen and Mickey Taylor and Jim and Sally Hill, had proved as popular as their Cinderella horse until the colt lost and trainer and jockey shake-ups were played out publicly. No matter how the racing world felt about Seattle Slew's connections, it was disturbing that the Triple Crown winner was booed in the paddock before the Marlboro Cup.

As the great dramas of two successive Triple Crowns played out, the well-traveled Exceller was making his mark as a racehorse, though perhaps less turbulently.

Hunt, who had campaigned Vaguely Noble in partnership, purchased Exceller at the 1974 Keeneland yearling sale for $25,000 and sent the colt to trainer Maurice Zilber in France. Exceller won important races in France, England, and Canada, then went to California-based trainer Charlie Whittingham late in his four-year-old season. Exceller thrived under the care of his new conditioner, winning major races on the dirt and turf. Whittingham sent him east for the big fall races, and despite Exceller's loss to Seattle Slew in the Woodward, his trainer had all the confidence in the world.

"I'm gonna win it," Whittingham was quoted as saying. "Exceller's a lot better horse than people think, and he is real good right now."

The public made Seattle Slew the favorite, with Affirmed second choice, and Exceller third. Two rabbits were entered to test the front-running Slew, but a downpour that turned the muddy track into a sloppy one left only speedster Life's Hope to attempt that task. One Cut Above and Great Contractor rounded out the field.

Exceller, with Bill Shoemaker aboard (left), gives his all in defeating an equally tenacious Seattle Slew (opposite)

Under Angel Cordero Jr., Seattle Slew burst to the lead from the inside post, with Life's Hope and Affirmed right there with him. Steve Cauthen had been instructed to run with Slew from the outset, then take back and see what unfolded. Unfortunately, Cauthen could not follow those orders when his saddle started slipping and Affirmed proved uncharacteristically rank. The younger colt stayed with the favorite through "suicidal" fractions of :22 3/5, :45 1/5, and 1:09 2/5. On the far turn Cauthen took Affirmed out of the frenzy, practically easing him to finish fifth. Meanwhile, Bill Shoemaker and Exceller were twenty-two lengths behind the leaders after a half-mile. "We were so far back, I couldn't see them, didn't know who was up there," Shoemaker told The Blood-Horse.

Shoemaker asked Exceller for his move at the three-eighths pole and the horse responded gamely. Inside the quarter pole, Exceller caught Slew and began to inch by him, grinding out a half-length advantage. Then the stubborn Slew, unused to competition in deep stretch, began to fight back. He came within inches of his rival at the wire, then surged past him just after the finish.

"I cried and cried and cried," co-owner Karen Taylor said, "not because he lost, but because he tried so hard."

Even Hunt conceded surprise at Exceller's victory. "I really didn't think he would get there."

In the Gold Cup both the winner and the vanquished performed at their finest. Seattle Slew would race once more, winning the Stuyvesant Handicap and earning the older horse championship over Exceller before embarking on a celebrated stud career. Exceller would race one more season, at six, before retiring to a less distinguished stallion career and an ignominious end in a Swedish slaughterhouse (See No. 64). JD

LITTLE SEPARATED Jaipur and Ridan as they took to the track for the 1962 Travers with bragging rights at stake. As leaders among the three-year-old colts, each had a firm grasp on the year-end championship. At the end of the mile and a quarter duel, the "little" had shrunk to a scant nose, and the 26,183 racing fans that poured through the turnstiles that warm August afternoon had witnessed one heck of a horse race, a Wild West showdown between two young gunslingers determined to settle things the old-fashioned way, a one-on-one shootout from gate to wire.

Both colts descended from the same sire line: Jaipur, a son of the powerful Nasrullah; Ridan, a grandson. Both had inherited the Nasrullah propensity for speed. Ridan was taller (16.2 to Jaipur's 16 hands); Jaipur, the more compact. Both possessed the tremendously deep girths and powerful rear engines so characteristic of the Nasrullah line. While both had inherited some of the physical characteristics of the family, only one had inherited the family temperament. Jaipur, the more direct Nasrullah descendant, was as mercurial as he was strikingly handsome. One moment he could be brilliant; the next, common. Ridan was much more tractable and consistent.

Both had been stellar juveniles. Precocious enough to win his first start in February, Mrs. Moody Jolley's Ridan ran undefeated through the rest of the year, winning two important juvenile fixtures: the Arlington Futurity and the Washington Park Futurity. A splint sidelined him before he could venture beyond the Midwest to test his mettle over longer distances against the best colts in the East.

Those best colts included George D. Widener's Jaipur, who had been slower to develop. After an impressive win in his first start, the handsome colt added the Flash Stakes, the historic Hopeful by a gaudy six lengths, and the Cowdin as well as suffering heartbreakingly narrow losses in the Futurity (a neck) and Champagne (a head).

Although both had accounted themselves well, neither won the juvenile championship. Crimson Satan had come on late in the year, taking the rich Garden State Stakes and the Pimlico Futurity. At year's end he not only was named champion but also was assigned top weight (126) on the Experimental Free Handicap, one pound ahead of Ridan and two more than Jaipur.

As three-year-olds, both had performed valiantly in the spring classics. As the favorite, Ridan had

79

Jaipur and Ridan's Travers Stakes

finished third in the Kentucky Derby. And the rangy son of Nantallah was on the hard-luck end of a nose behind Greek Money in one dogfight battle of a Preakness finish. Jaipur, who hadn't been put in the hunt for the Derby, prepped for the Preakness with a win in the Withers but sulked his way around the Pimlico oval, before fading to tenth of eleven.

Jaipur, too, would be battle tested. In the Jersey Derby, he engaged Crimson Satan and Admiral's Voyage in a hotly contested stretch run. Only noses separated the first three finishers as Crimson Satan sneaked by Jaipur, who edged out Admiral's Voyage. However, the stewards found Crimson Satan guilty of interfering with Jaipur and disqualified him to second. Jaipur rebounded to defeat Admiral's Voyage in a similar skirmish in the Belmont Stakes.

In the interim the rugged Ridan had won the one-mile Arlington Classic. The mile and a quarter American Derby may have lain on the periphery of his ability as he pressed a brisk pace but finished second.

While Ridan was dutiful in the Midwest, Jaipur yielded to some genetic tug on his bipolar temperament and refused to work on the main Belmont track while preparing for the Leonard Richards Stakes. Perhaps thinking that a change of scenery would help his erratic star, trainer Bert Mulholland switched Jaipur to the training track. Evidently that scenery didn't appeal to the colt either as he promptly dumped his exercise rider, ran through a temporary rail, and headed back to the barn. While Jaipur's antics might not have endeared him to the stable staff, they did earn the colt an all-expense paid trip to Widener's Erdenheim Farm for rest and relaxation.

With a championship well within reach, Ridan's trainer LeRoy Jolley eyed another trip to the proving ground of the East: Saratoga and its Midsummer Derby — the Travers. Ridan's fellow contender for the crown, Jaipur, would be there too as he had returned from his mental-health holiday to win the Choice Stakes at Monmouth.

Seven names were dropped into the entry box for the ninety-third running of the Travers,

Jaipur (in blinkers) and Ridan match steps in an unforgettable Travers

including the champion filly Cicada. Yet only two mattered. Equally weighted at 126 pounds, Ridan and Jaipur were battling for more than the gold cup and the $53,722 winner's purse. Bragging rights and a possible championship dwarfed everything else. With typical machismo, no quarter would be asked; none, given.

Lined up next to one another, the two colts sprang alertly as the starting gates opened. Ridan under Manuel Ycaza fired the first shot, taking the lead into the first turn with Jaipur drafting menacingly a half-length behind. A moderate pace through the first half-mile allowed the speedy Ridan to maintain a lead, but Bill Shoemaker edged Jaipur closer and the fervid head-to-head battle had begun in earnest. Through the next eight furlongs neither foe relented. Tiring but unyielding, Ridan, on the inside, carried Jaipur wide in the final turn. Unfazed, Jaipur matched Ridan stride for stride through the stretch. Only a photo could separate them.

Such a brilliant battle deserves no loser, and there was none. But there was a second-place finisher. At the wire Ridan had been gathering for the next stride while Jaipur had reached that part of a horse's stride that lengthens the neck and foreleg. Jaipur won by a nose, breaking Man o' War's stakes record and equaling the track record. Jaipur would be named the champion three-year-old colt.

Neither horse would win another race that year, but for a little more than two minutes each combined speed and stamina to provide a thrilling spectacle at the Spa. *TH*

80

The Broadcast of Man o' War's Funeral

WHEN MAN O' WAR DIED at age thirty, the public still adored him as much as it had twenty-seven years earlier in the heyday of his legend-making career. His funeral attracted a crowd of about five hundred, and untold thousands heard the national radio broadcast.

Man o' War had commanded center stage at ceremonies before, such as the day heavyweight champion Jack Dempsey joined the thousands who turned out to see the horse at the Rose Tree Hunt Club in Media, Pennsylvania. Rose Tree was sacred ground to Man o' War's owner, Samuel Riddle, so he arranged to have the champion shown there during the horse's train trip from the races to retirement in Kentucky. A number of years later, the horse's twenty-first birthday party had been broadcast nationally, with noted sports announcer Clem McCarthy mastering the ceremonies.

There might have been sentimental leanings to keep the funeral more private, but in the case of Man o' War, it would have been somewhat hard-headed of Riddle and a slap in the face of those who regarded Man o' War as a part of their lives. Since his retirement from the racetrack in

1920, the horse beloved as Big Red had segued from sports and public figure into national icon. Legend merged with, and was supported by, the facts of his racing and breeding career. All the while, his physical bearing bespoke nobility. To anyone touched by such qualities, Man o' War was hard to resist.

Always willing to summarize the big stallion's accomplishments was his long-time groom, Will Harbut, and at telling a tale this distinguished gentleman was as much Southern preacher as he was historian.

Central to his sonorous spiel to the thousands who traveled to Faraway Farm outside Lexington to gaze upon Man o' War was the tale of the 1920 Dwyer Stakes. This event had gone down as the one in which Man o' War was most thoroughly tested in a truly run race. As Harbut recalled Man o' War's race with Harry Payne Whitney's John P. Grier: "... and he looked over to that Whitney hoss and he said, 'Now you come on, Grier, iffin you can.'"

There were other repeated and repeatable standards to the soliloquy, such as "and a man comes here and offers a million dollars for him and Mr.

Riddle says, 'No, lots of men might have a million dollars, but only one man can have Man o' War.' " This might be punctuated by a terse "stand still, Red," to suggest that man was still the master.

With thousands of visitors, there were inevitably some questions Harbut regarded as unworthy. These might draw a response such as "No, ma'am, he ain't no trotter," while if it were requested that the horse be roused in his stall, Harbut would be quick to say, "Ma'am, that's Manny Wah. When he wants to git up, he gits up; when he wants to lie down, he lies down."

Harbut's closing stanza was described by former editor of *The Blood-Horse* Joe Estes as "with a rare felicity, denied to deliberate phrasemakers, he made a fine phrase," to wit, "He wuz de most-ess hoss that ever wuz."

The statistics on Man o' War as a racehorse were twenty wins in twenty-one races and record earnings for his day, $249,465. For the most part he not only won, but also won with flash and awesome finality. Harbut reduced this adroitly to "he beat all the records and he beat all the horses and there wasn't nothin' left for him to do."

So, Man o' War had been retired to Faraway Farm, which was owned in part by Riddle, the wealthy sportsman who had purchased him for five thousand dollars at a Saratoga yearling sale in 1918 (*See No. 18*). The son of Fair Play had been foaled in Kentucky, too, having been bred by August Belmont II.

Man o' War's death came on November 1, 1947. He had been pensioned from stud duty since 1943, although still made available to the public until a few months before his passing. Dr. William McGee understood when the old warrior's time had come and euthanized him.

The reputation among the greatest of the heroes of what is sometimes called the Golden Age of Sports had been enhanced by his stud record. Just how much that had to do with his continuing hold on the general public is difficult to discern, but he had sired a series of thrilling runners in their own right. The best was the Triple Crown winner War Admiral, but there were also Crusader, American Flag, and Battleship — glamorous horses with glorious names.

Although there were logistical problems to such a plan, Man o' War was embalmed in his entirety and placed in a huge casket, which had been ordered some time in advance of what was recognized as the inevitable need. The box was lined with black and yellow cloth, the colors of Riddle's silks. The body barely fit. The casket and horse were buried in a small, shady area of Faraway, which Riddle had deeded to Fayette County.

Lexington radioman Ted Grizzard provided listeners details of the event. Speakers who took their turns in eulogies included distinguished breeder A.B. Hancock Jr., who noted that "the name Man o' War is a household word wherever the Thoroughbred is loved."

Seven years before, Riddle had commissioned the distinguished sculptor Herbert Haseltine to create a larger-than-life statue of Man o' War. Wartime restrictions on materials delayed com-

Man o' War's funeral attracted many notables (opposite); his statue presides today over the Kentucky Horse Park

pletion of the heroic statue (20 hands), so it was not there looming over its ward during the funeral. Not until the next year was the three-thousand-pound bronze placed on a granite base over the grave.

Nearly three decades later, in 1976, the grave and statue were moved to the Kentucky Horse Park. There, Man o' War, a beacon and a sentry, is apt to catch the eye of all visitors. Sculptor Haseltine had said of the living subject, "There was something that emanated from that noble animal that took my breath away."

When one gazes at the statue all these years later, it takes but little imagination to feel a similar flight of breath. *ELB*

81

The Zev–Papyrus Match Race

IN 1923 MOST MATCH RACES could claim no uniqueness. There was nothing new about them. Horse racing had been born from match races, pitting the confidence of one man in his horse against the surety of another man in his. Many a famous match race had occupied its niche in American racing history, from American Eclipse pitted against Sir Charles in 1822 to the 70,000 spectators who witnessed the 1842 heats between Fashion and Boston. But a match race between Derby winners from each side of the Atlantic was indeed a singular event.

The idea of pitting the best English three-year-old against his American counterpart was hatched at historic Saratoga Racecourse. Billed as the "world championship," the race would take place on October 20 over the mile and a half dirt oval of Belmont Park, for a purse of $100,000 ($20,000 of which would go to the loser).

Although Rancocas Stable's Zev was the erst-while leader of the three-year-olds off his Kentucky Derby and Belmont Stakes victories, the United States' representative would be select-ed by The Jockey Club from among horses run-

ning in the Lawrence Realization Stakes and in the National Trial Sweepstakes, held only a week later. Included among the other lead-ing sophomores was Admiral Cary T. Grayson's My Own, undefeated on the year including a vic-tory over older horses in the Saratoga Cup.

Benjamin Irish's Papyrus, winner of the 1923 English Derby, represented the Union Jack.

The pressures inherent in such a transatlantic race rested solely in the Papyrus camp. Basil Jarvis, the colt's trainer, had the paramount logistical prob-lem of keeping his charge fit and content during an arduous four-thousand-mile voyage in the hold of a ship. He planned meticulously, addressing every possible problem. Accommodations: Papyrus trav-eled in a stall arranged in a light and airy D-deck baggage compartment, where the pitch and roll of the ship were less likely to affect him. His groom could exercise him by walking him around the deck, which had been covered with cork for safety and comfort. Different food: August Belmont, chairman of The Jockey Club, gained permission from the U.S. Department of Agriculture for Jarvis to import enough English hay and oats for the stay. Different water: Five tanks of English water were packed aboard. Unfamiliar surroundings: Papyrus was accompanied by his stable companion Bargold

Papyrus, followed by Zev, is led onto the track for the match race (opposite); Zev charges home first in the 1923 Kentucky Derby

and by Tinker, the familiar black stable cat.

Time, however, did not favor Papyrus. On September 12 the colt finished a brave second in the St. Leger to the good filly Tranquil, despite his suffering cuts to both hind legs when crowded during the running. Although the interference might have cost the son of Tracery the win, the injuries did not necessitate a break in his training regimen.

Meanwhile, Zev had won the Lawrence Realization by more than two lengths over Greentree's champion three-year-old filly Untidy but not without injury. During the mile and five-eighths race, he lost the protective padding on the bottom of his right front hoof (the frog). Sam Hildreth, Zev's trainer, discounted the injury and indicated that the Kentucky-bred son of The Finn would be able to proceed toward the showdown if fitted with a special pad and plate. Although Hildreth displayed confidence in his colt's participation, Zev had not yet been selected to oppose Papyrus.

The very next weekend Grayson's My Own won the National Trial Sweepstakes (like Zev, beating Untidy by more than two lengths), and the controversy heated up. Many racing aficionados took up the cause of this star on the rise, as he had won all of his starts at Saratoga that summer.

On September 22, the *Aquitania* sailed from Southampton, England; Papyrus, safely tucked in for the voyage, promptly ate his meal and lay down to nap, a sign of his tractable nature. Six days later the ship landed in New York, and upon disembarking down a specially built and specially fitted (matted with enclosed sides) eighty-foot gangplank, Papyrus shipped to Belmont Park, a very tired horse but otherwise healthy and happy. Only three weeks remained for him to recover and prepare for his debut on American soil.

Zev continued to train even though The Jockey Club had not made its final decision. On the evening of October 5, official word came from the selection committee: Zev, first choice; My Own, second; Untidy, third.

However, the rumor mill spread that all was not well with Zev. His unimpressive morning performances and Papyrus' splendid showing in his final prep for the match race did little to quell the talk that perhaps Zev was sub par. Fueled by the desire to pit the best against the English invader, The Jockey Club fitted a special rail car to rush My Own to Belmont the day before the race, just in case. But Hildreth was sanguine as he showed a healthy Zev to the committee, and Earl Sande, Zev's jockey, was confident that the colt had been performing only what was asked of him. Persuaded by the evidence, the committee allowed Zev the honor.

On the morning of the race, rain tattooed the stable roofs and pelted the grounds, turning dirt into goop. An undeterred crowd filled the grandstand and spilled over onto the infield. By race time sunshine had replaced the clouds but had done little to dry out the track. It was especially wet in the stretch, which untouched by the low late-autumn sun, lay in the shadow of the grandstand.

Jarvis, who had been so careful in foreseeing and allaying the problems of travel, was a bit less circumspect at the moment of truth. A.J. Joyner, who had trained H.P. Whitney's European horses, advised Jarvis to reshoe Papyrus with special plates designed for more traction in mud. Jarvis refused, citing the colt's unfamiliarity with such racing plates. Hildreth, on the other hand, had Zev reshod with shoes suited for a sloppy surface.

Under regular rider Steve Donoghue, Papyrus was first away and gained an easy lead, but Sande and Zev soon overcame the advantage and forged ahead. Down the backstretch the American pair was several lengths in front. When Donoghue asked for more run, all Papyrus could do was slip and slide on the slick surface. At the wire Zev was five lengths ahead and never really asked for run.

Although not the race that fans on either continent had hoped for, the event marked the first time that Derby winners from separate continents had met, and in some part, the race laid the foundation for future international races such as the Washington, D.C., International (*See No. 17*). *TH*

211

82 Dale Baird Trains 9,000 Winners

HIS CAREER DIDN'T START with a bang. In fact, winning wasn't that easy at first, nor was finding stalls for his small stable of horses.

On August 12, 1961, trainer Dale Baird won the first race of his career at Ellis Park in western Kentucky. Well, not quite. His horse, New York, was disqualified in the $1,250 claiming race.

Six days later the ten-year-old mare crossed the wire first, and this time it was official. Baird had won not only his first race, but the first of a mind-boggling number of wins that have made him the all-time leading trainer in Thoroughbred racing.

Forty-three years after that first victory, Baird on November 5, 2004, won his nine thousandth race, becoming the first trainer to crack that number. (At the time, his nearest competitor, Jack Van Berg, had 6,334 wins.) Appropriately, the milestone victory came at Mountaineer Race Track & Gaming Resort, the West Virginia track at which Baird has been based since the late 1960s.

Baird, born in Martinsville, Illinois, ended up in West Virginia by necessity. When he started his career in the Midwest, he was just another trainer looking for stalls — and they were hard to come by. There was no room for him at Fairmount Park in southern Illinois, so he traveled to West Virginia's northern panhandle, where Wheeling Downs is located. But he couldn't get stalls there, either, so he ended up at a training center in nearby Moundsville.

Once established, Baird found his key to success. He specialized in the bottom-level horses that filled the programs at Wheeling and at Waterford Park, which later became Mountaineer. With a year-round racing circuit, the wins piled up for Baird.

"Back then, I just kept reinvesting in the business," Baird told *The Blood-Horse*. "I drove an old truck or car, and lived as cheaply as I could. Whenever I made a little money, I used it to buy another horse. Once you get established, everybody's out to sell you a cheap horse."

At Wheeling and Waterford, thousand dollar purses were the norm in the late 1960s. So Baird needed to win a lot of races to make those six hundred dollar first-place purse checks worthwhile. That he did, and he owned most of the horses himself. In his busiest years, Baird would purchase about 250 horses privately and sell the same number. The idea was to maintain fresh horses that usually held a class edge when they shipped to West Virginia.

By the early 1990s, Baird had become a local legend. Legislation that authorized video gaming at West Virginia tracks greatly increased purses. Baird capitalized on the newfound revenue by upgrading his stock, either privately or at auctions, and continued to lead the standings at Mountaineer.

Baird won twenty straight leading trainer titles at Mountaineer through 2000. He won fifteen national leading trainer titles by wins, seventeen national owner titles by wins, and had eight years in which he won more than three hundred races.

In 2004, at the age of sixty-nine, Baird was honored with a Special Eclipse Award for "outstanding individual achievements in or contributions to the sport of Thoroughbred racing." He also remains a candidate for the Hall of Fame.

In 2005, as the year came to a close, Baird was back on top at Mountaineer. It looked like the old

Dale Baird is the first trainer to record 9,000 victories

days — more than three times as many victories as his nearest rival and more than three times the number of starters than any other trainer. His horses earned more than $2 million in 2005.

On a national scale, other trainers who have hundreds of horses in multiple strings around the country have taken over the top spots by number of annual victories. But Baird's accomplishments still speak for themselves.

Baird, whose father, John "J.I." Baird, was a horse trainer, has had some company at Mountaineer. His son, Bart, has trained there, as has his brother, John, and John Baird's son, J.M. Dale Baird said everything he does revolves around his racehorses, and that Mountaineer would be his home as long as it continues to offer year-round racing. *TL*

83 Bold Ruler and Round Table Born the Same Day

DURING CLAIBORNE FARM's heyday in the 1950s and '60s, every foal born at the Hancock family's famed nursery near Paris, Kentucky, was a potential champion. After all, Claiborne's philosophy of breeding the best mares to the world's leading sires was a formula that worked, and there was every reason to believe that the two foals born on April 6, 1954, could each blossom into something special.

But no one could have predicted how special both would become.

At 1:15 that morning, a son of Nasrullah was produced from the Discovery mare Miss Disco. Bred by Mrs. Henry Carnegie Phipps' Wheatley Stable, the colt would be named Bold Ruler.

Later that morning, at 8:15, a son of Princequillo was foaled from the mare Knight's Daughter. Bred by Claiborne, the colt would be named Round Table. Both would go on to live up to their potential, on the racetrack and in the breeding shed.

Arthur B. "Bull" Hancock Jr., who ran Claiborne on behalf of his ailing father, managed both

Princequillo and Nasrullah. He owned Knight's Daughter, having bought her at the Newmarket sale in England. Hancock also had owned Miss Disco, purchasing her for $27,500, then reselling her to Mrs. Phipps when the acquisition of another mare fell through.

"So Mrs. Phipps got Bold Ruler, and I didn't," Hancock succinctly described the turn of events.

Round Table began his career racing for Claiborne, but Hancock sold the colt in February of his three-year-old season to Oklahoman Travis Kerr for a figure reported to be near $145,000. Hancock retained 20 percent interest in Round Table for breeding purposes and used the proceeds to help pay estate taxes following the death of his father, Arthur B. Hancock Sr., in April of that year. The sale of Round Table "more or less held the farm together, paid the estate taxes, and so on," the younger Hancock said of the deal.

Meanwhile, Bold Ruler, who was trained by Sunny Jim Fitzsimmons, had raced primarily in New York at two, going with the Phipps stable to

214

Florida in the winter of 1956–57. Round Table, who was trained by William Molter following his purchase by Kerr, was campaigned mainly in the Midwest and California in the spring of his three-year-old year.

Both ran in the 1957 Kentucky Derby, with Round Table finishing third behind winner Iron Liege and runner-up Gallant Man, and Bold Ruler fourth. That year's Derby was memorable not only because of the rich supply of talented horses but also because the great Bill Shoemaker misjudged the finish line, arguably costing Gallant Man the victory.

Competing during a period when horses were burdened with large weight assignments, Bold Ruler and Round Table evolved into two of the best handicap runners of their generation.

Bold Ruler, whose career was plagued by chronic rheumatic conditions and a tender tongue that made it hard to rate him during a race, never carried less than 133 pounds during his four-year-old campaign, in which he won five of seven starts. At ages four and five, Round Table carried 130 pounds or more in twenty-three races.

Bold Ruler retired with twenty-three wins in thirty-three starts, including seventeen stakes victories, and earnings of $764,204. He was Horse of the Year and champion three-year-old male of 1957 and champion sprinter of 1958, primarily on the basis of a win in the seven-furlong Carter Handicap while carrying 135 pounds. He ranked nineteenth on *The Blood-Horse*'s list of the top one hundred racehorses of the twentieth century.

Round Table was retired in 1959 as the then all-time leading money earner with $1,749,869. He won forty-three of sixty-six starts, with thirteen additional second- or third-place finishes. His honors included Horse of the Year in 1958, three-time champion grass horse from 1957 to 1959, and two-time champion handicap horse in 1958–59. He ranked seventeenth on *The Blood-Horse*'s top one hundred list.

Both horses went on to illustrious stud careers while standing at Claiborne, with Bold Ruler the better at siring top progeny. Both belonged to an elite club of siring 20 percent stakes winners or more from total foals, with Bold Ruler having a 23 percent rate in that category and Round Table coming in with 21 percent.

Bold Ruler led the American general sire list for eight years (seven consecutively), with his eighty-two stakes winners including the great Secretariat (*See No. 41*). The broodmare sire of seven champions and 119 stakes winners, Bold Ruler has had a lasting impact on the breed, through the sire success of his great-great-grandson A.P. Indy. Bold Ruler died in 1971 at age seventeen after a battle with cancer and was buried at Claiborne.

Round Table was leading sire in 1972 and his eighty-three stakes winners included champion Apalachee and millionaire Royal Glint. He, too, continues to have an influence on the breed

Round Table (top) and Bold Ruler finish third and fourth in the 1957 Kentucky Derby (opposite)

through the successes of his daughters. Round Table lived to the ripe old age of thirty-three and he also was buried at Claiborne following his death in 1987.

In attempting to put April 6, 1954, into perspective, Turf writer Pete Axthelm wrote: "The coincidence of the birthdate is mind-boggling. The odds against two horses of such stature being born in the same year are considerable; the chances of their arriving on the same farm on the very same night infinitesimal." *RM*

84 The Miracle Million at Arlington Park

AS A SUCCESSFUL BUSINESSMAN who used part of his vast fortune to purchase Chicago's Arlington Park racetrack, Richard Duchossois gained a reputation as a risk taker. Not only did he take risks, but more often than not Duchossois' gambles succeeded against seemingly insurmountable odds.

Duchossois succeeded in perhaps his greatest gamble when he staged the 1985 Arlington Million less than a month after fire had destroyed the grandstand and clubhouse.

The horse-owning Duchossois had purchased 60 percent of Arlington Park in 1983. In the summer of 1985, he retired from his billion-dollar conglomerate, Duchossois Industries, to focus on his racetrack operation. With the blaze that consumed much of the track's front side on July 31, Duchossois and partners Joe Joyce, Ralph Ross, and Sheldon N. Robbins got more than they bargained for as racing was brought to an abrupt halt.

While the fire was a devastating blow to the Illinois racing community, the timing of the inferno could not have been worse: The track's premier event, the Arlington Million, was scheduled to be run on August 25, a mere twenty-five days after the fire.

With its main facility nothing but burned-out rubble (the barns were not damaged and the racetrack surface was unaffected by the fire), Arlington officials immediately transferred all live racing to nearby Hawthorne Racecourse.

But questions remained about the status of the Million, which was being renewed for the fifth year in 1985. Inaugurated in 1981, the Million was the first race in the world to offer a guaran-

teed purse of $1 million. The race was run on grass rather than the main dirt track to attract the world's best horses. In a short period, the Million had become a prestigious fixture on the international racing calendar and succeeded in luring the best grass horses from around the world.

Duchossois, known to his employees as "Mister D," and the Arlington management team were faced with the possibility that canceling the Million would interrupt the continuity of a race that had already cemented its place in racing history. On the other hand, readying the track for the race and the large number of international horses, fans, and horsemen it attracted would prove a daunting task.

Ever the risk-taker, Duchossois wanted to race. As did Joyce.

But some of the other partners were not as optimistic about the feasibility of having the debris removed and the temporary facilities in place in such a short period of time. They also were considering offers from five other racetracks interested in hosting the Million.

"When Joe (Joyce) recommended we run it at Arlington, for a minute or two I thought the fire had warped his mind," Ralph Ross said in an August 31, 1985, article in *The Blood-Horse*.

The other partners came around, and three days after the fire Arlington announced that the 1985 Million would be run at the burned-out track in a festival-type atmosphere with temporary bleachers for the fans and tents for other essential operations such as concessions, betting areas, and restrooms.

Demolition of the grandstand and clubhouse began immediately, with crews from Cleveland Wrecking Company working two ten-hour shifts a day and the other four hours used for maintenance and repair work. Using sixty-five pieces of heavy equipment, the wrecking crew hauled away the estimated seven thousand tons of steel and fourteen tons of debris in twelve days.

Meanwhile, the North American Construction Company began moving in to lay blacktop and erect tents on the cleared areas.

Thanks to the efforts of an estimated one thousand workers, Arlington Park was declared ready for the Million four days before the event.

The track was resplendent with blooming flowers and healthy shrubs in the infield and paddock (the plants had been tended to non-stop since the fire). A crowd of 35,651 was on hand to witness what was dubbed "The Miracle Million." The only remnant from the previous building was a large concrete slab behind the temporary stands upon which the old clubhouse and grandstand had stood a month earlier.

Reflecting its international appeal, the 1985 Million was won by British import Teleprompter, the first horse ever to race in the United States for Lord Derby.

The massive effort to stage the Million earned the track a Special Eclipse Award, racing's highest honor. It was the first track so awarded.

Having been run in 1988 at Woodbine Racecourse in Canada while Arlington was being rebuilt, the Million returned to its home in 1989 and continued to be a fixture on the international racing calendar. The scheduling of other top graded races on Million Day and the day preceding it has broadened its appeal.

But were it not for the willingness of the owners and management to make sure the "Miracle Million" was run, it could have been lost forever. *RM*

Fire engulfs Arlington Park, leading to construction of a new facility (opposite); temporary stands were in place for the 1985 Million, won by Teleprompter

85 Launch of Claiborne Farm

MANY IMPORTANT "MOMENTS," be they benign or bellicose, are not recognized as such at the precise time of occurrence. A singular incident may be looked upon in retrospect as having started, say, a world war or a flowering romance, but such judgment often requires perspective from after the fact.

The creation of Claiborne Farm as a Thoroughbred enterprise — arguably the most important in this country in the twentieth century — was a tentative activity, envisioned as a sideline, if that, by its very creator! Claiborne's powerful arsenal of stallions provided the leading sire in North America on twenty-eight occasions, including one run of fifteen years in succession (1955–69). Meanwhile, three generations of Claiborne's Hancock family led the breeders' list ten times, and seventeen Horsed of the Year were foaled at the Kentucky farm.

The tale begins in Virginia. Captain Richard Hancock of the Confederate Army suffered the third of his three Civil War wounds in a skirmish near Charlottesville and was taken in by the Harris family. In due course he not only recovered but took as his bride a daughter of the welcoming

rescuers. The estate, named Ellerslie, became the seat of the Hancock family's first Thoroughbred breeding, racing, and selling enterprise, and one of Hancock's sons, Arthur Boyd Hancock Sr., was so smitten by the activity that he determined to make it his career.

By early in the twentieth century, A.B. Hancock had taken over much of the responsibility of Ellerslie and developed an admirable reputation in the Thoroughbred world. This status led to his being invited by a distinguished horseman, U.S. Senator Johnson Camden, to travel to Kentucky to judge horse classes at the Bluegrass Fair in Lexington. While on that enjoyable mission, he was introduced to Nancy Clay, whose family had migrated from England to Virginia and thence to establish large land holdings in the western sections of that colony. When statehood was granted to that western part of Virginia, the Clays found themselves Kentuckians. Hancock and Miss Clay were married the following year, and they set up their household on one of the old houses back at Ellerslie.

In 1910 both of Nancy Clay Hancock's parents died within four days of each other, and Mrs. Hancock soon was designated as heiress of a sub-

chased the talented two-year-old Spendthrift, who would race with distinction for his new owner and then leave his mark at stud. Spendthrift sired Hastings, the sire of Fair Play, Colin's contemporary. Fair Play, in turn, would sire Man o' War.

Keene also raced the great Domino, who sired Colin's sire, Commando. Keene disliked the coarse, big-boned Commando but came around when the horse won the Belmont Stakes and other important races. Keene also initially disliked Colin, fearing a curb on the colt's hock would compromise Colin's racing chances.

Colin never knew he had a blemish, for in 1907 he fashioned perhaps the greatest juvenile season in American racing, winning all twelve of his starts and setting or equaling three track records.

"I fancy that Colin is the best I ever had in the stable," said Keene, who also had raced the once-defeated Sysonby among the 113 stakes winners he bred.

Fair Play had chased Colin in vain during their two-year-old season then lost to him again in the Withers Stakes, Colin's first race back as a three-year-old.

Bred by August Belmont II, Fair Play was a magnificent chestnut with the fiery temperament of Hastings. He won three times from ten starts at two but would not truly shine until Colin and then stablemate Celt left the picture. "Fair Play was a high-class racehorse, regarded by some racing men as the best colt to carry the scarlet and maroon Belmont silks," Edward L. Bowen writes in *Legacies of the Turf*.

The forty-second running of the Belmont unfolded during a deluge that made the track deep and tiring. In addition to Colin and Fair Play the field consisted of King James and Robert Cooper.

"The race was run in a driving rainstorm and the horses could not be distinguished until the stretch was reached," according to trip notes.

Colin had a five-length advantage, but Fair Play cut into his margin with every stride. The trip notes suggest that Colin's jockey, Joe Notter, began easing up at the wrong marker, misjudging the finish line for the mile and three-eighths race. But Notter would argue otherwise. It was all he could do, he would say, to hold off Fair Play with a horse tiring under the impost and terrible conditions.

Colin (left and opposite) faced his sternest test from Fair Play (below) in the 1908 Belmont

Colin held on for a head victory. "Fair Play ran a wonderfully game race and stood a long stretch drive in the most resolute fashion imaginable," the trip notes said.

The lack of visibility precluded timing the race.

With a ban on gambling in New York imminent, Colin raced just twice more in America, once in a betless competition his arrogant owner thought would matter not to devoted racegoers. It did, with less than a capacity crowd on hand at Sheepshead Bay.

Colin went to England to continue racing but fell lame after winning a trial and was retired. In all he won fifteen of fifteen races and $178,110 to become the only major racehorse to retire undefeated until Personal Ensign replicated the feat in 1988 after a perfect thirteen-for-thirteen career.

Colin had limited fertility and did not achieve the same success at stud as his rival Fair Play, but he nevertheless perpetuated the important Domino line. *JD*

88 Swaps' Record-Breaking Season

JUST BEFORE HE GAVE JOCKEY Willie Shoemaker a leg up for the 1956 Hollywood Gold Cup, trainer Meshach "Mesh" Tenney had these instructions: "Well, Bill, it's the same old thing. The slower you take it the first part of the race, the better I'll like it."

Those were easy words to understand but hard words to obey, for Swaps wanted to do nothing but run. And in that race and his others in the spring and summer of that year, Swaps was perhaps the greatest racehorse ever seen in California.

Brilliance in the racehorse has taken many forms in California, embodied in the likes of Seabiscuit, Citation, Native Diver, and Affirmed. But in Swaps, brilliance burned at a higher sheen during those glorious months of 1956.

Not only did his wins come at California tracks, but the son of Khaled was bred, owned, trained, and ridden by top California-based horsemen. For California racing fans during that era, Swaps belonged to them. The East could have its Nashua.

Swaps had beaten Nashua in the previous year's Kentucky Derby, then lost to his rival in a match race at Washington Park that summer. But his defeat was all but forgotten when Swaps embarked on the 1956 racing season with a vengeance, leaving track and world records, and the previous year's memories, in his wake.

Swaps, bred and owned by Rex Ellsworth, made ten starts in 1956 from February 17 to September 3 and won eight, despite a chronic foot problem that eventually ended his career. Of those eight victories, four were in world-record time, another equaled a world record, and two were in track-record time. In Swaps' two defeats at four, one came in his only start of the year on turf, while in the other the chart caller noted he was "eased by mistake." In all ten races Swaps started as the odds-on favorite.

Swaps winning the Hollywood Gold Cup during his sensational 1956 season

After his match race with Nashua the last day of August 1955, Swaps, reportedly unsound for the running, received a much-needed break. Six months later he made his first start of 1956 in an overnight handicap at Santa Anita. Swaps won easily under Bill Shoemaker, who would be aboard each time the chestnut colt went to the post that year.

Shipped to Gulfstream Park for what would be the only start of his twenty-five-race career in Florida, he carried 130 pounds in the Broward Handicap and set a world record of 1:39 3/5 for the mile and seventy yards.

Returned to California, Swaps made his next six starts at Hollywood Park and set or equaled a record in five of them:

• He set a world record in the Argonaut Handicap, going a mile under 128 pounds in 1:33 1/5. Swaps was "in hand" at the finish.

• In the Inglewood Handicap two weeks later, he was "eased in the final sixteenth" while setting a world record of 1:39 for a mile and one-sixteenth while again carrying 130 pounds.

• Less than two weeks later, to help celebrate the Fourth of July, he equaled the world record for a mile and one-eighth in the American Handicap. Carrying 130, he could have broken the record, but he was "eased in the final stages" while crossing the teletimer in 1:46 4/5.

• Ten days later, in the mile and a quarter Hollywood Gold Cup, he opened up a four-length lead, was "eased at the finish" to win by two, carrying 130 pounds to a track record of 1:58 3/5.

(Years later fans would lament how Alydar would have been a Triple Crown winner had Affirmed not been in his crop. It should be noted that in the Inglewood, American, and Hollywood Gold Cup handicaps, Mister Gus ran second in all three races to Swaps.)

• Eleven days hence, again under 130 pounds, Swaps set a world record of 2:38 1/5 in the mile and five-eighths Sunset Handicap.

Swaps would make two more starts, both at Washington Park in Chicago, where he had lost that celebrated match race with Nashua. He ran seventh in the Arch Ward Memorial Handicap on grass, and then just for good measure in the final race of his career, he carried 130 pounds to set a track record for a mile of 1:33 2/5 in the Washington Park Handicap.

A foot problem kept Swaps from an intended start in the United Nations Handicap. He was to meet Nashua again in the Jockey Club Gold Cup, but he fractured a bone in his left hind leg while galloping one morning and luckily was saved for stud duty.

Swaps retired with nineteen wins in twenty-five starts, was named 1956 Horse of the Year, and lives on in the memory of racing fans, in particular Californians, to this day. *DL*

WHEN SIR IVOR UNLEASHED his electrifying run to win the 1968 Epsom Derby, not only did he validate the quality of American horses, he helped internationalize Thoroughbred racing. His emphatic victory in England's venerated classic beckoned European sportsmen and, later, Arab sheikhs to Kentucky yearling sales and breeding farms. Soon, the Bluegrass would become the heart of a global industry.

Kentuckian Alice Headley Chandler bred Sir Ivor, a son of Sir Gaylord and the stakes-placed mare Attica, a descendant of the Headley family's foundation mare, Alcibiades. Chandler was a daughter of legendary horseman Hal Price Headley, master of Beaumont Farm and a founder of the Keeneland Association. Headley died in 1962, leaving his daughter a portion of Beaumont she would develop into her own Mill Ridge Farm. Chandler was taking her first solo steps as a breeder when Attica foaled the dark bay colt in 1965.

Chandler wanted to keep the sturdy youngster, but circumstances prevented it. "I had to sell Sir Ivor, because when Daddy died, there wasn't any

89 Sir Ivor Wins the Epsom Derby

money," Chandler recalled in the book *Women in Racing: In Their Own Words*.

The colt was consigned to the 1966 Keeneland summer sale, where Claiborne Farm owner A.B. "Bull" Hancock paid $42,000 for him on behalf of Raymond Guest, a former U.S. ambassador to Ireland. Guest maintained a stud and a racing stable in Ireland and sent Sir Ivor to champion trainer Vincent O'Brien, known as the Wizard of Tipperary.

Sir Ivor made a forgettable first start as a two-year-old at The Curragh, then won Ireland's National Stakes and France's Grand Criterium and was champion two-year-old in Ireland. Bookmakers installed Sir Ivor the early favorite for the Derby, and the colt confirmed his high regard by winning the Two Thousand Guineas Trial Stakes and the Guineas itself.

Sir Ivor appeared hopelessly beaten in the Derby but managed to break free of a bottleneck and storm into the clear in the final furlongs. Under Lester Piggott's masterful handling, the Kentucky colt ran down Connaught to win by a length and a half to become Guest's second Epsom Derby winner after Larkspur in 1962.

The brilliant, nerveless Piggott was winning his fourth Derby in 1968 and had many more classic victories to come, including his run aboard the 1970 English Triple Crown winner Nijinsky II. But he would insist over the years that Sir Ivor, with the colt's tenaciousness and turn of foot, was the best horse he had ridden. "He was the complete professional," Piggott said in his autobiography.

Sir Ivor went winless his next four starts, including a second-place finish to the classy Vaguely Noble in the Prix de l'Arc de Triomphe, then rebounded in the Champion Stakes at Newmarket. Owner Guest wanted to give his star a swan song on native soil and gamely sent him to contest the Washington, D.C., International at

Mrs. Raymond Guest leads in Sir Ivor after the Epsom Derby (opposite); Alice Chandler (left, with father Hal Price Headley) bred the champion

Laurel in November 1968. In its sixteen-year existence, the International had become an important turf fixture, attracting the best runners from around the world.

Sir Ivor vindicated his favoritism with a dazzling finishing punch, besting a field that included Paul Mellon's turf star Fort Marcy. Deep going kept his margin of victory to three-quarters of a length; otherwise, he would have won by ten, according to Piggott.

The transcontinental traveler retired to Claiborne Farm, where he enjoyed a distinguished stallion career. But his influence went far beyond the breeding shed. Buyers beat a path to the Keeneland sales pavilion, O'Brien among them, and they plucked such dazzling stars as The Minstrel, Nureyev, Storm Bird, and Alleged to dominate the once-sacrosanct racecourses of Europe.

"The biggest difference Sir Ivor made was in the Keeneland sales, because he was the first really good horse that had ever been bought there and gone across the ocean and succeeded," Chandler said. "That's what brought the people — the Europeans, later the Arabs, the Japanese, many other people — to the Keeneland sales. That's what really happened." *JD*

IN 1913 HORSE RACING IN NEW YORK re-emerged from a three-year darkness imposed by anti-gambling legislation. In those early moments of rejuvenated racing, a repatriated, seasoned veteran, H.P. Whitney's Whisk Broom II, illuminated the handicap ranks with impressive victories in the Metropolitan, Brooklyn, and Suburban handicaps, three races that would later be inextricably linked as the handicap triple crown and prove far more elusive than the Triple Crown for three-year-olds.

Passage of the 1908 Hart-Agnew Act outlawed professional bookmaking that used written bets. A few tracks managed to stay open for "sporting" purposes, but by 1910 the act had been extended to cover oral bets, effectively shutting down racing in New York — as well as in several other states. The East's venerated tracks extinguished their lights, locked their gates, and abandoned their facilities to dust and cobwebs. Forsaken, the patriarchs of racing removed their stables, either to the

90

Whisk Broom II Sweeps Handicap Triple Crown

hinterlands or, for those rich enough, to Europe.

Harry Payne Whitney embodied those able to take refuge in the cradle of racing tradition, England. Having sensed the coming change, he had already shipped a string of horses abroad. One of Whitney's favorites among that contingent was Whisk Broom II, a chestnut son of Broomstick—Audience, by Sir Dixon, whom the wealthy sportsman had bought from his trainer Andrew Jackson Joyner.

Joyner had been impressed with the colt when he saw him among the yearlings being offered for sale as part of the estate dispersal of Captain Sam S. Brown's Senorita Stud, held at the Sheepshead Bay paddocks. His primary concern was the colt's knees, which were scuffed and worn. Having been assured they resulted from spirited horseplay (kneeling to get at a fellow yearling in an adjoining paddock) and had been treated with tar, Joyner purchased him for a bargain price.

But the experienced horseman made a mistake in showing Whitney the Broomstick yearling. Whitney had already bought the colt's sire from the

Brown estate (a fortuitous purchase as Broomstick would sire Regret, Whitney's first Kentucky Derby winner). From the moment Whitney first laid eyes on the colt, he had liked him; but when the colt worked a quarter-mile in twenty-four seconds flat, he loved him and immediately accepted Joyner's ill-timed offer to buy the colt for the same $2,500 the trainer had paid for him. (Joyner, perhaps intending to keep the colt for himself, had instructed the rider to work the colt in twenty-five seconds, but the jockey was unable to restrain the exuberant youth.) And, thus, Whisk Broom II was destined to sport the Eton blue and chocolate silks of the Whitney stable.

Whisk Broom II performed ably enough on England's undulating grass courses. He broke his maiden in his second start at two and at three earned classic black type by finishing third in the Two Thousand Guineas over Newmarket's Rowley Mile. At four and five he bore the burden of more and more weight (up to 138 pounds), and by the end of his English sojourn, he had earned the reputation as one of the fastest horses in England at distances up to a mile.

However, a combination of events on separate sides of the Atlantic foreshadowed the repatriation of Whisk Broom II. In England the handicappers assigned him more and more weight (145 pounds for one start), and Whitney bristled at such imposts. In America, attitudes were changing.

The moral pendulum that had pushed horse racing into those dark years entered its backward arc, and racing resumed. On opening day at Belmont Park on May 30, 1913, 30,000 race-starved fans roared their approval as the staccato strains of the bugle welcomed the runners to the post. Westchester Racing Association had carded the Metropolitan Handicap as the day's centerpiece. Having disembarked a mere five weeks earlier (to the barn of Whitney's trainer James Rowe Sr.), Whisk Broom II relished his new surroundings and easily won the mile event under jockey Joe Notter.

Removed from England's turf, Whisk Broom II evidently thrived on New York's dirt ovals. Less than a month later he and Notter successfully negotiated the mile and a quarter of the Brooklyn Handicap (his first success at a distance more

Whisk Broom II leads the field in the 1913 Metropolitan Handicap

than a mile), carrying 130 pounds and besting the old track record by nearly a second.

Perhaps the transition to dirt allowed him to carry his speed farther than ever before; seven days after the Brooklyn, the Whitney colt carried a staggering 139 pounds over the ten furlongs of the Suburban Handicap in the official (although highly disputed) time of 2:00, setting a world record. (The record would last until 1939 when St. Andrews II, carrying 133 pounds, ran the distance in 1:59 4/5 in Brighton, England.)

While preparing for the Saratoga Handicap, Whisk Broom II injured himself and was retired to stud. What his future accomplishments might have been can only be surmised, but winning the handicap triple crown — the Metropolitan, Brooklyn, and Suburban — in the same year has proved an elusive accomplishment for other horses. (A 1932 reference in the *New York Times* refers to these three handicap races as "the triple crown": "Once, years ago, the important triple on the Eastern turf included the Metropolitan, Suburban and Brooklyn, all handicaps, and future books were made on each. Now the 'triple crown' is the Kentucky Derby, Preakness and Belmont, all three-year-old specials.")

While eleven horses have claimed the Triple Crown for three-year-olds, only three have managed to duplicate Whisk Broom II's feat: Tom Fool (1953), Kelso (1961), and Fit to Fight (1984). *TH*

Smarty Jones: the People's Horse

JAY LENO INVITED HIM to appear on his show. President Bush gave him an open invitation to the Rose Garden at the White House. Two jockeys wrote a song in his honor.

But not even his celebrity status and the record crowd of 120,139 that turned out at the 2004 Belmont Stakes to support Smarty Jones' bid for the Triple Crown — the largest crowd ever to see a sporting event in New York — could lend the beloved Thoroughbred what he needed to cross the finish line first. Deep in the stretch Smarty had nothing left to give as Birdstone ate away at his lead, overtaking the 3-10 favorite to win by a length and crushing the nation's hope for another Secretariat.

Everyone had had such good feelings about this colt. They knew his story, admired his chutzpah, and saw the opportunity for something wonderful to happen.

Smarty Jones was bred at Someday Farm near Philadelphia by his owners, Roy and Patricia

Chapman, and was foaled February 28, 2001. The Chapmans' veteran trainer, Bob Camac, had planned the mating, combining the talents of the stallion Elusive Quality, who performed best at distances up to a mile, with the sprinting ability of I'll Get Along. The rambunctious result was named after Patricia Chapman's late mother, Mildred, who shared a birthday with the colt and whose nickname as a child had been Smarty Jones.

Several months after Smarty was foaled, Camac and his wife, Maryann, were shot to death at their New Jersey farm by her son from a previous marriage. After the murders Roy Chapman, a retired auto dealer in his mid-seventies who was battling emphysema, considered getting out of the horse business. He sold all of his horses except for two, one of which was Smarty Jones. The horse had a look in his eye that Chapman and his farm manager liked. Chapman sent the colt to Florida to be broken for racing and then returned him to Philadelphia, to the barn of trainer John Servis.

we have a winter home, they talk about the obeah man, and the obeah woman," she said in the interview. "If the obeah is around, you go for a wand to protect yourself."

The filly was trained by Bill Badgett Jr. and ran to her pedigree from the start. She won three of her four races as a two-year-old, including the Breeders' Cup Juvenile Fillies to clinch her division championship. She didn't debut as a three-year-old until April, but when she did, she picked up where she had left off. She won her next two races, under Randy Romero, the only jockey she would ever know, in large fashion, taking the Beaumont at Keeneland by eight lengths and the Ashland Stakes by five lengths in a wire-to-wire victory.

In her next start, the Kentucky Oaks, she struggled in the mud at Churchill Downs and finished second to Seaside Attraction. Back at home at Belmont Park she won the Mother Goose, the first of five consecutive grade I wins. Not regarded as a sprinter, she showed a new dimension in the seven-furlong Test at Saratoga, winning by two lengths in 1:21 and equaling the stakes record. Nine days later she won the mile and a quarter Alabama, leading all the way to score by seven lengths, setting a stakes record of 2:00 4/5 for the distance, and clinching her division. She followed the Alabama with two stunning victories over older fillies and mares at Belmont. She won the Maskette by two and a half lengths and the Beldame by nearly five lengths at 1-10 odds. In the latter, she came within two clicks of Secretariat's track record with a time of 1:45 4/5 and set a filly record for nine furlongs.

As the 1990 Breeders' Cup approached, many wondered whether Badgett would run Go for Wand in the Classic against males in a bid for Horse of the Year. Badgett stuck with his plan to run her in the Distaff, remarking that she would have many chances to take on the males as a four-year-old.

If only it were to be. The race that was hailed to be the event of the year started out as exciting as everyone had anticipated, with the champion Bayakoa seeking to defend her title in the Distaff against Go for Wand. Go for Wand took an early

Go for Wand in her fatal showdown with Bayakoa (opposite); trainer Billy Badgett, jockey Randy Romero, and owner Jane du Pont Lunger

lead with Bayakoa right behind her. With a furlong left, the pair had opened up six lengths on the field and Go for Wand hung tightly to a narrow lead. As the two hit the sixteenth pole, Go for Wand went down, got back up, and then crumpled, as did every heart in the place. A collective sob went up from the crowd. Romero, who had been thrown to the ground, was taken away by ambulance but returned later that day to ride, while a screen appeared before Go for Wand and she was put down on racing's darkest day. *RB*

94 Breeders' Cup Pick 6 Scandal

THREE FRATERNITY BROTHERS tried to orchestrate one of the biggest scams in racing when they hit the Breeders' Cup Ultra Pick 6 on October 26, 2002. But there was no payoff, because the nature of their selections immediately sent up red flags to pari-mutuel officials.

After a quick investigation, it was determined the tote system had been compromised in the Ultra Pick 6, and the winning tickets, valued at more than $3 million, were deemed fraudulent. The incident led to calls for tote-system upgrades and the formation of the National Office of Wagering Security.

The scheme, which attracted attention from the U.S. Justice Department and Federal Bureau of Investigation, was masterminded by Chris Harn, a former Autotote software engineer; the other Drexel University fraternity brothers were Derrick Davis, who owned the winning tickets, and Glen DaSilva, who said he had made money on previous schemes.

Harn was sentenced March 20, 2003, to a year and a day — the least amount of prison time for the three fraternity brothers involved in the case because he helped authorities in the investigation. DaSilva was sentenced to two years in prison, while Davis received thirty-seven months.

A total of $4,646,289 was wagered on the Ultra Pick 6. The six winning tickets, all purchased through Catskill Off-Track Betting Corporation in New York, each paid $428,392.

Each of the winning tickets involved single selections for the first four Ultra Pick 6 races, followed by "all" selections for the final two races. The unusual nature of the winning wagers prompted the request for a review, which deter-

mined Harn had been able to access the pool after wagering had closed. The computerized bets were made via the account wagering system operated by Catskill.

At the time, selections on a pick-six ticket submitted through an outside betting hub such as Catskill weren't revealed to the host track, in this case Arlington Park, until after the fifth race in the sequence. Thus, someone with access could change the selections in the first four legs before data was sent to the host.

The six winners were Domedriver ($54 to win), Orientate ($7.40), Starine ($28.40), Vindication ($10.20), High Chaparral ($3.80), and Volponi ($89).

The scam, unusual in that it involved computer tampering rather than race-fixing, was just the tip of the iceberg for the pari-mutuel industry, which had been and still is fighting in Washington, D.C., to protect its right to conduct simulcasting and account wagering. (The U.S. Justice Department has questioned that right under the federal Wire Act, which governs transmissions using communications equipment.) The fraud put the spotlight on the industry, which in turn adopted a series of stopgap measures to protect the integrity of the pari-mutuel system.

There were wagering cutoffs at zero minutes to post time or when the first horse was loaded into the gate, and changes in tote protocol were implemented. The biggest development was the forma-tion of a task force by the National Thoroughbred Racing Association and the hiring of former New York City Mayor Rudolph Giuliani's company, Giuliani Partners, to develop a security plan.

Giuliani's key recommendation was formation of a National Office of Wagering Security.

Given the many factions and organizations in pari-mutuel racing, development of the National Office of Wagering Security was no easy task. In 2004 the NTRA announced it had hired a banking executive to run the office; she declined before she started the job. In April 2005 regulators from around North America weighed in.

Meanwhile, major racing companies and associations set to work on upgrading the industry's tote system, something The Jockey Club has been pushing for years. As of late 2005, only the framework for the National Office of Wagering Security was in place, while the tote upgrade was expected to take at least another year.

The need for tighter security was magnified yet again in early 2005 when an eighty-eight-count federal indictment charged seventeen defendants with operating an illegal gambling business that involved wagers made offshore. Though most of the betting services named in the indictment weren't charged, the indictments placed under scrutiny offshore wagering companies that are believed to account for about 10 percent of the total pari-mutuel handle in the United States each year. *TL*

95

The Theft of Fanfreluche

LATE IN THE AFTERNOON on Saturday, June 25, 1977, a horse farm owner's worst fears materialized when the champion mare Fanfreluche was stolen from the Hancock family's famed Claiborne Farm near Paris, Kentucky.

Owned by Canadian industrialist Jean-Louis Levesque, Fanfreluche had been a standout on the racetrack, finishing first, second, or third in nineteen of twenty-one starts. The Northern Dancer mare's stellar race record had earned her the title of champion three-year-old filly in North America in 1970, the same year she was crowned Canadian Horse of the Year.

Boarded at Claiborne at the time of the theft, Fanfreluche was in foal to the outstanding racehorse and budding young sire Secretariat. As a broodmare, Fanfreluche had gotten off to a great start, producing the champion L'Enjoleur, Canada's Horse of the Year in 1974 and 1975.

No one witnessed the horse-napping, but a night watchman placed the time of the heist after 4 p.m., when he did a head count and accounted for nine broodmares, including Fanfreluche, in the paddock. A similar check four hours later revealed only eight horses, but the watchman assumed one was out of his sight. It was not until the next morning that a section of fence was found dismantled and Fanfreluche missing.

The theft made national headlines, with *Sports Illustrated* magazine labeling the mare the "most famous missing female since Patty Hearst."

With no immediate arrest or suspect, speculation centered around whether the thief (or thieves) targeted the expensive Fanfreluche or whether she was plucked from the field at random. In the days following the theft, law enforcement officials waited for a ransom note that never materialized. The lack of a motive and the silence from whoever took Fanfreluche led to speculation that someone might try to fabricate registration papers, necessary for the mare to be entered in a race or have her offspring registered with The Jockey Club.

Fanfreluche had a value of $500,000, though her owner did not have the mare insured. A $25,000 reward was offered for her recovery.

Within a month of the theft, the Kentucky State Police issued a warrant for the arrest of William Michael McCandless, a former exercise rider and self-described gambler, in connection with Fanfreluche's disappearance. After turning himself in, McCandless was charged with felony theft and released on bond. However, McCandless disappeared, forfeiting his bond. He would be the only person charged in the case.

Acting on a tip, the FBI located Fanfreluche in December, some five months after her disappearance, on a farm in southwestern Kentucky. The farm owner, who said he had found the mare standing on a roadside, had renamed her Brandy and was using her as a pleasure horse. The FBI determined the farm owner was not involved in the theft.

Despite the time lapse between her theft and discovery, Fanfreluche was still in foal and the following year produced a Secretariat colt aptly named Sain Et Sauf, which is French for "safe and sound."

McCandless was arrested in Tennessee in 1981 and charged with directing a tractor-trailer theft ring. He was serving a ten-year prison sentence in that case when he was tried and convicted in June 1983 — six years after the theft — for the abduction of Fanfreluche. Convicted of theft by unlawful taking, McCandless was sentenced to four years in prison, to be served concurrently with one year for bail jumping. He would serve the Kentucky sentence after completing his Tennessee sentence.

Meanwhile, Fanfreluche was sold to Bert Firestone for $1.3 million in 1978 and resumed her life as a successful broodmare, producing the grade II winner D'Accord (by Secretariat).

In an interesting twist, McCandless later surfaced in connection with another horse-racing related crime — the intentional "sponging" of horses at Kentucky tracks in the mid- to late-1990s.

The act of sponging, not to be confused with the bathing of a horse following exercise or a race, entails the placement of a piece of sponge — the size of an egg — in a horse's nostrils. Since horses breathe only through their noses, the sponging has the effect of reducing oxygen supply by up to 50 percent.

The first sponging incidents were detected in five claiming horses that ran at Churchill Downs during the spring 1996 meet. With the assistance of another convicted felon, authorities concluded that McCandless was responsible for the sponging of one or more horses in three different races at Churchill Downs. In 1998, more than twenty years after Fanfreluche was taken, the man convicted of her theft was indicted on six charges of wire fraud and interstate travel to aid in racketeering.

As of late 2005 McCandless had never been located to stand trial on those charges.

Fanfreluche, named Canadian Broodmare of the Year in 1978, was retired from breeding in 1991 and died in the summer of 1999 at age thirty-two. She left behind a stellar legacy on the track and in the breeding shed. *RM*

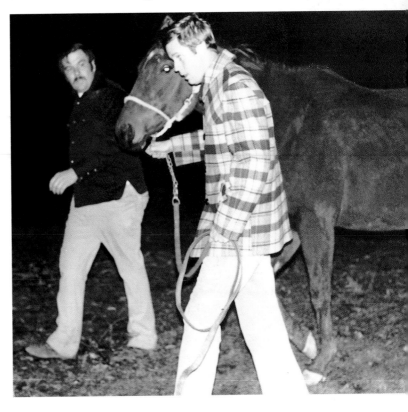

Claiborne's Seth Hancock retrieves Fanfreluche after the mare's discovery

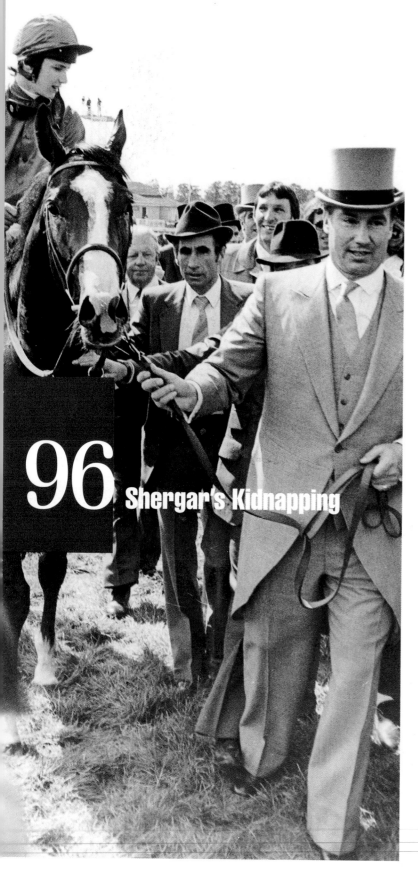

THE BRAZEN KIDNAPPING of champion Shergar and his disappearance without a trace remain one of the Turf's most baffling mysteries. Only the kidnappers know for sure whether the crime was motivated by spite, politics, or prank.

Shergar, bred by the Aga Khan and reared at Sheshoon Stud in County Kildare, Ireland, was a young, highly prized stallion at the time of his disappearance in 1983. The blaze-faced bay had won the 1981 Epsom Derby by a record ten lengths, the Irish Derby by four, and the King George VI and Queen Elizabeth Stakes against older horses by the same margin. His six victories in eight starts earned him European Horse of the Year honors. Shergar's dazzling credentials attracted offers from American breeders, but the Aga Khan turned them down and syndicated his star for $18.3 million. Shergar would stand in Ireland.

The stallion's second season was about to begin, and by February 8, mares already had arrived at Ballymany Stud to visit his court. That afternoon a heavy fog descended on the farm, obscuring visibility and heightening the sense of isolation. Little in the way of security existed at the time.

Jim Fitzgerald, Ballymany's head groom, secured Shergar in his stall before going home for dinner. At 8:30 p.m., five, possibly six, armed and masked gunmen burst into Fitzgerald's home and terrorized him and his family.

"We've come for Shergar, and we want two million quid for him," Fitzgerald said one of the intruders demanded. "Call the police and he's dead."

Fitzgerald was forced to take the gunmen to the stable then watched helplessly as Shergar was loaded onto a shabby horse van. The groom himself was blindfolded and taken as well, driven around for several hours, and deposited some forty miles from the stud.

The following day Ballymany manager Ghislain Drion received a ransom demand for $3 million from an anonymous caller. The Gardai Siochana, Ireland's police force, became involved, with Superintendent Jim "Spud" Murphy leading the investigation. He ordered a massive horse hunt while he and his staff fielded calls from people all over the country, including psychics and clairvoyants.

By Friday, three days after the kidnapping, the

Dublin *Evening Herald* reported that Shergar was dead, this information based on anonymous calls to news outlets earlier in the day. Police, however, did not confirm that assertion and various individuals, including journalists and a shareholder, were reportedly contacted by kidnappers weeks after the horse disappeared.

But by May, police finally conceded that Shergar was dead. In June, Lloyds of London settled approximately $10.5 million in claims with shareholders, who had insured their pieces in the horse.

Theories abounded about who took Shergar and why. Suspects included the IRA, Libyan leader Colonel Muammar el-Quadaffi, and various and sundry individuals who allegedly disliked the Aga Khan. Some speculated that it was a simple horse heist gone awry.

Nearly ten years after Shergar's disappearance,

(Opposite) The Aga Khan leads in Shergar after his 1981 Epsom Derby victory, pictured below

the London *Sunday Times* published a sensational interview with Sean O'Callaghan, a high-ranking IRA leader turned police informant. O'Callaghan claimed the IRA indeed had kidnapped Shergar, but the theft did not go according to plan.

"The horse threw himself into a frenzy in the horsebox, damaging a leg and proving impossible for the team to control," O'Callaghan told the newspaper.

"He was killed within days even though the IRA kept up the pretence that he was alive and demanded a £5 million pound (sic) ransom for his safe return."

The kidnappers dug a pit in a desolate mountain area, disposed of Shergar's body, and left no markers, according to O'Callaghan.

However, no evidence ever emerged to support this claim or any other theory surrounding Shergar's fate. His disappearance remains as shrouded as the February night he last was seen alive. *JD*

97 The Jockey Club Begins DNA Typing

THOROUGHBRED OWNERS, who sometimes invest millions of dollars in their horses, want assurance that the horse they own really has the pedigree it shows on paper. And through The Jockey Club's required DNA testing, implemented early in the twenty-first century, they can know with certainty.

Owners and breeders rely on a horse's pedigree to make many decisions, ranging from buying the animal to choosing its mate. After all, one of the most important components of how fast or far a horse can run is its genetics. In addition, a horse's DNA (deoxyribonucleic acid) makeup can also determine important factors, such as conformation flaws that lead to unsoundness or a predisposition to health issues, such as respiratory problems. Therefore, the reliability of the information pertaining to the horse's lineage is paramount.

In the late 1970s The Jockey Club took steps to confirm the accuracy of the sire and dam information provided for horses registered with the organization by requiring blood-typing as part of the registration process. In 1977 blood-typing was required for all stallions standing at stud in North America. That was followed by required blood-typing verification for broodmares, starting in 1979, and for foals, beginning in 1987.

While blood-typing was considered a reliable test for verification of a horse's breeding, The Jockey Club, as well as registries for other breeds, wanted to improve on the 96 percent accuracy rate of the blood tests. The ultimate goal is a test providing 100 percent verification; DNA testing with its 99.9 percent accuracy rate nearly achieves that goal. The high accuracy rate stems from the fact DNA contains the genetic makeup of each individual animal, with no two alike. The testing involves technology that is akin to using a fingerprint for verifying a person's identity.

Although The Jockey Club set 1994 as the target for introducing DNA testing into the registration process, it was a long road from concept to reality. Obtaining DNA samples was as simple as taking small swab samples from the animal's nostrils or pulling hair roots. But processing the large number of samples posed a more daunting challenge for the company initially contracted to perform the services, dealing a setback to implementation of DNA verification.

The Jockey Club invested in the testing company — which had successfully performed the same services for the huge American Quarter Horse Association — and proceeded with plans to have testing mandatory for the 1994 foal crop. Toward that goal, The Jockey Club began field tests of the DNA techniques in 1993, but those plans came untracked.

While there reportedly were "problems with adapting testing techniques to the production-line environment of a laboratory that would be required to verify the parentage of thousands of foals," according to an article in *The Blood-Horse*, the testing program was also impaired by a decision to pursue "emerging technologies" for DNA testing procedures rather than rely on the techniques that had worked for the AQHA.

The Jockey Club ended its partnership with the DNA company and returned to the drawing board. By the late 1990s sufficient progress had

been made. DNA testing was again on track, this time to be implemented in 2001, a goal achieved with the foal crop of that year.

In the first step, more than 20,000 stallions and broodmares were DNA-typed, using frozen blood samples that had been retained by the genetic-typing laboratories under contract with The Jockey Club. For those stallions and broodmares whose blood samples could not be tested, their owners were sent DNA typing kits in late 2000.

DNA typing was officially incorporated into The Jockey Club's registration process in 2001. The organization's Web site provided breeders with background on the scientific and financial benefits of the switch to DNA-typing as well as illustrated instructions on obtaining the DNA hair root sample.

As a result of adopting DNA testing, The Jockey Club can assure buyers of horses at auction or through private transactions that they are 99.9 percent certain the horse's breeding is accurate. And that is a figure any prospective buyer would use to bid on. *RM*

A hair root sample is pulled and then attached to a DNA-typing kit. The hair is tested to verify parentage

THOROUGHBRED RACING AND BREEDING are data-driven industries. From race records for individual horses, to statistics for jockeys, trainers, owners, and breeders, to lists on how the progeny of stallions are doing, the importance of numbers cannot be overstated.

So it was with some puzzlement that horse racing and breeding went so long without a central clearinghouse for information and statistics until Equibase Company was formed in 1990. Based in Lexington, Kentucky, Equibase is a partnership of The Jockey Club, the horse industry's breed registry that also compiles and disseminates breeding data, and the Thoroughbred Racing Associations, the trade organization of North American racetracks.

Equibase Is Formed

While Equibase was formed to "provide the Thoroughbred racetracks of North America with a uniform, industry-owned database of racing information and statistics," its partners also pointed to the promotion and "betterment" of racing as another goal.

"It is essential to the future of Thoroughbred racing's statistical records that the industry own and maintain control of its own database," said James E. "Ted" Bassett III, Equibase's first chairman, shortly after the service began. "We are extremely optimistic over the future of Equibase."

Before the establishment of Equibase, the racing industry relied upon data compiled and published by various trade publications. The *Daily Racing Form* was considered the most reliable source of racing data and served as racing's unofficial clearinghouse. Even with the reliance upon

the *Form* as the primary source for racing stats, however, discrepancies persisted in the compiling of numbers and the methods of reporting.

Once Equibase was established, the company used its personnel to compile charts at racetracks, a task already being performed by *Daily Racing Form*. Equibase's own ways of compiling information sometimes put it at odds with the numbers kept by the *Form*. Many North American tracks began to use Equibase information for the past-performance data published in the tracks' daily programs, essentially making the company partners with the tracks. Using Equibase's data, tracks were also able to upgrade the amount and quality of handicapping data provided patrons in the daily programs, with the resulting product positioned to compete with the *Form*.

With two primary sources for racing information, however, inconsistencies occurred among the running lines published in the Equibase-generated past performances, those published in the *Form*, and those in another leading daily publisher — *Sports Eye*.

Equibase was not an overnight success as it underwent some growing pains in its infancy.

"Frankly, we did not anticipate the enormous complexity not only of obtaining the information, but also in getting it in a format to be given back to them (tracks)," Bassett said two years after Equibase was established.

But company officials persevered and in 1998 entered into an agreement with the *Form*. As a result, Equibase became the sole data-collection agency and supplier of information to the *Form* and other industry groups.

Equibase now relies upon its chart callers to compile information from all North American tracks. The information is processed and stored in the company's database and is available for retrieval by those involved in the daily operations at some one hundred racetracks and more than a thousand simulcast outlets, as well as at *Daily Racing Form* and *Sports Eye*.

As it has evolved, Equibase has expanded its operations, with emphasis on new products to assist handicappers and racetracks, taking advantage of the timely distribution of information via the Internet. The company now has a wholly owned subsidiary, TrackMaster, which provides a comprehensive menu of handicapping products not only for Thoroughbred racing fans, but also for the Quarter Horse and Standardbred industries. In 1994 Equibase established an automated system to track and send reports to media about personal milestones of trainers and jockeys, with the alerts sent before and after the events.

In an effort to provide more access to racing entries, results, scratches, and other information pertinent to daily racing, Equibase established a condensed version of its Web site that can be accessed through wireless devices.

Other expanded services include Equibase Virtual Stable, through which an estimated 100,000 race fans receive e-mail notifications of real-time entries, results, and workouts for horses included in their individual "stables." Virtual Stable participants also receive daily e-mail reports leading up to the Triple Crown races and the Breeders' Cup World Thoroughbred Championships.

According to *The Jockey Club Fact Book*, dividends totaling $2.4 million were distributed in 2004 to Equibase's partners — Equibase Holding Partners and The Jockey Club Racing Services. *RM*

Equibase past performances in an Aqueduct program

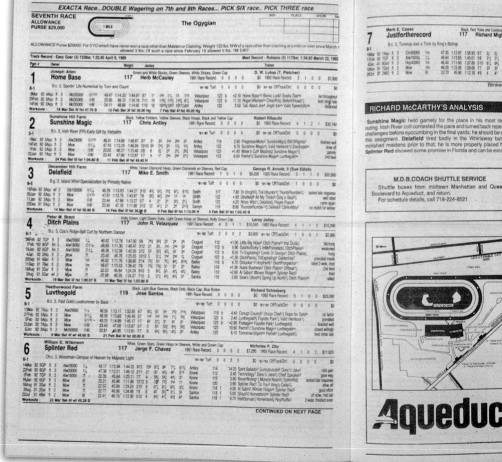

William Woodward Jr. Is Shot

IT WAS THE STORY that inspired Dominick Dunne's *The Two Mrs. Grenvilles* and left many torn over whether Ann Woodward intentionally killed her husband, William Woodward Jr., or, as she told police, mistook him for a prowler and shot him dead in their Long Island home.

Her name had been Ann Crowell when she came to New York City in the early 1940s at age twenty-two. A tall, pretty blonde from a small town in Kansas, she found work as a showgirl and radio actress, and later as a dancer in the Monte Carlo nightclub. It was there that the young woman who had grown up with little money but plenty of brains and ambition met the prominent and wealthy William Woodward and his only son, William Jr.

The senior Woodward had taken over the powerful Hanover Bank of New York nearly twenty years earlier when his bachelor uncle, James, had died. In addition to his duties as bank president, Woodward also served as a director of the Federal Reserve Board and chairman of The Jockey Club. His status as Eastern aristocracy was as solid as the foundation beneath his five residences, and he was well known in the horse racing world for the success of his famous Belair Stud.

It was speculated but never proven that Ann Crowell might have started out as the senior Woodward's mistress before falling in love with his son, who was five years her junior. William Woodward Jr., known to friends and family as Billy, went to Groton and then Harvard, just as his father had. After graduation, and with the advent of World War II, he entered the Navy and earned the rank of lieutenant. During this time he also married Ann Crowell, a union his mother, Elsie Cryder Woodward, strenuously opposed. She was widely quoted as once saying, "These girls from nowhere can be dangerous to (good) families."

After the war the senior Woodward gave his son the rest of a trust consisting of blue-chip stocks, helping set up the young couple financially. Billy served on the boards of several businesses and stayed busy pursuing his sporting interests. He was an avid tennis player and big-game hunter, but he seemingly had little interest in Thoroughbreds despite his father's success with Belair Stud.

Billy's marriage to Ann, meanwhile, had its ups and downs. The couple constantly fought and at one point, in 1948, separated and considered divorce. During their separation the two still saw each other and, reportedly, other people. They continued to fight, at times their altercations drawing enough alarm for neighbors to call the police. The Woodwards reconciled a year later, and Ann began to join Billy on his big-game hunting trips, becoming an active convert to the sport. Ann's interest in hunting prompted Billy to have a shotgun custom made for her in England.

When William Woodward Sr. died in 1953, Billy inherited a million dollars and Belair Stud. Ann successfully encouraged her husband to take an interest in what had been his father's passion. The senior Woodward had died when Nashua (Nasrullah—Segula, by Johnstown) was just a yearling. Nashua's burgeoning success as a two-year-old drew Billy and Ann to the racing scene. Ann was frequently photographed at the track and pictured in magazines, garnering a spread on her racetrack outfits in *Sports Illustrated* and the chagrin of her mother-in-law.

When Nashua, as a three-year-old, beat Swaps in a much-anticipated match race (*See No. 6*), Billy and Ann Woodward were pictured in newspapers all over the country — the handsome couple smiling as they stood next to Nashua.

Two months later, on October 30, 1955, Billy Woodward was dead and she was the one who had shot him in their Oyster Bay, Long Island, home, known as "The Playhouse."

The couple had been at a nearby party for the visiting Duchess of Windsor. According to several guests later interviewed by police, the Woodwards mentioned that a prowler had been trying to get into their home.

Ann Woodward told police that when the couple arrived home from the party at about 1 a.m., they searched the house to make sure no one else was in it, except their two young sons and the maid, who were all asleep. The couple then retired to separate bedrooms, she said, Billy arming himself with an automatic pistol (which police subsequently found in a bureau in his bedroom) and she with the shotgun Billy had given her as a present. They agreed that either one of them who heard the prowler would go after him with a gun.

Not long after the couple had gone to bed, Ann told police she heard her dog bark, grabbed the shotgun, opened her bedroom door, and saw a figure down the dark hallway. Acting instinctively,

William and Ann Woodward in the winner's circle with trainer Sunny Jim Fitzsimmons and jockey Eddie Arcaro; Woodward leading in Nashua (opposite)

she said, she raised the gun and quickly pulled both triggers. Almost immediately, she said, she realized she had shot her husband. One of the pellets had hit him in the head and killed him. It was 2:08 when the operator received a call from the Woodward number and heard a woman screaming incoherently. When police arrived, they found Ann on the floor embracing her husband's nude body.

A couple of days later police picked up twenty-two-year-old Paul Wirth near a stolen car that contained a gun. He admitted to having attempted to break into the Woodward's mansion the previous week and later admitted he had been trying to break in at the time of the shooting. When he had heard the gunfire in the house, he said it had scared him off.

On November 25, Ann Woodward told her story to the Nassau County Grand Jury, which had also heard testimony from twenty-five other witnesses. The jury deliberated for thirty minutes before telling the judge it would not indict Ann Woodward on the grounds that no crime had been committed. *RB*

100 Mary Hirsch Becomes First Licensed Female Trainer

MARY ELIZABETH HIRSCH wasn't the first woman trainer, but she was the first licensed by The Jockey Club. That took place in 1935 and took some doing because the New York-based organization didn't license women. Of course, refusing to license women trainers defied all logic because a woman had been elected to Congress as early as 1916 and women had gotten the right to vote in 1920.

Hirsch wasn't just anybody. Her father was veteran trainer Max Hirsch, but he didn't help matters much. Training was a man's game and a hard life, he explained. Besides, Hirsch hoped his daughter, an accomplished pianist and a successful rider, would pursue a more refined career.

Although women had been refused licenses as trainers, they played other important roles in racing.

The 1904 Derby winner, Elwood, was the first Derby winner bred by a woman and the first owned by a woman. Bred by Mrs. J.B. Prather, Elwood won as the longest shot on the board for owner Laska Durnell, whose husband, Charles, trained the colt.

Years later Rosa Hoots witnessed an impossible dream. Hoots' husband, Alfred, had dreamed of sending his humble broodmare Useeit to E.R. Bradley's blue-blooded stallion Black Toney. Alfred Hoots got his wish but died before the resultant foal, Black Gold, won the 1924 Derby as a homebred for Rosa Hoots.

Four years after Black Gold's victory, Fannie Hertz won the Derby with Reigh Count. In 1931 Helen Hay Whitney, a major owner for years in the name of her Greentree Stable, won the Derby and Belmont Stakes with homebred Twenty Grand. And just a year before The Jockey Club gave its approval to Mary Hirsch, Isabel Dodge Sloane of Brookmeade Stable won the Derby with Cavalcade.

Hirsch's intention to apply to The Jockey Club was made public in December 1932, when she was twenty. Hirsch had been assisting her father for several years but she was advised by The Jockey Club that submitting her application would be a waste of time. Midway through the following year, the publication *Daily Running Horses* wrote that Hirsch "knows more about spread hoofs, splints, bowed tendons, bog spavins, etc., than the several persons now training horses here under license from The Jockey Club, despite the fact that their knowledge of the horse was obtained in the back room of a cigar store."

The article also stated that "if the precedent of a licensed woman trainer had been set in 1732 or some other medieval time most likely the stewards of The Jockey Club would have been happy to have granted her permission to train horses."

What made The Jockey Club's rejection seem so misguided was the common knowledge that Hirsch was training some of her father's horses on her own and doing well. But when the horses were entered to race, they were listed as trained by Max Hirsch or Mary Hirsch's brother, William J. "Buddy" Hirsch.

She once said, "Dad taught me all I know, and I think that's enough."

Although women weren't licensed in New York,

Mary Hirsch, shown in the winner's circle with Sir Bede Clifford (left), jockey Jack Westrope, and Joseph E. Widener, saddled the stakes winner No Sir (below)

they were licensed as trainers in other states. Out West, Hilda Bauer, Ruth Parton, and M.E. Henderson were licensed, and Elizabeth Bosley was training horses in Maryland. Hirsch herself was licensed in 1934 in both Illinois and Michigan. She finally got the go-ahead from The Jockey Club in the spring of 1935 when the organization bowed to pressure. A short time later Judy Johnson was given permission to train in New York.

Hirsch was the first woman to saddle a horse in the Kentucky Derby. Her charge, No Sir, finished thirteenth in War Admiral's 1937 triumph. Hirsch earlier had sent out No Sir to win the 1936 East View Stakes at Empire City in New York and the 1937 Bahama Handicap at Hialeah in Florida. In 1938 Hirsch and Mrs. Parker Corning became the first women to train and own a Travers Stakes winner, Thanksgiving. Johnson became the first woman to saddle a horse in the Preakness Stakes when she sent out Sir Beau in the 1968 running, won by Forward Pass. Sir Beau finished seventh.

Hirsch married Hialeah racing secretary Charles McLennan in 1940 and gave up training but continued to follow the sport. *DS*

Top 100 Lists

BY CATEGORY

TOP MOMENTS / Racing

1. SEABISCUIT VS. WAR ADMIRAL
2. KELSO'S FIVE HORSE OF THE YEAR TITLES
3. SECRETARIAT'S BELMONT
4. NASHUA VS. SWAPS
5. DR. FAGER'S WORLD-RECORD MILE
6. AFFIRMED AND ALYDAR'S BELMONT
7. WOODY STEPHENS' FIVE BELMONTS
8. REGRET WINS THE KENTUCKY DERBY
9. D. WAYNE LUKAS WINS SIX STRAIGHT TRIPLE CROWN RACES
10. MATT J. WINN SAVES CHURCHILL DOWNS AND THE DERBY
11. NATIVE DANCER'S DERBY UPSET
12. LAFFIT PINCAY JR. BECOMES ALL-TIME LEADING RIDER
13. RUFFIAN'S BREAKDOWN
14. FOREGO'S MARLBORO CUP
15. TOM FOOL'S PIMLICO SPECIAL
16. MAN O' WAR'S UPSET
17. JOHN HENRY WINS INAUGURAL ARLINGTON MILLION
18. BELMONT PARK OPENS
19. COUNT FLEET'S BELMONT
20. BARBARA JO RUBIN'S HISTORIC RIDING VICTORY
21. THE JERSEY ACT IS RESCINDED
22. THE 1967 WOODWARD STAKES
23. CIGAR WINS THE FIRST DUBAI WORLD CUP
24. PERSONAL ENSIGN'S BREEDERS' CUP DISTAFF
25. CITATION BECOMES RACING'S FIRST MILLIONAIRE
26. THE "FIGHTING FINISH" DERBY
27. CARL NAFZGER'S FAMOUS DERBY "CALL"
28. JOHN LONGDEN'S DERBY DOUBLE
29. KEENELAND OPENS
30. AFLEET ALEX'S PREAKNESS
31. JULIE KRONE WINS THE BELMONT STAKES
32. JIM DANDY UPSETS GALLANT FOX
33. HIALEAH PARK POPULARIZES WINTER RACING
34. DANCER'S IMAGE'S DERBY DISQUALIFICATION
35. SIR BARTON CAPTURES THE FIRST TRIPLE CROWN
36. RICHARD MANDELLA'S BREEDERS' CUP FEAT
37. SEABISCUIT AND RED POLLARD MAKE THEIR COMEBACK
38. CITATION'S SIXTEEN-RACE WIN STREAK
39. EASY GOER AND SUNDAY SILENCE'S PREAKNESS
40. RIBOT WINS BACK-TO-BACK ARCS
41. THE FIRST MEETING OF TRIPLE CROWN WINNERS
42. DAHLIA'S INTERNATIONAL ACHIEVEMENT
43. EXCELLER AND SEATTLE SLEW'S JOCKEY CLUB GOLD CUP
44. JAIPUR AND RIDAN'S TRAVERS STAKES
45. THE ZEV-PAPYRUS MATCH RACE
46. DALE BAIRD TRAINS 9,000 WINNERS
47. THE MIRACLE MILLION AT ARLINGTON PARK
48. COLIN HOLDS OFF FAIR PLAY IN THE 1908 BELMONT
49. SWAPS' RECORD-BREAKING SEASON
50. SIR IVOR WINS THE EPSOM DERBY
51. WHISK BROOM II'S HANDICAP TRIPLE CROWN
52. SMARTY JONES: THE PEOPLE'S HORSE
53. SPECTACULAR BID'S WALKOVER CAPS UNDEFEATED SEASON
54. GO FOR WAND'S BREAKDOWN
55. MARY HIRSCH BECOMES FIRST LICENSED FEMALE TRAINER

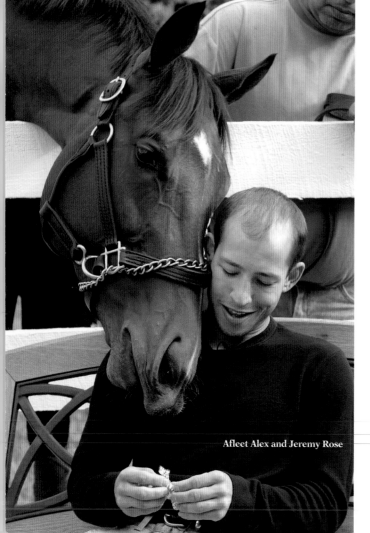

Afleet Alex and Jeremy Rose

TOP MOMENTS / Oddities

1. CALUMET FARM FILES FOR BANKRUPTCY
2. THE LEGEND OF PHAR LAP
3. BEST-SELLER SPARKS SEABISCUIT MANIA
4. EXCELLER'S DEATH MOBILIZES HORSE RESCUE GROUPS
5. ALYDAR'S DEATH
6. THE BROADCAST OF MAN O' WAR'S FUNERAL
7. BOLD RULER AND ROUND TABLE BORN THE SAME DAY
8. BREEDERS' CUP PICK 6 SCANDAL
9. THE THEFT OF FANFRELUCHE
10. SHERGAR'S KIDNAPPING
11. WILLIAM WOODWARD JR. IS SHOT

BY CATEGORY

TOP MOMENTS / Innovations

1. THE INAUGURAL BREEDERS' CUP
2. HOLLYWOOD PARK INTRODUCES FIRST FILM PATROL
3. THE FIRST PHOTO FINISH CAMERA
4. LIP TATTOOS IMPROVE RACEHORSE IDENTIFICATION
5. THE ARRIVAL OF INTERTRACK WAGERING
6. THE MODERN STARTING GATE OPENS ITS DOORS
7. KENTUCKY TRACKS INSTITUTE PARI-MUTUEL BETTING
8. THE FIRST WASHINGTON, D.C., INTERNATIONAL
9. THE NEW YORK RACING ASSOCIATION IS CREATED
10. RACING COMES TO TELEVISION
11. DRUG TESTING OF HORSES BEGINS
12. THE CALIENTE SAFETY HELMET IS INTRODUCED
13. THE ADVENT OF ARTHROSCOPIC SURGERY
14. FIRST NETWORK RADIO DERBY BROADCAST
15. THE FIRST TRANSCONTINENTAL FLIGHT OF THOROUGHBREDS
16. THE FIRST RACE CALL
17. THOROUGHBRED RETIREMENT FOUNDATION IS CREATED
18. THE JOCKEY CLUB BEGINS DNA TYPING
19. EQUIBASE IS FORMED

TOP MOMENTS / Auctions

1. SAMUEL D. RIDDLE PURCHASES MAN O' WAR
2. CALUMET FARM PURCHASES BULL LEA
3. KEENELAND CONDUCTS FIRST SUMMER YEARLING SALE
4. SEATTLE SLEW SELLS FOR $17,500
5. THE TRIUMVIRATE OF ROBERT SANGSTER, VINCENT O'BRIEN, AND JOHN MAGNIER
6. FIRST TWO-YEAR-OLDS IN TRAINING SALE

TOP MOMENTS / Breeding

1. LA TROIENNE IS IMPORTED
2. NASRULLAH IS IMPORTED FROM ENGLAND
3. SIR GALLAHAD III IS IMPORTED
4. NORTHERN DANCER ENTERS STUD
5. BOLD RULER LEADS SIRE LIST A RECORD EIGHT TIMES
6. MR. PROSPECTOR MOVES TO CLAIBORNE FARM
7. THE DIVISION OF E.R. BRADLEY'S BLOODSTOCK
8. PRINCEQUILLO MOVES TO CLAIBORNE FARM
9. LAUNCH OF CLAIBORNE FARM

BY DECADE

TOP MOMENTS / 1900–1909

1. MATT J. WINN SAVES CHURCHILL DOWNS AND THE DERBY
2. BELMONT PARK OPENS
3. COLIN HOLDS OFF FAIR PLAY IN THE 1908 BELMONT

TOP MOMENTS / 1910–1919

1. REGRET WINS THE KENTUCKY DERBY
2. KENTUCKY TRACKS INSTITUTE PARI-MUTUEL BETTING
3. SAMUEL D. RIDDLE PURCHASES MAN O' WAR
4. MAN O' WAR'S UPSET
5. SIR BARTON CAPTURES THE FIRST TRIPLE CROWN
6. LAUNCH OF CLAIBORNE FARM
7. WHISK BROOM II'S HANDICAP TRIPLE CROWN

TOP MOMENTS / 1920–1929

1. SIR GALLAHAD III IS IMPORTED
2. THE FIRST NETWORK RADIO DERBY BROADCAST
3. THE FIRST RACE CALL
4. THE ZEV-PAPYRUS MATCH RACE

TOP MOMENTS / 1930–1939

1. SEABISCUIT VS. WAR ADMIRAL
2. THE FIRST PHOTO FINISH CAMERA
3. THE MODERN STARTING GATE OPENS ITS DOORS
4. LA TROIENNE IS IMPORTED
5. CALUMET FARM PURCHASES BULL LEA
6. DRUG TESTING OF HORSES BEGINS
7. THE "FIGHTING FINISH" DERBY
8. THE LEGEND OF PHAR LAP
9. KEENELAND OPENS
10. JIM DANDY UPSETS GALLANT FOX
11. HIALEAH PARK POPULARIZES WINTER RACING
12. MARY HIRSCH BECOMES FIRST LICENSED FEMALE TRAINER

TOP MOMENTS / 1940–1949

1. HOLLYWOOD PARK INTRODUCES FIRST FILM PATROL
2. LIP TATTOOS IMPROVE RACEHORSE IDENTIFICATION
3. COUNT FLEET'S BELMONT
4. THE JERSEY ACT IS RESCINDED
5. KEENELAND CONDUCTS FIRST SUMMER YEARLING SALE
6. THE FIRST TRANSCONTINENTAL FLIGHT OF THOROUGHBREDS
7. SEABISCUIT AND RED POLLARD MAKE THEIR COMEBACK
8. THE DIVISION OF E.R. BRADLEY'S BLOODSTOCK
9. PRINCEQUILLO MOVES TO CLAIBORNE FARM
10. THE BROADCAST OF MAN O' WAR'S FUNERAL

BY DECADE

TOP MOMENTS / 1950–1959

1. NASHUA VS. SWAPS
2. THE FIRST WASHINGTON, D.C., INTERNATIONAL
3. NATIVE DANCER'S DERBY UPSET
4. NASRULLAH IS IMPORTED FROM ENGLAND
5. TOM FOOL'S PIMLICO SPECIAL
6. THE NEW YORK RACING ASSOCIATION IS CREATED
7. RACING COMES TO TELEVISION
8. CITATION BECOMES RACING'S FIRST MILLIONAIRE
9. THE CALIENTE SAFETY HELMET IS INTRODUCED
10. CITATION'S SIXTEEN-RACE WIN STREAK
11. RIBOT'S BACK-TO-BACK ARCS
12. BOLD RULER AND ROUND TABLE BORN SAME DAY
13. FIRST TWO-YEAR-OLDS IN TRAINING SALE
14. SWAPS' RECORD-SETTING SEASON
15. WILLIAM WOODWARD JR. IS SHOT

Citation

TOP MOMENTS / 1960–1969

1. KELSO'S FIVE HORSE OF THE YEAR TITLES
2. DR. FAGER'S WORLD-RECORD MILE
3. NORTHERN DANCER ENTERS STUD
4. BARBARA JO RUBIN'S HISTORIC RIDING VICTORY
5. THE 1967 WOODWARD STAKES
6. JOHN LONGDEN'S DERBY DOUBLE
7. DANCER'S IMAGE'S DERBY DISQUALIFICATION
8. JAIPUR AND RIDAN'S TRAVERS STAKES
9. SIR IVOR WINS THE EPSOM DERBY

TOP MOMENTS / 1970–1979

1. SECRETARIAT'S BELMONT
2. AFFIRMED AND ALYDAR'S BELMONT
3. RUFFIAN'S BREAKDOWN
4. FOREGO'S MARLBORO CUP
5. BOLD RULER LEADS SIRE LIST A RECORD EIGHT TIMES
6. SEATTLE SLEW SELLS FOR $17,500
7. THE FIRST MEETING OF TRIPLE CROWN WINNERS
8. THE TRIUMVIRATE OF ROBERT SANGSTER, VINCENT O'BRIEN, AND JOHN MAGNIER
9. DAHLIA'S INTERNATIONAL ACHIEVEMENT
10. EXCELLER AND SEATTLE SLEW'S JOCKEY CLUB GOLD CUP
11. THE THEFT OF FANFRELUCHE

TOP MOMENTS / 1980–1989

1. THE INAUGURAL BREEDERS' CUP
2. WOODY STEPHENS' FIVE BELMONTS
3. THE ARRIVAL OF INTERTRACK WAGERING
4. JOHN HENRY WINS INAUGURAL ARLINGTON MILLION
5. PERSONAL ENSIGN'S BREEDERS' CUP DISTAFF
6. THE ADVENT OF ARTHROSCOPIC SURGERY
7. MR. PROSPECTOR MOVES TO CLAIBORNE FARM
8. EASY GOER AND SUNDAY SILENCE'S PREAKNESS
9. THOROUGHBRED RETIREMENT FOUNDATION IS CREATED
10. THE MIRACLE MILLION AT ARLINGTON PARK
11. SPECTACULAR BID'S WALKOVER CAPS UNDEFEATED SEASON
12. SHERGAR'S KIDNAPPING

Shergar

BY DECADE

TOP MOMENTS / 1990–1999

1. D. WAYNE LUKAS WINS SIX STRAIGHT TRIPLE CROWN RACES
2. LAFFIT PINCAY JR. BECOMES ALL-TIME LEADING RIDER
3. CIGAR WINS FIRST DUBAI WORLD CUP
4. CARL NAFZGER'S FAMOUS DERBY "CALL"
5. CALUMET FARM FILES FOR BANKRUPTCY
6. JULIE KRONE WINS THE BELMONT STAKES
7. EXCELLER'S DEATH MOBILIZES HORSE RESCUE GROUPS
8. ALYDAR'S DEATH
9. GO FOR WAND'S BREAKDOWN
10. EQUIBASE IS FORMED

TOP MOMENTS / 2000–Present

1. AFLEET ALEX'S PREAKNESS
2. BEST-SELLER SPARKS SEABISCUIT MANIA
3. RICHARD MANDELLA'S BREEDERS' CUP FEAT
4. DALE BAIRD TRAINS 9,000 WINNERS
5. SMARTY JONES: THE PEOPLE'S HORSE
6. BREEDERS' CUP PICK 6 SCANDAL
7. THE JOCKEY CLUB BEGINS DNA TYPING

BY DERBY WINNERS

TOP MOMENTS / Derby Winners

1. SEABISCUIT VS. WAR ADMIRAL
2. SECRETARIAT'S BELMONT
3. NASHUA VS. SWAPS
4. AFFIRMED AND ALYDAR'S BELMONT
5. REGRET WINS THE KENTUCKY DERBY
6. NORTHERN DANCER ENTERS STUD
7. COUNT FLEET'S BELMONT
8. CITATION BECOMES RACING'S FIRST MILLIONAIRE
9. THE "FIGHTING FINISH" DERBY
10. CARL NAFZGER'S FAMOUS DERBY "CALL"
11. JOHN LONGDEN'S DERBY DOUBLE
12. JIM DANDY UPSETS GALLANT FOX
13. DANCER'S IMAGE'S DERBY DISQUALIFICATION
14. SIR BARTON CAPTURES THE FIRST TRIPLE CROWN
15. CITATION'S SIXTEEN-RACE WIN STREAK
16. SEATTLE SLEW SELLS FOR $17,500
17. EASY GOER AND SUNDAY SILENCE'S PREAKNESS
18. THE FIRST MEETING OF TRIPLE CROWN WINNERS
19. EXCELLER AND SEATTLE SLEW'S JOCKEY CLUB GOLD CUP
20. THE ZEV-PAPYRUS MATCH RACE
21. SWAPS' RECORD-BREAKING SEASON
22. SMARTY JONES: THE PEOPLE'S HORSE
23. SPECTACULAR BID'S WALKOVER CAPS UNDEFEATED SEASON

Spectacular Bid

PHOTO CREDITS IN LIST SECTION
Afleet Alex and Jeremy Rose (Barbara D. Livingston); Citation (Hollywood Park); Shergar (Sport & General); Spectacular Bid (The Blood-Horse); Tiznow (Rob Moskal).

TOP MOMENTS / Honorable Mentions: NUMBERS 101–125

101. RACING FLOURISHES IN ILLINOIS IN THE 1920S AND EXPANDS WEST TO CALIFORNIA IN THE 1930S

102. CIGAR RETIRES IN 1996 AS THE WORLD'S RICHEST RACEHORSE WITH $9,999,815 IN EARNINGS

103. MARE REPRODUCTIVE LOSS SYNDROME HITS KENTUCKY FARMS IN SPRING 2001

104. SPENDTHRIFT FARM IS LEADING KEENELAND CONSIGNOR IN 1949 FOR FIRST OF SIXTEEN CONSECUTIVE YEARS

105. SADLER'S WELLS ENTERS STUD AT COOLMORE IN 1985

106. SEATTLE DANCER SELLS FOR $13.1 MILLION AT THE 1985 KEENELAND JULY YEARLING SALE

107. SANTA ANITA HANDICAP IN 1935 IS FIRST U.S. RACE TO OFFER $100,000 PURSE

108. HORSEMEN'S BENEVOLENT AND PROTECTIVE ASSOCIATION IS FOUNDED IN 1941

109. GENUINE RISK WINS THE 1980 KENTUCKY DERBY AND PLACES IN THE PREAKNESS AND BELMONT

110. SHUG MCGAUGHEY WINS SIX OF TEN RACES ON BREEDERS' CUP PREVIEW DAY IN 1993

111. H.P. WHITNEY DIES IN 1930 AND SON C.V. WHITNEY TAKES OWNERSHIP OF EQUIPOISE AND THE REST OF HIS FATHER'S BLOODSTOCK

112. TIZNOW BECOMES FIRST BACK-TO-BACK WINNER OF THE BREEDERS' CUP CLASSIC IN 2000-01

113. SEATTLE SLEW WINS THE TRIPLE CROWN WHILE UNDEFEATED

114. THE 1944 CARTER HANDICAP'S TRIPLE DEAD HEAT

115. STABLEMATES SECRETARIAT AND RIVA RIDGE GO HEAD TO HEAD IN INAUGURAL MARLBORO CUP IN 1973

116. POLYTRACK IS INSTALLED AT TURFWAY PARK IN 2005

117. NASHUA BECOMES FIRST MILLION-DOLLAR SYNDICATION IN DECEMBER 1955

118. NIJINSKY II SWEEPS 1970 ENGLISH TRIPLE CROWN

119. ARAZI'S 1991 BREEDERS' CUP JUVENILE

120. KEENELAND INTRODUCES VETERINARY REPOSITORY IN 1996

121. EQUINE VIRAL ARTERITIS HALTS 1984 BREEDING SEASON IN KENTUCKY

122. SHEIKH MOHAMMED PAYS $3.3 MILLION FOR SHAREEF DANCER AT KEENELAND IN 1981

123. BILL SHOEMAKER'S FINISH-LINE ERROR IN THE 1957 KENTUCKY DERBY

124. CALUMET FARM WINS EIGHTH KENTUCKY DERBY WITH FORWARD PASS IN 1968

125. KENTUCKY DERBY WINNER SPEND A BUCK PASSES THE 1985 PREAKNESS FOR JERSEY DERBY AND $2-MILLION BONUS

Tiznow holding off Giant's Causeway in the Breeders' Cup Classic

1) The Inaugural Breeders' Cup (*William Strode, p. 10; The Blood-Horse, p. 11; Anne M. Eberhardt, p. 12; Wally Skalij, p. 13*); 2) Seabiscuit vs. War Admiral (*Joe Fleischer, pp. 14-17*); 3) Kelso's Five Horse of the Year Titles (*NYRA/Mike Sirico, p. 18; NYRA/Bob Coglianese, p. 19; The Blood-Horse, p. 19; Bert and Richard Morgan, p. 20; Mike Sirico, p. 20; The Blood-Horse, p. 21*); 4) Secretariat's Belmont (*Ray Woolfe Jr., pp. 22-23.; The Blood-Horse, p. 24; NYRA/Bob Coglianese, p. 25*); 5) First Film Patrol (*Powell Press Service, p. 26, 28; The Blood-Horse, p. 27; Lexington Herald-Leader, p. 29*); 6) Nashua vs. Swaps (*Keeneland-Morgan, p. 30; Courier-Journal and Louisville Times, p. 30; Bernie Metzroth, p. 32; Baltimore Sun, p. 33*); 7) Dr. Fager's World-Record Mile (*The Blood-Horse, pp. 34-35; Paul Schafer, p. 35; Bob Coglianese, p. 36; Arthur Kunkel, p. 37*); 8) The First Photo Finish Camera (*Jones Precision Photo, p. 38; The Blood-Horse, p. 39; Churchill Downs, p. 40; D&S Photo, p. 41*); 9) Affirmed and Alydar's Belmont (*NYRA/Bob Coglianese, p. 42; NYRA, p. 43; Kinetic Corporation, p. 44; Jerry Frutkoff, p. 45*); 10) Woody Stephens' Five Belmonts (*Barbara D. Livingston, p. 46 ; The Blood-Horse, p. 47; Tony Leonard, pp. 47-49*); 11) Regret Wins the Kentucky Derby (*National Museum of Racing, p. 50; Kinetic Corporation, p. 51; Keeneland-Cook, p. 52; Lexington Herald-Leader, p. 53*); 12) D. Wayne Lukas Wins Six Straight Triple Crown Races (*Skip Dickstein, pp. 54-56; Barbara D. Livingston, p. 57*); 13) Lip Tattoos Improve Racehorse Identification (*The Blood-Horse, pp. 58-59; Bill Straus, pp. 60-61*); 14) Arrival of Intertrack Wagering (*Anne M. Eberhardt, pp. 62-65*); 15) Modern Starting Gate (*Courtesy True Center Gate Company, pp. 66-69*); 16) Kentucky Tracks Institute Pari-Mutuel Betting (*Keeneland, p. 70; Keeneland-Hemment, p. 71; Churchill Downs, p. 72*); 17) The First Washington D.C., International (*Francis DiGennaro, pp. 74-75; Empire City Photo, p. 76*); 18) Samuel D. Riddle Purchases Man o' War (*Keeneland-McClure, p. 78; The Blood-Horse, p. 79, 80; NYRA, p. 80; Keeneland, p. 81*); 19) Matt Winn Saves Churchill Downs and the Derby (*R.G. Potter, p. 82; Caufield & Shook Inc., pp. 83-84; Kinetic Corporation, p. 85*); 20) La Troienne Is Imported (*The Blood-Horse, p. 86; J.A. Estes, p. 87; L.S. Sutcliffe, p. 88; H.C. Ashby, p. 89*)

21) Native Dancer's Derby Upset (*Kinetic Corporation, p. 90; Caufield & Shook Inc., p. 91; Churchill Downs, p. 91*); 22) Laffit Pincay's Riding Record (*Benoit & Associates, pp. 92-93*); 23) Nasrullah Imported (*Skeets Meadors, p. 94, 95; The Blood-Horse, p. 95*); 24) Sir Gallahad III Imported (*The Blood-Horse, p. 96; H.C. Ashby, p. 97*); 25) Ruffian's Breakdown (*Roland J. Chenard, p. 98; New York Daily News, p. 99*); 26) Forego's Marlboro Cup (*The Blood-Horse, p. 100; Jones Precision/NYRA, p. 101*); 27) Tom Fool's Pimlico Special (*The Blood-Horse, p. 102; Keeneland-Morgan, p. 103*); 28) Northern Dancer Enters Stud (*The Blood-Horse, p. 104; Winants Bros., p. 105*); 29) Man o' War's Upset (*Keeneland-Cook, p. 106, 107; The Blood-Horse, p. 107*); 30) John Henry Wins Inaugural Arlington Million (*The Blood-Horse, p. 108; Katey Barrett, p. 109*); 31) Belmont Park Opens (*NYRA, p. 110; Courtesy Ken Grayson, p. 111*); 32) Calumet Purchases Bull Lea (*The Blood-Horse, p. 112; Skeets Meadors, p. 113*); 33) Count Fleet's Belmont (*Bert Morgan, pp. 114-115; The Blood-Horse, p. 115*); 34) Barbara Jo Rubin's Historic Riding Victory (*Tropical Park/Leo Frutkoff, p. 116; NYRA/Bob Coglianese, p. 117*); 35) The New York Racing Association Is Created (*The Blood-Horse, p. 118; John C. Wyatt, p. 119; Paul Schafer, p. 119*); 36) Racing Comes to Television (*Bert Morgan, p. 120; The Blood-Horse, p. 120; Rob Moskal, p. 121*); 37) Drug Testing of Horses Begins (*Anne M. Eberhardt, p. 122; Tom Hall, p. 123*); 38) Jersey Act Is Rescinded (*Skeets Meadors, p. 124; Sport & General, p. 125*); 39) The 1967 Woodward Stakes (*NYRA/Bob Coglianese, p. 126; The Blood-Horse, p. 127*); 40) Cigar Wins First Dubai World Cup (*Trevor Jones, pp. 128-129*); 41) Bold Ruler Leads Sire List a Record Eight Times (*NYRA/Mike Sirico, p. 130; The Blood-Horse, p. 131*); 42) Personal Ensign's Breeders' Cup Distaff (*Skip Dickstein, p. 132; E. Martin Jessee, p. 133*); 43) Citation Becomes Racing's First Millionaire (*Hollywood Park, pp. 134-135*); 44) The "Fighting Finish" Derby (*Wallace Lowry/Courier-Journal, p. 136; Turf Pix, p. 137; Courier-Journal, p. 137*); 45) Caliente Safety Helmet Introduced (*The Blood-Horse, p. 138; Courtesy David Jimenez Beltran, p. 138; Anne M. Eberhardt, p. 139*); 46) Carl Nafzger's Famous Derby "Call" (*Skip Dickstein, p. 140; Kinetic Corporation, p. 140; Dan Johnson, p. 141*); 47) Keeneland's First Summer Yearling Sale (*Skeets Meadors, p. 142; Kinetic Corporation, p. 143*); 48) Calumet Farm Files for Bankruptcy (*Barbara D. Livingston, p. 144; Morgan Photo Service, p. 144; Anne M. Eberhardt, p. 145*); 49) Advent of Arthroscopic Surgery (*Anne M. Eberhardt, p. 146; The Blood-Horse, p. 147*); 50) First Network Radio Derby Broadcast (*H.C. Ashby, p. 148; Bert Clark Thayer, p. 149*)

51) John Longden's Derby Double (*Bert Morgan, p. 150; Winants Bros., p. 151; The Blood-Horse, p. 151*); 52) The Legend of Phar Lap (*The Blood-Horse, p. 152; Courtesy David Jimenez Beltran, p. 153; Keeneland-Cook, p. 153*); 53 Keeneland Opens (*Audio Visual Archives, Special Collections & Archives, U of K Libraries, p. 154; Keeneland, pp. 154-155*); 54) Afleet Alex's Preakness (*Horsephotos/NTRA, p. 156; Rick Samuels, p. 156; Barbara D. Livingston, p. 157*); 55) Julie Krone Wins the Belmont (*The Blood-Horse, p. 158; Barbara D. Livingston, p. 159*); 56) Jim Dandy Upsets Gallant Fox (*The Blood-Horse, p. 160; NYRA, p. 161*); 57) Hialeah Popularizes Winter Racing (*C.C. Cook, p. 162; Turf Pix, p. 163*); 58) The First Transcontinental Flight of Thoroughbreds (*Fred A. Boschetto/Hollywood Park, p. 164; The Blood-Horse, p. 165*); 59) Mr. Prospector Moves to Claiborne (*Shigeki Kikkawa, p. 166; John C. Wyatt, p. 167*); 60) Dancer's Image's Derby Disqualification (*Kinetic Corporation, p. 168; Winants Bros., p. 169*); 61) Best-Seller Sparks Seabiscuit Mania (*Courtesy Laura Hillenbrand, p. 170; Random House, p. 170; Keeneland-Cook, p. 171*); 62) First Race Call (*San Diego Historical Society, p. 172; The Blood-Horse, p. 172; Barbara D. Livingston, p. 173; Shigeki Kikkawa, p. 173*); 63) Sir Barton Wins First Triple Crown (*Keeneland-Cook, p. 174; R.L. McClure, p. 175*); 64) Exceller's Death Mobilizes Horse Rescue Groups (*Santa Anita Photo, p. 175; Arrow Stud Photo, p. 176*); 65) Richard Mandella's Breeders' Cup Feat (*Anne M. Eberhardt, p. 178; Mike Corrado, p. 179; Barbara D. Livingston, p. 179; Skip Dickstein, p. 179*); 66) Seabiscuit and Red Pollard Make Their Comeback (*Keeneland-Morgan, p. 180; H.C. Ashby, p. 181*); 67) Citation's Sixteen-Win Race Streak (*The Blood-Horse, pp. 182-183*); 68) Division of E.R. Bradley's Bloodstock (*Bert Morgan, p. 184; Lexington Herald-Leader, p. 185; NYRA, p. 185; The Blood-Horse, p. 185; Marshall P. Hawkins, p. 185*); 69) Seattle Slew Sells for $17,500 (*NYRA, p. 186; NYRA/Bob Coglianese, p. 187*); 70) Easy Goer and Sunday Silence's Preakness (*Skip Dickstein, pp. 188-189; Four Footed Fotos, p. 189*); 71) Ribot Wins Back-to-Back Arcs (*Perrucci Foto Agenzia, p. 190; Skeets Meadors, p. 191*); 72) First Meeting of Triple Crown Winners (*NYRA, p. 192; NYRA/Bob Coglianese, p. 193*); 73) Alydar's Death (*Anne M. Eberhardt, p. 194; Barbara D. Livingston, p. 195*); 74) Princequillo Moves to Claiborne (*Skeets Meadors, pp. 196-197*); 75) Triumvirate of Sangster, O'Brien, and Magnier (*Anne M. Eberhardt, p. 198; John C. Wyatt, p. 199*); 76) Thoroughbred Retirement Foundation Is Created (*Courtesy TRF, pp. 200-201*); 77) Dahlia's International Achievement (*Alec Russell, p. 202; Ray Woolfe Jr., p. 203*); 78) Exceller and Seattle Slew's Jockey Club Gold Cup (*NYRA/Bob Coglianese, pp. 204-205*); 79) Ridan and Jaipur's Travers (*NYRA/Bob Coglianese, p. 206; Jones Precision Photo, p. 207*); 80) Man o' War's Funeral (*Barbara D. Livingston/James W. Sames III Collection, p. 208; The Blood-Horse, p. 209*); 81) Zev-Papyrus Match Race (*Keeneland-Cook, p. 210; The Blood-Horse, p. 211*); 82) Dale Baird Trains 9,000 Winners (*Chuck Saus/Mountaineer Race Track, p. 212; Tim Cooley, p. 213*); 83) Bold Ruler and Round Table Born Same Day (*Kinetic Corporation, p. 214; Allen F. Brewer Jr., p. 215; The Blood-Horse, p. 215*); 84) Arlington Park's "Miracle Million" (*Thomas Grieger, p. 216; Matt Goins/EquiPix, p. 216; Milt Toby, p. 217; The Blood-Horse, p. 217*); 85) Launch of Claiborne Farm (*The Blood-Horse, p. 218, 219; Anne M. Eberhardt, p. 219*); 86) First Two-Year-Olds in Training Sale (*Jim Raftery/Turfotos, pp. 220-221*); 87) Colin Holds Off Fair Play (*C.C. Cook, p. 222; Widener Collection, p. 223; The Blood-Horse, p. 223*); 88) Swaps' Record-Breaking Season (*Hollywood Park, p. 224; The Blood-Horse, p. 225*); 89) Sir Ivor's Epsom Derby (*John Slater, p. 226; Delaware Park, p. 227*); 90) Whisk Broom II Sweeps New York Handicap Triple Crown (*Widener Collection, pp. 228-229*); 91) Smarty Jones: the People's Horse (*Barbara D. Livingston, p. 230; Bill Denver/Equi-Photo, p. 231*); 92) Spectacular Bid's undefeated season (*The Blood-Horse, p. 232; Turfotos, p. 233*); 93) Go for Wand's Breakdown (*Dan Johnson, p. 234; Anne M. Eberhardt, p. 235; Barbara D. Livingston, p. 235*); 94) Breeders' Cup Pick 6 Scandal (*AP Photo/Louis Lanzano, p. 236; John Filer Design, p. 236; Rick Samuels, p. 237*); 95) The Theft of Fanfreluche (*Anne M. Eberhardt, p. 238; The Blood-Horse, p. 239*); 96) Shergar's Kidnapping (*Sport & General, p. 240, 241; W.W. Rouch & Co., p. 241*); 97) The Jockey Club Uses DNA-Typing (*Anne M. Eberhardt, pp. 242-243*); 98) Equibase Is Formed (*Courtesy Equibase Company, pp. 244-245*); 99) William Woodward Jr. Is Shot (*Belmont Park, p. 246; The Blood-Horse, p. 247*); 100) Mary Hirsch Becomes First Female Licensed Trainer (*Morgan Photo Service, p. 248; The Blood-Horse, p. 249*)

Panelists / Contributors

PANELISTS

Edward L. Bowen
is president of the
Grayson-Jockey
Club Research
Foundation and
the author of sev-
enteen books,
including *Legacies
of the Turf* and
biographies of
Man o' War, Bold
Ruler, and Nashua.

Timothy T. Capps
has served as
editor of *The
Thoroughbred
Record* and as an
executive for the
Maryland Jockey
Club. He is the
author of a
biography of
Affirmed and
Alydar.

Morton Cathro
is a former
reporter, editor,
and columnist for
the Oakland
Tribune and a
contributor to *The
Blood-Horse*
magazine.

Alice Chandler,
who has raised
champions and a
Kentucky Derby
winner on her Mill
Ridge Farm, is
active in many
Thoroughbred
organizations,
including The
Jockey Club and
the Keeneland
Association.

Steve Haskin
is the award-
winning senior
correspondent for
The Blood-Horse
magazine and the
author of several
books about horse
racing, including
*Holy Grail: The Epic
Quest for the
Kentucky Derby*.

Joe Hirsch,
whose venerated
Turf-writing career
spanned five
decades, is known
as the dean of horse
racing journalism.
He has authored or
co-authored five
books about
Thoroughbred
racing.

John McEvoy,
former Midwest
editor of *Daily
Racing Form*, is the
author of *Great
Horse Racing
Mysteries* and a
biography of
Round Table.

Multiple Eclipse
Award winner
William Nack, a
longtime writer for
Sports Illustrated, is
the author of
*Secretariat: The
Making of a
Champion* and *My
Turf: Horses, Boxers,
Blood Money and
the Sporting Life*.

CONTRIBUTORS

Rena Baer

Edward L. Bowen

Stephanie L. Church

Pat Dolan (fact checker)

Jacqueline Duke

Tom Hall

Evan Hammonds

Steve Haskin

Avalyn Hunter

Tom LaMarra

Dan Liebman

Judy Marchman

Eliza McGraw

Eric Mitchell

Ron Mitchell

Penny Mullinix

Ray Paulick

David Schmitz

Mary Schweitzer (fact checker)

Brian Turner (designer)

Diane Viert (fact checker)

David Young (photo technician)